THE TRIUMPH OF CAPITALISM

THE
TRIUMPH OF
CAPITALISM

ROBERT A. DEGEN

Transaction Publishers
New Brunswick (U.S.A.) and London (U.K.)

Library of Congress Catalog Number: 2007037779
ISBN: 978-1-4128-0689-3
Printed in the United States of America

Library of Congress Cataloging-in-Publication Data

Degen, Robert A.
   The triumph of capitalism / Robert A. Degen.
        p. cm.
   Includes bibliographical references and index.
   ISBN 978-1-4128-0689-3
     1. Capitalism—History. I. Title.

HB501.D415   2008
330.122—dc22   2007037779

For Karin, Christina, and Maire Caitlin

Contents

List of Abbreviations

AFDC	Aid to Families with Dependent Children
AFL	American Federation of Labor
BBC	British Broadcasting Corporation
B.C.E.	Before the Common Era
CAP	Community Action Program
C.E.	Common Era
CEO	Chief executive officer
CFC	Chlorofluorocarbons
CFO	Chief financial officer
CIO	Congress of Industrial Organizations
DARPA	Defense Advance Research Projects Agency
DEA	Department of Economic Affairs
EPA	Environmental Protection Agency
FDIC	Federal Deposit Insurance Corporation
FERC	Federal Energy Regulatory Commission
FLA	Fair Labor Association
FTC	Federal Trade Commission
GATT	General Agreement on Tariffs and Trade
GDP	Gross domestic product
IBM	International Business Machines
IMF	International Monetary Fund
IPO	Initial public offering
JOBS	Job Opportunities in the Business Sector

MITI	Ministry of International Trade and Industry
M.P.	Member of Parliament
NACA	National Advisory Committee for Aeronautics
NASD	National Association of Securities Dealers
NBER	National Bureau of Economic Research
NEDC	National Economic Development Council
NEP	New Economic Policy
NHS	National Health Service
NUM	National Union of Miners
OECD	Organization for Economic Cooperation and Development
PATCO	Professional Air Traffic Controllers Organization
PCAST	President's Council of Advisers on Science and Technology
RCA	Radio Corporation of America
RFC	Reconstruction Finance Corporation
SEC	Securities and Exchange Commission
SEIU	Service Employees International Union
SSI	Supplemental Security Income
TANF	Temporary Assistance for Needy Families
UAW	United Auto Workers
UK	United Kingdom
USSR	Union of Soviet Socialist Republics
VISTA	Volunteers in Service to America
WRC	Worker Rights Consortium
WTO	World Trade Organization

Foreword:

A Summary of *The Triumph of Capitalism*

There is today widespread recognition that capitalism is the socio-economic system of choice. Its preeminence is conducive to admiration that may encourage conformity to an idealized model but be inattentive to emerging problems. The purpose of this book is to contribute to an understanding of the historic role of capitalism, particularly during the past century, taking into account political and social circumstances.

Chapter 1 reviews the gradual growth in influence of market forces until, in the eighteenth century, systemic capitalism arrived giving rise to unprecedented expansion of production. Progress came at a high human cost to workers living in industrial slums that led to a backlash in the form of socialism, trade unionism, and middle-class reform movements. In general, however, the capitalist system and its cultural values grew rapidly during the nineteenth century, making it the unchallenged form of social organization in the West until war came in 1914.

Chapter 2 explains how the world wars of 1914-1918 and 1939-1945, the Great Depression of the 1930s, and competing ideologies threatened capitalism and brought about major reforms to provide greater economic stability and security. Keynesian economics and the welfare state transformed capitalism.

Chapter 3 covers the era from the time wartime recovery was completed until the late 1970s. The welfare state was enlarged and government spending rose relative to national output. Governments experimented with public ownership of major industries, economic planning, and regulation. By the late 1970s, however, the combination of inflation and slow economic growth led to disillusionment with the postwar policy mix.

In Chapter 4, the resurgence of capitalism that began about 1980 is analyzed. A wave of privatization of industry occurred and planning died out. Regulation was reduced in some areas but increased in others, especially with the new awareness of danger to the ecosystem from pollution, and in the areas of health, consumer protection, and worker rights. A major phenomenon was the spread of globalization by which trade, investment, and outsourcing of production raised world output while also bringing problems of financial risk, economic dislocation, and income and wealth inequality. After the boom of the late 1990s collapsed in 2000, the need for greater regulatory oversight of corporate financial practices became clear.

Chapter 5 summarizes the rise to dominance—the triumph—of capitalism as well as the weaknesses of and challenges to it. In the course of the past century, socialism as a system has been generally rejected as an alternative to capitalism, but in gaining ascendancy, capitalism has found it necessary to embrace important discrete elements from socialist doctrine.

Preface

In 1989 the economist Robert L. Heilbroner, a perceptive student of capitalism and socialism for decades, proclaimed "the triumph of capitalism." The contest of economic systems was over and the victory of capitalism was unambiguous. Fifteen years later, C. Fred Bergsten, Director of the Institute for International Economics, reinforced this view: "The U.S. model of capitalism and globalization dominates thinking around the world." The writer Russell Baker, dismayed by perceived degrading effects of market-obsessed management on journalism, observed, "belief in the virtue of maximized profits has acquired something like sanctity in American life." Capitalist values so permeate modern culture in America that to question them seems like heresy.

That capitalism has triumphed and brought progress is true, but repeating a mantra could encourage mindless acceptance of dogma. The success of the market mechanism in solving some problems may tempt many to consider it the solution to all social issues. Such a mind-set would judge policy by the litmus test of how well it conforms to an ideal form of capitalism. Experience, however, strongly suggests that the temptation should be resisted.

Some appreciation of economic and social history, and the attendant clash of ideas, is helpful in providing a context in which ongoing developments may be evaluated. In particular, it is important to know that what is understood to be capitalism has changed very significantly over time. The purpose of this book is to provide such context. In Pasteur's neat dictum, "chance favors the mind prepared."

1

The Gestation and Birth
of the Capitalist System

Capitalism is a natural form of social behavior. It developed spontaneously and gradually over the long course of history until it reached a climax in the nineteenth century. It was not conceptualized in advance. There is no Archimedes, Galileo, or Edison to honor as the inventor of capitalism; it came to be appreciated only after it had evolved into a working institution. No council of savants, no royal society or academy of science, and no commission of religious or lay leaders proclaimed to some clutch of ancient and honorable guild of reporters that a private enterprise market system was the wave of the future and should be embraced by right-thinking people. Instead, the market system had a long struggle to gain acceptance, for it constituted a challenge to tradition and to generally accepted ideas of morality and even of common sense.

A Glimmer of Capitalism in Primitive and Ancient Societies

Peoples in primitive societies of the northwest coasts of Canada and Alaska, of Polynesia and Melanesia, as well as the Andaman Islanders and the Maori of New Zealand, exchanged gifts as a form of trade. Such exchanges were not primarily economic, but had significance of a social, religious, moral, magic, or other character. The French social anthropologist Claude Levi-Strauss long ago pointed out that such exchanges are different from commercial transactions in a modern society, for profit in the modern market sense is absent. They involve power, status, and influence achieved through a set of maneuvers calculated to enhance the security and place in society of the participants. Yet some embryonic market behavior lurks within the web of custom and tradition, for each

1

party must consider the tastes and expectations of the other for the gifts to be deemed worthy and acceptable.[1]

For four millennia preceding the Christian Era, highly structured empires controlled the great river valleys of Mesopotamia, Egypt, India, and China. Anthropologist Marvin Harris described all of these ancient dynasties as having similar economic systems based on complex and extensive networks of dams, canals, ditches, sluice gates, and levees to control river water. Agro-managerial bureaucracies concentrated power in a supreme ruler; every village was answerable to provincial and national centers; bureaucrats high and low exploited the peasant populations. Labor was conscripted to serve in "antlike armies" to build the huge hydraulic networks as well as pyramids, palaces, tombs, the Great Wall, and the Grand Canal. Although these "hydraulic societies" had archetypically command economies, they contained some private enterprises. China permitted private ownership of land, markets existed for agricultural and manufactured goods, and there were banks and wealthy merchants. But private entities were subservient; licenses to trade were subject to arbitrary suspension, government might take over the more remunerative businesses, and corrupt officials could readily siphon off profits. Rulers viewed capitalist enterprise as a useful garden.[2]

The invention of money in the form of ingots of silver or gold has been traced to Mesopotamia before 2000 B.C.E.; the first coins date from the seventh century B.C.E. when the discovery of the touchstone enabled the rulers of Lydia to assay the quality of gold by the streak left on the black stone when metal was rubbed against it. Money stimulated wealth accumulation via the financing of larger trading and construction projects through lending and charging interest, and by fostering banking and the bill of exchange. Businessmen emerged to provide the services of storing money savings and lending to profit-making enterprises. Capitalism was present although greatly confined.[3]

Babylonia, in the southern part of Mesopotamia, where industry and commerce were well developed, maintained extensive trade with many of the areas of the Middle East. The prosperous class in Babylon enjoyed a very comfortable and refined lifestyle with beautifully furnished houses, fine clothes and jewelry, entertainments, and the services of physicians and dentists. The Bible condemns Babylon and announces its fall, but in doing so calls attention graphically to the success of its economy.

And the merchants of the earth shall weep and mourn over her; for no man buyeth their merchandise any more:
  The merchandise of gold, and silver, and precious stones, and of pearls, and fine linen, and purple, and silk, and scarlet, and all thyine wood, and all manner vessels of ivory, and all manner vessels of most precious wood, and of brass, and iron, and marble,
  And cinnamon, and odours, and ointments, and frankincense, and wine, and oil, and fine flour, and wheat, and beasts, and sheep, and horses, and chariots, and slaves and souls of men.
  And the fruits that thy soul lusted after are departed from thee, and all things which were dainty and goodly are departed from thee, and thou shalt find them no more at all.[4]

The Bible views the destruction of the great but sinful city by an avenging God as inevitable. It is interesting to note, en passant, the parallel between the biblical view of Babylon's fall and Marx's view of the future of capitalism. Marx asserts that capitalism must inevitably collapse and, as the Bible does for Babylon, calls attention to the wealth it has created. Of course, Marx attributes capitalism's future doom to the system's inner contradictions, rather than to immorality.

Hammurabi, the greatest king of the First Dynasty of the Babylonian empire, promulgated the celebrated legal code bearing his name around 1700 B.C.E. Among its numerous topics were business affairs: employee rights and duties as well as business/customer relations were covered; limitations were placed on interest charges for various types of loans; maximum prices and minimum wages were set. Although important, the economy was not considered a sphere of activity distinct from political, social, and ethical norms: economic life was incorporated along with other socioreligious concerns into a unified whole. An autonomous market system may have been germinating, but it would require a different world far in the future for the nascent plant to emerge generally free of inhibiting institutions.

In considering the influence of ancient Greece on economic thought, the writings of Plato (427-347 B.C.E.) and Aristotle (384-322 B.C.E.) are relevant for what they considered to be the proper role and status in society of those who provided the material conditions of life. The framework of Greek thought was human life and problems within the city-state, and political philosophy was the medium of interpretation. As in earlier centuries, economic activity was not viewed separately, but was part of society seen as a unified whole; the state was the institution that gave direction to society. In The Republic, economics is part of Plato's vision of what the ideal city-state should be, what would later be called a Utopia. This approach centered on how to arrange for the good and just life that would provide wisdom and satisfaction for humankind. An upper caste of rulers (guardians) to whom government would be entrusted, would not own property individually or be concerned with pecuniary gain. Instead, there would be communism for the elite, a notion far from the Marxian concept. Joseph A. Schumpeter, one of the twentieth century's greatest (although pessimistic) scholarly champions of capitalism, saw little point in pinning a modern ideological label on Plato, but if forced to do so preferred fascist to communist because private property was permitted except to the crème de la crème, life including speech was strictly regulated, and the society was essentially corporative.[5] Unlike the guardians, the numerous farmers, artisans, and other producers would be free to pursue monetary rewards and to accumulate property, presumably without exciting the envy of their supposedly wise aristocratic masters.

Aristotle's Politics also divides society into two distinct groups. The "officer class" or citizens would serve in turn as warriors, priests, and rulers as they progressed through life. They would be expected to use their freedom from the mundane work of producing goods and services to expand their knowledge and refine their political skills. The subordinate class, who would not qualify for citizenship, would consist of merchants, artisans, husbandmen, and so forth. Their lives were considered to be ignoble, did not allow for the development of "virtue," and did not qualify them for the performance of political duties. Furthermore, Aristotle distinguished between production to satisfy needs, which he considered natural and therefore legitimate, and production to gratify desires, seen as unnatural. Market activity was approved only when needs were being satisfied; the pursuit of monetary gain was not sanctioned. In his version of the ideal republic, Aristotle rejected Plato's communism. Communal property lacked the incentive to care for it; in addition, it was necessary for differences in individual ability and effort to be appropriately rewarded to avoid quarrels. Yet, like the philosophers before him, Aristotle was not an individualist in the modern sense but viewed men as elements of a collective community.

Clearly Plato and Aristotle discouraged the development of the capitalistic spirit and took a very condescending attitude toward economic activity. Such activity was recognized as necessary, but of low status and in need of supervision and control by the higher orders of society. However, not all Greek philosophers placed so low a value on the contributions of businessmen.

A study of the evolution of business standards among the ancient Greeks found that traditionally agriculture alone was a suitable occupation for citizens of Athens. At the same time, trade and a variety of industries provided wealth necessary for the good life. Following the Peloponnesian War (431-404 B.C.E.), "the capitalist, the merchant, and the manufacturer came to be thought of as really respectable members of society," for they were needed to recover from the loss of wealth over many years of warfare. Fourth-century Athenians continued to view small-scale trade with contempt, but those who commanded substantial capital became influential, and business success led to social and political success. It was found that whereas the contributions of ancient Greece to government are well known, "they also developed and applied, for the first time in history, the principles of economic freedom . . . what is probably the most important single step in the whole course of economic evolution . . ." This emphatic claim is modified by the observation that wealth was not something its possessor might use without respect for its social consequences. The possession of wealth carried responsibilities; the idea that there was something sacred about private property was unacceptable. What was taking place was the development of practices tending toward the formation of a capitalist market economy within strong cultural and institutional constraints. This elevated status for the business community was exceptional, for democratic Athens was not typical of the ancient world.[6]

In Rome, commercial enterprises were not a matter of much interest to citizens, for foreigners generally controlled commerce, and the workers in shops and factories were usually slaves or ex-slaves. During the early empire the state did not control or participate significantly in trade; merchants could import freely. However, the government did intervene to secure ample food by granting citizenship rights and legal privileges to traders to induce them to enter contracts for transporting grain purchased by the state. Subsidies were given ship owners during periods of scarcity to keep wheat prices low. While state policy allowed and even encouraged the retail grain dealers, it consistently watched prices; Augustus and Tiberius sought to control prices in the interests of farmers and merchants as well as the consuming public. Indeed, "it is not unlikely that the state always regulated prices." In explaining why manufacturing on a large scale did not develop in the city of Rome, Helen Jefferson Loane cites a lack of local sources of metals and fuel, the absence of patent rights, partnership law discouraging to the concentration of capital, "and especially the lack of respect that prevailed in ancient society for the success won from commerce and trade."[7]

Some major features of economic life in the Greco-Roman world as a whole provide a general view of the nature of that major segment of antiquity. Private ownership of land was widespread, ranging from a few acres to huge estates of the ruling classes; trade and the production of manufactured goods was primarily in private hands. Corporations were absent as were long-term partnerships. The acquisition of wealth was a strong motive, but it failed to result in systemic capital creation, for the mental set focused on acquisition itself rather than on production. Strong social and political attitudes constrained economic behavior. Entrepreneurs, in particular the large maritime traders and moneylenders to the rich, failed to seize the opportunities open to them to be innovative. Large landholders had even greater potential due to their accumulation, but they lacked the incentive to develop as capitalists.

The authority of the state was ubiquitous in the ancient world. There was considerable freedom of speech, of business, and of religion, but the principle of inalienable rights was inconceivable. Nor, in the words of the Cambridge historian M. I. Finley, could "any specific instance of non-interference in the economy be explained by a theory of laissez faire," a doctrine that could not come into existence in the absence of "the prior concept of 'the economy,'" defined as "an enormous conglomeration of interdependent markets."[8]

Some summary remarks will complete our consideration of antiquity. To explain any economy, it is necessary to understand how the system resolves three fundamental questions: (1) What different kinds and amounts of commodities and services are produced?; (2) How is production carried on in terms of the personnel, resources, and technology employed?; (3) For whom does production take place, or how is the productive pie shared or distributed among the varied members of society?

In antiquity, these questions were decided basically by tradition and command rather than by markets, which had only a limited role. Primarily rural, the mass of producers in these economies had little contact with markets. At the same time, the commerce of the larger urban centers of Egypt, Greece, and Rome bore some resemblance to the modern capitalist world. What differentiates them from the present is the limited role of the ancient city markets. Trading mainly involved basic provisions for urban consumption and luxuries for the wealthy. The cities were, in Robert Heilbroner's description, "enclosures of economic life rather than nourishing components of integrated rural-urban economies." Furthermore, while the cities bustled with commercial activity, slavery provided a major share of the economy's labor power. So while there was unquestionably a capitalist component, "Nothing like the free exercise and interplay of self-interest guided the basic economic effort of antiquity." As for the distribution of wealth, those who controlled society—the military, religious, and political elites—were the chief beneficiaries. Some merchants and bankers became wealthy, but, in general, economic activity, lacking in prestige, was not well rewarded.[9]

Thousand-Year Bridge: Antiquity to Early Modern Times

The Roman Empire in the West collapsed at the beginning of the fifth century at the hands of invading Germanic tribes, setting off a political implosion or fragmentation of government and society into a mosaic of small, generally isolated political and economic units. Despite many significant developments over the centuries, it took about a thousand years before forces of cohesion and integration brought the modern era into being.

During the early medieval period, 500-1000 C.E., trade survived on a small scale and over long routes. Long-distance commerce was carried on with the Orient in silks, textiles, spices, timber, iron, and slaves, activities requiring capitalist merchants. But aside from these exotic fringe activities, feudal life was dominated by the manorial system under the control of a lord, with the bulk of the population bound to the manor, an arrangement in which markets had no place. The economy of the manor did not produce goods for "export," and its labor force consisted of serfs. Each manorial estate was essentially a self-sufficient community.

The medieval attitude toward economic life emanated from the Roman Catholic Church which implemented its decrees through watchful guidance by ecclesiastical "proctors." A figurative organizational chart for humanity assigned each individual a place with functions to be performed appropriate to the person's station in the overall scheme of things. Attempts to rise above one's station, to accumulate wealth or higher social status, was to risk damnation; trade, which was not considered to be a productive activity, and the receipt of interest on loans, seen as a reward for lending "sterile" money, were considered particularly damnable. Some trading was recognized as necessary, but should take place at a "just price" that was "fair" to both parties to the trade. The condemnation of interest (usury) was not new to Christianity, for money-lending had been considered a parasitic activity ever since Aristotle opposed it on the grounds that money is barren. But the church made usury a mortal sin with severe earthly consequences also, including being declared a social pariah ineligible for confession, religious burial, or even the ability to rent a house. Such severe strictures should be seen in the light of harsh lending practices that took advantage of dire need, such as extremely high interest rates on loans for bread during famines.

The decline of the cities following the fifth century Barbarian invasion, together with the social, political, and economic preeminence of the church, resulted by the ninth century in the emasculation of urban life, for the towns had lost their independence as well as their communities of free men pursuing various crafts and trading activities.

Around 1100 the population of northern Europe began to grow rapidly, a consequence of greater food production due to innovations including the three-field system, equipping horses with shoes and collars, and a heavier plow. Near the end of the twelfth century the horizontal-axel windmill added to the power capabilities of the lowlands along the North Sea. As the population grew, it spilled out of the manorial estates and provided labor for other purposes and lifestyles. Towns again grew as commercial and industrial relationships were formed based on increased specialization and exchange which enriched and gradually transformed the European economy. Additional land was cleared from the eleventh to the thirteenth centuries for which contractors and subcontractors were engaged. On the whole the peasants gained from the new employment opportunities. The self-sufficient manor with its crude agricultural methods experienced change as techniques improved, "and after the twelfth century there was a trend toward farming for a profit—toward capitalistic agriculture."[10]

By the eleventh century Italian cities, Venice most prominently, were in the forefront of a commercial revitalization linking East and West via the Mediterranean. Further north, the fairs of Champagne evolved by the twelfth and thirteenth centuries into trading centers for merchants attracted from a wide area. Merchants from the Mediterranean moved north to settle in cities of northwest Europe including England; by the end of the thirteenth century, the fairs, having performed a key role but now under competition from sea routes and the greater number of manufacturing towns, became less important. Clearly both trade fairs and towns were essential features of the economic transformation of the Middle Ages.

Efficient business conduct requires record keeping; accounting records were used by traders and agents of estates as far back as ancient Egypt. The basis for modern accounting, double-entry bookkeeping, was devised by the merchants of Venice in the 1200s, and in 1494 was made known to the world by the published work of Luca Pacioli, an Italian monk. It is evident that business activity was widespread and sophisticated in both accounting and banking before the Protestant Reformation, although it is equally clear that the Protestant countries of northern Europe surged well ahead in economic development following the Reformation.

British historian J. M. Roberts considers the appearance of the bill of exchange along with the first real bankers in the thirteenth century, and the introduction of limited liability in Florence in 1408, to mark the imminent arrival of modern capitalism. While highly significant, these and concurrent commercial and technological innovations were a small beginning: "For all the magnificence of its palaces, the goods shipped by medieval Venice in a year could all have fitted comfortably into one large modern ship."[11]

The rapidly emerging towns of the north sprouted from a nucleus of merchants around whom various craftsmen tended to cluster. The latter were provided with materials by the merchants who also marketed the finished products.

Another factor that stimulated economic life was the series of crusades extending over a period of about two hundred years beginning shortly before 1100 and continuing until nearly 1300. Motivated by religious zeal to capture the Holy Land as well as by expected opportunities for adventure, military glory, and the acquisition of wealth through trade and land acquisition, these invasions had an important impact on the feudal system of Europe as contact with the richer, more money-oriented, and more vibrant East introduced new ideas that gave added impetus to the commercial transformation in progress.

The pronounced economic growth dating from about 1000 was cruelly halted by the onset of the Black Death starting in 1348; it took about a century before forward momentum was resumed.[12]

By the latter part of the fifteenth century, the European industrial areas contained numerous workshops with craftsmen equipped with machinery powered by natural forces. The substitution of power machinery for human energy was a gradual long-term process; it was not a phenomenon that appeared suddenly in the eighteenth century under the banner of the Industrial Revolution.

Innovations stemming from scientific discoveries revolutionized the cloth-making industry in thirteenth century England. The method of fulling was greatly improved by the invention of the mechanical fulling mill. This fundamental change in one of the major stages of cloth manufacturing engendered opposition by the traditional handworkers. Fulling was now performed at the mill instead of in homes where the guilds had exercised control. The industry became much more capital intensive and shifted geographically to regions with good supplies of water power. Often the lords of the manor, lay or ecclesiastical, were the "capitalist" sources of the new equipment which brought substantial profits to them. The manorial system was at its peak, the lords possessing seigniorial rights that included monopolies on the fulling process. Resentment on the part of those obliged to patronize monopolies led to bitter resistance, a particular instance being an insurrection in 1274 at St. Albans when a zealous abbot had houses entered and seizures made to enforce his monopoly against recalcitrants who refused to use his mills.[13]

Thus, industrial progress was associated with the profit motive and burdened with ethical questions. Recent historical research reveals that Catholic monasteries introduced the preconditions of capitalism in rural areas during the late Middle Ages. Monastic orders, like modern corporations, have perpetual life that allows for sustained organized activity and the accumulation of capital over the long run. They fostered intellectual attainment, the acquisition of specialized skills, and a spirit of innovation and enterprise. The church was immensely rich, holding over one-third of all European land, and it accumulated capital steadily by plowing back profits from its manufacturing and agricultural pursuits. Administration of its enormous properties, located throughout a continent that was fragmented into a great number of jurisdictions, both secular and religious, required some ordering mechanism, and this the church developed by means of the rule of law. Among the entrepreneurial religious orders the Cistercians were particularly important and have even been credited with "the Protestant ethic" long before there were Protestants. In interpreting the role of Christianity in the Middle Ages, the scholar Michael Novak reached the following judgment: "Literacy and study were the main engines of such medieval monasteries; human capital, moral and intellectual, was their primary economic advantage."[14]

For some four centuries, from about 1100 to 1500, guilds played a very prominent role in certain areas, especially in England, some of them continuing until the late 1700s. They consisted of men who were economic composites: the master craftsman, a capitalist of sorts, was also a worker engaged in day-to-day manufacturing and marketing. He either purchased raw material or accepted it from clients and disposed of the finished product by sales from his shop. It has been called, in its ideal form, a perfect industrial democracy because collectively the masters, acting through guild officials, controlled prices, work processes and quality, and even the workers' standard of living. Apprentices, after years learning the trade and perhaps working as journeymen for a time, became masters.

Eileen E. Power found that by the fourteenth century there were industries in towns where capitalism existed in an advanced state; capitalists emerged in the climate of steadily expanding markets for goods during the later Middle Ages. The guild system worked well in towns where markets were stable and quite small, and where the master craftsmen were of similar size. When the markets of London and other larger towns widened considerably, some masters grew rather rich and then, specializing in distribution, grew even richer. They came to dominate the craft guilds by transforming them from democracies into oligarchies, thereby limiting competition by restricting the entry of apprentices into the guilds, as well as by keeping trained apprentices from establishing their own shops. The result was a growing population of permanent wage workers and a separation between capital and labor. The journeymen workers responded by forming yeoman guilds to maintain wages—and the strike weapon was forged. By the fourteenth century the guild system was succumbing to the growing force of capitalism although the guilds held their ground in the smaller towns and among the crafts for which the markets were small.[15]

Strategically located as a commercial hub linking Germany, France, and England, the Netherlands played a unique role in medieval European economic history. Commercial enterprise developed there in a setting of personal freedom. As early as the twelfth century there were highly successful merchants who used their considerable wealth to buy land, a process that culminated by about 1200 in the merchant class becoming also the landowning class. Some of the rich merchants became financiers who provided loans to many borrowers, the King of England among them. To expiate their sins for receiving much usury, many good works were performed by these capitalists, such as building hospitals and institutions to care for the aged. However, by mid-thirteenth century these indigenous capitalists were displaced in the field of finance by the

"Lombards," i.e. by Italians, who brought improved methods of credit and foreign exchange.

This region produced fine quality manufactured goods, notably metal products and the woolen cloth for which Flanders was renowned. Industry gravitated to the towns; as early as the thirteenth century the Netherlands became the most urbanized area of northern Europe resulting in the demise of the manorial system. By about 1300, the Netherlands had forged ahead of its neighbors in international competition, as England was to do some five hundred years later.

The worker in the woolen industry for the most part differed from the typical small medieval artisan who was an independent small businessman. Despite membership in a craft association, he was simply a wage worker who worked at home on material provided by an employer. As described by Henri Pirenne, the export industries presented "a clearly capitalist character, and the artisans depended closely on the merchants who provided them with raw material and fixed their wages." The merchants also dominated politically; they controlled the municipal governments which established the rules of industrial regulation so that "both in law and in fact, labour was subordinated to capital." The powerful, wealthy men of the towns held the reins, but this aristocracy was opposed, beginning in the thirteenth century, by the wage earning class and those better-off citizens who had been excluded from positions of power. Resentment over grievances, economic and social, bred strikes and physical clashes. The bitterness engendered notions of communism, and rebellion broke out in many towns. The struggle continued for more than a century until the town plutocracies were broken up. By the early 1400s, power came to be shared in an arrangement giving representation to various segments of the social order, but the dichotomy between wage earners and capitalist merchants remained.

During the course of the fifteenth century, conditions changed as England developed woolen manufactures; the Flemish towns that tried to protect their positions by strict regulation lost out to rural areas which were freer from control and encouraged by both capitalists and the court. During this period, a time of political unification under the Dukes of Burgundy, the Netherlands were transformed economically as modern economic organization replaced the medieval one. The general interest replaced the old local privileges. Greater economic freedom and rapid maritime expansion, notably involving Antwerp followed by Amsterdam, were features of the new era.[16]

A fascinatingly bizarre illustration of what Adam Smith later called "a certain propensity in human nature . . . to truck, barter, and exchange one thing for another" came to the attention of Portugal's Prince Henry the Navigator early in the fifteenth century as a result of a crusade against Muslims in North Africa. It was "the silent trade" between peoples unable to understand each other's language.

> The Muslim caravans that went southward from Morocco across the Atlas Mountains arrived after twenty days at the shores of the Senegal River. There the Moroccan traders laid out separate piles of salt, of beads from Ceutan coral, and cheap manufactured goods. Then they retreated out of sight. The local tribesmen, who lived in the strip mines where they dug their gold, came to the shore and put a heap of gold beside each pile of Moroccan goods. Then they, in turn, went out of view, leaving the Moroccan traders either to take the gold offered for a particular pile or to reduce the pile of their merchandise to suit the offered price in gold. Once again the Moroccan traders withdrew, and the process went on. By this system of commercial etiquette the Moroccans collected their gold.[17]

Our summary so far has dealt with major developments that transpired up to the beginning of the modern era when the nature of Western economies reached the stage known as mercantilism. It is convenient to take the year 1500 as a reference point to suggest the start of the modern era.

Professor Kenneth Boulding called the transformation from feudalism to capitalism "a classic example of evolutionary transformation." It is not possible to date the end of the former and the start of the latter; they were not "two clearly identifiable systems in dialectical conflict at any time." Incremental and imperceptible changes occurred in behavior, the structure of organizations, and technology.[18]

Mercantilism

A combination of powerful forces transformed the Western world during the sixteenth, seventeenth, and eighteenth centuries. The period of roughly 250 years (1500-1750) is known as the age of mercantilism, or commercial capitalism, to distinguish the era from feudalism, which was on the way out, and industrial capitalism, which emerged as the dominant economic motif of the nineteenth century. Mercantilism comprised a new set of concepts, policies, and behavior based on a worldview brought about as a result of the Renaissance, the great voyages of discovery, the centralization of power in the state, and the Protestant Reformation. It brought capitalists to the fore as leading actors in human affairs as never before, but it did so in the context of state regulation of economic activity. So while capitalists now sat at the high table of society sharing the status, influence, wealth, and power of the elite, capitalism, viewed as a self-regulating competitive system that functioned naturally and freely without control by the state, had not arrived.

Beginning in northern Italy and spreading throughout Western Europe from the fourteenth to the sixteenth century, a fundamental change occurred in the way the world was perceived. Nineteenth-century scholars were so impressed by their examination of that period that they wrote of a rebirth of learning, or Renaissance. Scholars turned their attention to the study of ancient Greece and Rome; the art and literature of those earlier civilizations became of interest to wealthy men of business and government. The medieval focus on religion diminished and was largely replaced by concern with the way the world works. Emphasis on the secular opened the way to empirical study, experimentation, and a wide range of thought; the confining limits to education that had been dominated by religious concerns were removed, making room for humanism, the study of humanity. Greater knowledge of the physical world resulted in important inventions including the clock, microscope, and the Gutenberg press. By the close of the period, c. 1600, modern science was on a firm basis while, in the political realm, power and wealth were in the process of transfer from the church to princes.

The great voyages of discovery beginning with those of Columbus in the 1490s followed in the 1500s by Magellan and other adventurers, under royal sponsorship, opened the way to trade, colonization, and innovation. A huge flow of gold and silver from the New World greatly invigorated investment, production, and commerce throughout the Old World and between the two worlds. Vast new markets were opened to merchants whose enterprises were further enhanced by rising prices (and lagging wages) that followed from the flood of money.

The political fragmentation that followed the collapse of the Roman Empire was gradually replaced by greater centralization of authority resulting, by the sixteenth century, in the formation of modern nation states. These states provided territorial unification, encouraged commerce by reducing internal obstacles to trade, both legal and financial, and directly stimulated economic activity by purchases of goods and services.

As a result of the Protestant Reformation of the sixteenth century that fundamentally changed the outlook of much of northern Europe, religious encouragement was given to productive economic activity. Most strikingly exemplified by Calvinism, this powerful force emphasized saving and investment. It has been credited with infusing a fresh spirit into capitalism that motivated a strong work ethic and urge to innovate. Early in the twentieth century, the German sociologist Max Weber put forward in The Protestant Ethic and the Spirit of Capitalism the thesis that by its emphasis on individualism, Protestantism shaped capitalist thinking and therefore is primarily responsible for the nature of capitalism.

In Religion and the Rise of Capitalism, published in 1926, the English economic historian R. H. Tawney argued that in its early years Puritanism rejected economic individualism. At this stage, Puritanism, like Catholicism, viewed all human affairs, including economic activity, as requiring approved rules of behavior. But the task of regulating conduct by applying rules of ethics failed, overwhelmed both by a virile commercial environment and by the "soul of Puritanism itself." Tawney viewed the capitalist spirit as old as history, not something that appeared as a result of the religious mutation associated with Luther and Calvin. "But it found in certain aspects of later Puritanism a tonic which braced its energies and fortified its already vigorous temper."

Tawney explained that Calvin had combined two incompatible elements: (1) approval of business, instead of the traditional religious view that it was morally doubtful and dangerous, and (2) "the restraining hand of an inquisitorial discipline." In Geneva discipline could be effective, but in the wider, more varied English setting, it was not. At the end of the sixteenth and the beginning of the seventeenth centuries came "the wave of commercial and financial expansion—companies, colonies, capitalism in textiles, capitalism in mining, capitalism in finance—on the crest of which the English commercial classes . . . had climbed to a position of dignity and affluence." The collectivist component of Puritanism fell away and the "individualism congenial to the world of business became the distinctive characteristic of a Puritanism which had arrived." In its later phases, Puritanism offered a moral creed which reconciled business and religion: "money making, if not free from spiritual dangers . . . could be and ought to be, carried on for the greater glory of God."[19]

Apart from powerful religious influences, a small but perhaps representative challenge to the established stratified social culture may be seen in the behavior of Shakespearean actors in the Elizabethan/Jacobean era as they lolled and pranced about London in their fine clothes. "Representing nascent capitalism, they were a menace to older systems of authority" in the view of some historians.[20]

The principal policy-makers and writers of the mercantilist period, the movers and shakers of the time, were merchant businessmen and public officials. Notable examples are Sir Josiah Child, the wealthiest Englishman of the seventeenth century, and Sir Thomas Mun—both of whom held leading positions in the East India Company. Chartered companies of two types were created for trade and colonization, joint-stock companies, early versions of modern corporations, and regulated companies whose members traded on their own. Unabashedly promoting policies to gain profits for their enterprises, yet well aware of the need to show that they were contributing to the power of their royal masters and accepting the need for state regulation to direct individual acquisitiveness in their nation's interest, these writers dealt with specific practical aspects of economic life and did not attempt a comprehensive or unified account of the economy as a whole. Strengthening the power of the nation was the supreme end to be pursued in a world of rival, generally hostile, states that coexisted in an environment of supposedly fixed resources, so that one country's gain was another's loss, a zero-sum game. Issues were presented in terms of cause and effect relations, a rational albeit self-interested approach. To increase the strength of the state, militarily and politically, it was necessary to acquire wealth, and precious metals were seen as the most important form of wealth. One way to get precious metals was through discovery and mining, another was by raiding the convoys of rivals. A more basic, dependable, long-run method was through a "favorable balance of trade" by which the country with a surplus of exports over imports would receive an inflow of gold and silver.

A favorable balance of trade became the focal point of mercantilist doctrine. A variety of policies were devised, all of which required government supervision and regulation. They included regulation of foreign trade, of domestic economic activity including labor markets, and of colonial policy. Monopoly privileges were standard practice in foreign trade. Within the domestic economy, monopolies and special privileges were granted to favored producers of certain goods.

The power of the enterprising spirit to lift even a relatively small nation to a high level of prosperity is evident by the emergence of the Dutch as the strongest commercial nation of Europe in the seventeenth century. Growth was so rapid that historians have been amazed by what was accomplished. Basic to the achievement was ingenuity in designing and building efficient, low-cost cargo ships. The Dutch East India Company and the Dutch West India Company, both founded in the seventeenth century, "brought home the riches to enlarge the tax base and provide the government with more money for building and manning more merchant fleets with enlarged scope for expansion. The process was watched resentfully by other nations who, to soothe their envy, endowed the Dutch with a reputation as money grubbers. Certainly moneymaking was a primary national interest and, combined with a strong sense of freedom and independence grown in a long revolt, was the key to the extraordinary Dutch enterprise."[21]

Based on its commerce and shipping, Holland built the most urbanized and cosmopolitan European state of the second half of the seventeenth century. It attracted young men from other Protestant countries who came to acquire knowledge of the country's commercial and financial techniques. Probably the most famous person to seek to learn from it came from the east, the young Peter the Great, who in 1697 traveled from Russia in search of methods of modernization for his realm.

Certain characteristic features of the mercantilist era are of particular interest: (1) emphasis on economic gain by prototypical capitalists, men who drove a hard bargain; (2) the imperative of reconciling individual and state interests; and (3) acceptance of the need for regulation of economic affairs. While the old guild system was being replaced, it is reasonable to view the change as a transfer of guild regulations and restrictions to the whole nation.

The Flowering of Systemic Capitalism

Mercantilism began to be transmuted into industrial (or fully developed) capitalism late in the eighteenth century in England when a series of new production techniques including the steam engine, coke-smelting, the spinning jenny, and the spinning frame resulted in increased production at lower cost enabling Britain to "take off" into sustained growth as the leading manufacturing nation of the world. Breakthroughs in technological innovation were based on the experience and skills acquired by craftsmen over many earlier generations. Remarkable industrial developments were possible at this time and place because the gradual accumulation of wealth through agriculture and commerce provided investment capital.

There were important political arguments in support of capitalism prior to its great advance, a theme cogently developed by Albert O. Hirschman in his The Passions and the Interests. Traditionally, human actions had been considered to be subject to destructive passions: St. Augustine (354-430) had identified three egregious sins, lust for power, sexual lust, and lust for money and possessions. The intended role of religion and moral philosophy was to restrain these dangerous passions, but by the seventeenth century, leading thinkers became convinced that the passions were too powerful to be contained. By the eighteenth century the idea that certain passions could be employed to neutralize those that were more vicious became prominent—a way of engineering desirable social behavior. David Hume (1711-1776) contended that since the passions were impervious to reason, the only way of negating or retarding a passion was by the use of another. It became necessary to choose the right set of passions to be encouraged and strengthened so as to tame those that were truly harmful. The terms "interest" and "interests" emerged to refer specifically to economic advantage or acquisitiveness. Eventually it developed "that one set of passions, hitherto known variously as greed, avarice, or love of lucre, could be usefully employed to oppose and bridle such other passions as ambition, lust for power, or sexual lust." This strategy led Hume to praise capitalism on the theory that it stimulated benign human propensities while deterring malignant ones, thereby improving human nature.

The pursuit of material gain came to be seen as innocuous. In the words of Dr. Samuel Johnson, "There are few ways in which a man can be more innocently employed than in getting money." Economic affairs were viewed as mundane, not important enough to affect the human condition in a major way, and so were not to be feared. In France the idea that commerce promoted gentleness, sweetness, and calm was much discussed. Baron Montesquieu (1689-1755) was the most important thinker to advance this point of view by observing that commerce and gentle ways go together, and that it can be seen daily that commerce softens barbarian ways. Montesquieu's works were influential among intellectuals in the early years of the United States. Alexander Hamilton, however, sharply disagreed with this diagnosis, as shown by the following quotation from The Federalist, No. 6, of November 14, 1787:

> Has commerce hitherto done any thing more than change the objects of war? Is not the love of wealth as domineering and enterprising a passion as that of power or glory? Have there not been as many wars founded upon commercial motives, since that has become the prevailing system of nations, as were before occasioned by the cupidity of territory or dominion? Has not the spirit of commerce in many instances administered new incentives to the appetite both for the one and for the other?[22]

Sir James Steuart (1712-1780), a Scottish contemporary of Hume, was influenced by Montesquieu's thinking, but he added the observation that trade improved the position of the middle classes vis-à-vis the lords and the king. He also compared the economy to a delicate and complicated watch which could be broken by arbitrary interference.

The sound running of the economy was of great value to the nation and its leaders; its complicated nature and delicacy served "against the folly of despotism."[23]

Adam Smith, the celebrated Scottish moral philosopher and economist, saw marvelous benefits deriving from individual self-interest, but not by making people less aggressive. In his view, people pursue economic gain in order to achieve respect and position in society. Ambition, power, and status are not alternatives to, but are achieved through, riches; the interests and the passions join together. Yet the competitive struggle brings about a harmonious result, for society as a whole reaps material benefits.

> It is thus that the private interests and passions of individuals dispose them to turn their stock towards the employments which in ordinary cases are most advantageous to the society. But if from this natural preference they should turn too much of it towards those employments, the fall of profit in them and the rise of it in all others immediately dispose them to alter this faulty distribution. Without any intervention of law, therefore, the private interests and passions of men naturally lead them to divide and distribute the stock of every society, among all the different employments carried on in it, as nearly as possible in the proportion which is most agreeable to the interest of the whole society.[24]

With the passage of time and the expansion of capitalism, the soothing notion that commerce brought gentleness to human affairs was discarded. Capitalism brought changes that benefited many, some enormously, but brought harshness in the form of social dislocation, unemployment, and poverty to others.

The concept of an autonomous self-adjusting market mechanism that determines prices, allocates resources, and distributes income efficiently through the uninhibited activity of private participants that is so central to capitalism, was discovered, not invented. It was advanced in France during the third quarter of the eighteenth century by the Physiocrats, a group of prominent intellectuals who were intent on reforming the French economic system that existed within a social order dominated by the monarchy and landed aristocracy, an order they did not propose to overthrow. Physiocracy meant the law of natural order, and was the application to economic life of the physical laws described earlier by Sir Isaac Newton that had become an accepted part of European thought. It was not through research that the Physiocrats formed their radical view of desirable human behavior, but by observation and insight. Well educated, rational, and confident of their powers of comprehension, they were self-appointed guides who saw themselves uniquely equipped to remove society's blinders. As people became enlightened by these mentors, the natural order would, they believed, be adopted for they considered it to be obvious once recognized.

The contributions of the Physiocrats constitute the first stage of economics as a discipline. Their leader, a physician, Dr. Francois Quesnay, pioneered macroeconomic analysis by describing the circulation of goods and money as analogous to the circulation of blood. They focused on the net product or surplus generated by productive activity to expand national output. Agriculture, by far the predominant economic activity of the time, suffered from inefficiency and lack of capital due to neglect by large absentee proprietors, seigneurial dues that drained the resources of peasants, and the poverty of sharecroppers. But hope lay in the northern provinces where progressive agricultural entrepreneurs were showing the way to reform and prosperity. The Physiocrats wanted to unblock the system by eliminating all taxes, except for a single tax on land rent, and by eliminating monopolistic privileges in manufacturing. Enterprise would be encouraged and capital accumulated; it was particularly important for capital to flow into the efficient entrepreneurial sector of agriculture. They were so impressed by the importance of agriculture that they erroneously considered it to be the sole source of the net product.

An egregious example of a rigged market in pre-revolutionary France was the salt industry, one of the sectors controlled by the harsh and detested "tax farmers," the Farmers-General, a quasi-government organization with some thirty thousand personnel. Salt was regulated from its production in the salt marshes to its sale to consumers with prices controlled and heavy taxes levied. "Even had the Farmers not had the right to set the price of salt, the sheer bureaucratic weight of its official distribution would have enormously increased its price. Few households could have conceived of doing without this most basic commodity, but they were not even given the possibility of forgoing it, since they were legally required to buy a minimum annual amount, determined by individual assessment." Salt was smuggled in at close to one-tenth of its official price.[25]

By recognizing the advantages of the free market mechanism, the Physiocrats strengthened the forces of capitalism. The advocacy of a policy of government abstention from interference in economic life entered our language in their encapsulating phrase laissez faire ("allow to do").

From the perspective of French history, the enthusiasm for the free market evinced by the Physiocrats and repeated around 1860 is something of an anomaly. A characteristic feature of France is the "etatist tradition," i.e., a strong role for the central government exercised by a relatively few people, an elite considered qualified by education and ability to guide national policy.

The case made by the Physiocrats in favor of the free market turned out to be a warm-up act for Adam Smith's masterpiece, The Wealth of Nations, published in 1776. Although Smith did not devise any new analytic concepts, he nevertheless presented a revolutionary doctrine by combining ideas, factual information, and interpretive insight into a comprehensive understanding of how the system worked and what was needed for economic growth. His book was an immediate success and had a powerful impact; its message was favorably received by businessmen for it sanctioned their activities in pursuit of profits and called for government generally to get out of their way. He came to this position, and developed his elaborate system of thought to justify it, as a result of a strong reaction against the existing network of government controls over economic life that either were instituted under mercantilism or had survived from the feudal era. The thrust of his argument was that if these shackles were removed, the standard of living of the peoples of the world would rise. Smith presented his case persuasively in a fine, flowing literary style with memorable phrases and engaging anecdotes. Theory, history, and institutional description are blended in a tone that evokes confidence in the reasonableness, relevance, and logic of the economic/social/political worldview being expounded. David Ricardo, the highly successful stockbroker who became the next-generation successor to Smith as the foremost British classical economist, picked up and read The Wealth of Nations while on vacation in the resort city of Bath. This fortuitous introduction to the study of political economy fascinated Ricardo and set him on the way to developing his highly abstract views on economic growth, income distribution, and international trade that restated Smith's concepts in terms of rigorous theorems.

Because Smith needed to overcome the formidable bastion of mercantilist ideology and practice, he argued the case for its opposite, the free market, very strongly. Yet he candidly recognized that "the obvious and simple system of natural liberty" had its own weaknesses and dark aspects, and he therefore acknowledged duties appropriate to government. His was a balanced version of the political/economic universe, not the stance of a doctrinaire free marketeer dedicated to an extreme laissez faire position. Today professional economists across a broad liberal/conservative spectrum appreciate this quality in Smith. He is viewed as the father of economics, a man of great wisdom whose understanding of the process by which societies raise their living standards remains relevant. Economists generally repudiate the inaccurate but nevertheless popular image of Smith—the icon that appeared on the ties of aides to President Reagan in the 1980s—who is supposed to have championed pure laissez faire and given his blessing to greed. Smith recognized that self-interest motivated people to work, save, and invest, as a result of which the common welfare is served—but there was more to the philosophy of this moral philosopher. He observed ironically that the pursuit of wealth could be "a necessary deception," and he identified flaws in the natural order: employers have a preponderance of bargaining power vis-à-vis employees; producers conspire to raise prices; repetitive tasks required by division of labor adversely affect those who perform them. Nobel laureate Professor Paul Samuelson observed, "My Adam Smith isn't the guy on the ties. He was for trade unions, he believed in public works and he was very suspicious of businessmen."[26]

Smith assigned three important tasks to government: national defense, justice, and the maintenance of certain public institutions and public works. He did not, however, draw a clear-cut line between the activities that government should and should not perform. Among the functions that he specifically included as appropriate for government to provide under the rubric of public works are highways, bridges, and harbors. Government should also be involved in the provision of general education and ought to act to prevent the spread of infectious diseases. Whether government should be relied upon to perform any particular task was a practical matter depending on circumstances that included the competence and honesty of government administration. The range of appropriate government activity in and interference with the economy was elastic, not prescribed in a creed. Clearly, the extent to which government is involved in the economy is a key question for capitalism. The crux of the ideological struggle over economic policy in the West for the past century has turned on what should be included in the third of Smith's boxes of appropriate government functions. In an informative and dispassionate article still entirely relevant, University of Chicago economist Jacob Viner observed in 1927 that while contending positions are taken by those convinced that they alone know the correct economic path, "how refreshing it is to return to The Wealth of Nations with its eclecticism, its good temper, its common sense." To the father of economics, laissez faire was not always good or always bad, but depended on circumstances, and he set an example by taking into account all the circumstances he could find.[27]

Among Smith's memorable observations we note:

> It is not from the benevolence of the butcher, the brewer, or the baker that we expect our dinner, but from regard to their own interest.
>
> People of the same trade seldom meet together, even for merriment and diversion, but the conversation ends in a conspiracy against the public, or in some contrivance to raise prices.
>
> Monopoly of one kind or another, indeed, seems to be the sole engine of the mercantile system.
>
> Consumption is the sole end and purpose of all production; and the interest of the producer ought to be attended to, only so far as it may be necessary for promoting that of the consumer. . . . But in the mercantile system, the interest of the consumer is almost constantly sacrificed to that of the producer; and it seems to consider production, and not consumption, as the ultimate end and object of all industry and commerce.
>
> By . . . directing . . . industry in such a manner as its produce may be of the greatest value, he intends only his own gain, and he is in this, and in many other cases, led by an invisible hand to promote an end which was no part of his intention. . . . By pursuing his own interest he frequently promotes that of the society more effectually than when he really intends to promote it.[28]

A review of the economic literature of the early years of the nineteenth century suggests that "we owe the phrase 'supply and demand' to Adam Smith."[29]

At the time Smith wrote, the English economy was evolving from its commercial base into industrial capitalism. Indeed the late eighteenth century was a turning point in world history as the Western world, led by Britain, began the great transformation that came to be known as the Industrial Revolution. There is general agreement among scholars that a distinct rise in agricultural productivity was a necessary precondition for industrial capitalism to develop; the increase in agricultural output per worker released labor for employment in industry. The workers in the manufacturing sector required the products of the farms, and those in farming demanded goods from the towns.

A leading thesis, presented by historian Robert Brenner, explaining why Britain was the first nation to experience this economic mutation, is that its agricultural land became consolidated into large estates resulting in a leap forward in agricultural productivity. This explanation emphasizes the class structure: landowners (lordly squires) leased their fields to tenants (capitalists interested in technology and efficiency) who employed landless laborers for wages. Large-scale capitalist farming in Britain is contrasted with generally fragmented as well as feudal organization on the Continent. Advances in agricultural technology, economies of scale, and class relationships all contributed to advances in productivity.

In the (then) young country of the U.S., capitalism clearly did not grow from the soil of a landlord/tenant/laborer class structure. How the small-scale family farms of New England increased their productivity enough to fuel the rise of capitalism has been a topic of major interest to historians. The fruits of much of their research, encapsulated by Professor Gordon S. Wood, whose work is drawn upon here, provide insight into the quite sudden rise of capitalism among small farmers on stony land.[30]

The traditional (pre-World War I) view held that agriculture in colonial New England was locked into a mere subsistence mode; wasteful, ignorant, conservative farmers; plentiful land scratched by relatively little labor; and the absence of local markets for agricultural output. According to research following World War II, however, colonial agriculture included many farmers who sold surpluses and had the true capitalist acquisitive attitudes toward product marketing and speculative land dealing. The entrepreneurial spirit was found to be widespread in America from its earliest days; the image of the staid yeoman was supplemented by that of go-getting individualists. If they were so inclined, however, it took a long time for them to make much progress.

By the 1970s, another set of historians discovered that colonial New England was far from a hotbed of enterprising and speculative capitalists after all. According to those who visited the subject from an anthropological perspective, this was a land of stable, self-sufficient peasant villages, corporate communities in which people lived according to strict religious precepts and were hostile to uncontrolled individualistic money-making activities. Studies of the economies of these villages by "social" or "moral" historians found them to be precapitalist. This version of our early history held that farmers had market opportunities, but contrary to the findings of the "market" historians, were deaf to the enticement of the capitalist ethos with its lure of profits. According to this interpretation, the northern farmers intentionally produced mainly for the purpose of providing for the maintenance of their households rather than for sale. They wished to perpetuate their way of life through successive generations. To the extent that trade occurred, it did so on the basis of customary or "just" prices, a practice evocative of the Middle Ages. This vision of early American life is quite agreeable to many of its depicters for they are themselves averse to capitalism.

From what has been presented to this point, with each of the diametrically opposed views supported by evidence adduced by qualified experts, the mindset of colonial New England was strongly capitalist or strongly anticapitalist (or precapitalist), or perhaps the two views coexisted in a state of social ambivalence. When even more recent research is put on the scales, the case in favor of the commercial activity interpretation is strengthened, for weighty evidence of land speculation has been brought to bear on the issue. Successful land speculation brought political success as well as riches. Indeed the appetite for land acquisition and the pursuit of gain generally have been shown as key motivating forces in America from its inception. Yet what is characteristic of part of society may not hold for all or most of society. Economic historian Winifred Barr Rothenberg recalls that market activity of some degree existed for thousands of years, so it is not strange that it was practiced in our early national history. But as long as the participants were a small segment of the population, consisting of merchants, bankers, and various entrepreneurs, but did not involve the majority of the population, then a true market economy (capitalism) did not exist. Just as a political system is not a democracy if only ten or twenty percent of the population qualifies as voters, an economy does not truly constitute capitalism if most people fail to participate in market activity.

A key feature identifying the arrival of capitalism historically is the integration of markets in the sense that prices of particular goods tend toward uniformity throughout some fairly wide area. A critical mass of buyers and sellers is needed to constitute an integrated market. Perhaps most important, economic growth becomes an integral part of life for most people. Rothenberg collected data to identify the time when such a market economy emerged in rural New England, when productivity growth rose enough to enable resources to shift out of agriculture to other sectors. She attributes the pronounced increase in farm productivity to farmers working harder and more efficiently. Market integration was found to have occurred in the 1780s. Capital markets, necessary for the industrialization that followed, also developed during that decade. The finding that increased rural market activity began shortly after the American Revolution, thereby advancing the development of a capitalist society, is so persuasive that the moral economy historians have embraced it.

Out of all the research and debate, a major conclusion is suggested: in explaining the creation of capitalism on these shores, the key event may well have been the American Revolution. As it had been throughout history, work was still considered drudgery. For ordinary folk in Puritan culture, hard work was thought to be good for the soul and has performed the same function vis-à-vis the devil as apples are said to do with regard to the doctor. Work was necessary but degrading, and those who labored were more likely to be treated with contempt than respect by those fortunate enough to be able to avoid it themselves. Leisure was prestigious, enjoyable, and desired, whereas work was demeaning and therefore tended to be performed perfunctorily. Gentlemen either did no work or were of the learned professions; those who toiled with their hands or were engaged in trade were consigned to the lower classes where Aristotle had placed them two millennia earlier. The distinction is nicely made in the mid-eighteenth-century English novel Tom Jones where the start of a new day is described: "Those members of the society, who are born to furnish the blessings of life, now began to light their candles, in order to pursue their daily labours, for the use of those who are born to enjoy these blessings."[31]

This ancient cake of custom was at last crumbling, for during the eighteenth century those who farmed, traded, worked lathes, kept shops, and so forth asserted a claim to status and influence. Their aspirations took form in a higher standard of consumption. Ordinary people were eager to emulate the "people of quality" by acquiring better quality household goods, equipment, and education. Indeed, the rise in consumption standards has been recognized as a "consumer revolution." The prospect of getting these finer (luxury) goods, to "come up in the world," motivated a large part of the population to apply themselves to their work more vigorously than when common folk had very limited expectations. As their prosperity grew so did the value of their labor. So the case has been made that the 1780s were the "most critical moment" in this nation's history—a modern society imbued with democratic along with business and consumer values emerged at last from the bonds of tradition. A great burst of energy was let loose by the American Revolution for it really had become "self-evident, that all men are created equal; that they are endowed by their Creator with certain inalienable rights; that among these are life, liberty, and the pursuit of happiness" as proclaimed by the Continental Congress.

The eighteenth century set humanity for the first time on a path of rising living standards as rationalism and the application of science opened the way for the Industrial Revolution. In earlier times, improved technology only temporarily raised the standard of life before being swamped by increased population pressing on limited resources. But along with the great boon of rising output came a cost, the modern business cycle. As Paul Krugman observed: "Preindustrial economies could not have recessions as we know them, both because of the simplicity of their monetary systems and because they consisted mostly of farmers who respond to a drop in demand mainly by cutting prices rather than by growing less."[32] Thus, it was that when the Napoleonic Wars ended in 1815, Britain, the first nation to industrialize, became the first to experience a modern recession with cuts in production and layoffs of wage workers.

The term "Industrial Revolution" entered the vocabulary in the 1880s when it was introduced by the English economic historian Arnold Toynbee. It applies to developments in Britain during the late eighteenth and early nineteenth centuries, beginning about 1760. The concept has continued to be used despite debate concerning its causes and timing.

Modern industrial (cum-commercial) capitalism developed during the nineteenth century as great manufacturing, mining, and steam-powered transportation brought enormous increases in wealth and provided the means for a vast increase in population. At last, after a gestation period extending far back in historical time, fully capitalist economies were born "when capitalism combined with industrialism to create what is now the modern world."[33]

We, of course, are the legatees of this historically unprecedented growth of material riches. It is ironic that Karl Marx, history's foremost critic of capitalism, bestowed on it the highest of enconiums, lauding its creative powers as virtually miraculous, and did so in 1848 before the much more impressive achievements that followed over the next 150 years.

> The bourgeoisie, during its rule of scarce one hundred years, has created more massive and more colossal forces than have all preceding generations together. Subjection of Nature's forces to man, machinery, application of chemistry to industry and agriculture, steam-navigation, railways, electric telegraphs, clearing of whole continents for cultivation, canalization of rivers, whole populations conjured out of the ground—what earlier century had even a presentiment that such productive forces slumbered in the lap of social labor.[34]

The Industrial Revolution spread to Western Europe, North America, and eventually around the globe. Napoleon had conquered much of Europe temporarily, but the "conquering forces" of industrial capitalism suffered no effective counterrevolution until the Russian Revolution of 1917. After 1815, in the words of G. D. H. Cole, "Free enterprise and nationalism were in the air, and men had to breathe the air of capitalism whether they liked it or not." By the middle of the nineteenth century, "the greatest revolution of all—the new power of steam had been successfully applied to the transport of men and goods by both land and sea as well as to production."[35]

A dark side of industrial capitalism—inhumane working and living conditions—soon became a massively ugly blot calling the system into question and giving rise to movements to check its sway. Reactions against industrial capitalism will be discussed later in these pages when the emergence of socialism is considered, but one striking fact will be noted now. Humanitarians succeeded in getting Parliament to abolish slavery in the British Empire in 1833, but despite graphic accounts of horrendous conditions in mines, factories, and industrial towns, remedies were long delayed for the working class within Britain. Slavery was considered immoral, but a system based on freedom of contract, whatever its result, was deemed virtuous. "Slavery, it was alleged, not only produced evil material conditions and an inhumane and unchristian type of civilization but also violated the principle of laissez faire which contemporary opinion regarded as the essential driving force of material progress."[36]

While the shift from a predominantly rural to an urban industrial society constituted progress, the problem was that the policy shapers and makers of the time were so hostile to government intervention that provision for sanitation and municipal governance was long neglected, and workers were exploited. Effective public health services date from the 1870s and representative local government began in the next decade.

By the early twentieth century, the U.S. and Germany had come to challenge Britain's industrial supremacy. In the U.S., industrial capitalism emerged from 1815 to 1860. After the Civil War ended in 1865, the influence of the agrarian South, politically powerful nationally in the antebellum era, was much reduced, and the nation's northern states moved rapidly and enthusiastically into the industrial capitalist system. The Civil War determined that North America would be dominated by a single great nation which would develop the enormously abundant natural resources of the continent. The nation's strength came to be determining in two world wars in the next century. The triumph of the Union had set its political system securely in the democratic mode of majority rule and had the effect also "of linking democracy and material well-being closely in the minds of Americans; industrial capitalism in the U.S. would have a great pool of ideological commitment to draw upon when it faced its later critics."[37]

Germany lagged far behind Britain for most of the nineteenth century. After unification of the separate German states into the German Empire following success in the Franco-Prussian War of 1870-1871, a great burst of industrial growth made Germany a powerful rival to Britain. Their industries were quite similar and competitive, but their national economic policies were different. In contrast to Britain's devotion to laissez faire principles, the fervently nationalistic German state directly encouraged and guided German industry. The rules of capitalism differed in two other main ways between the leading countries. Germany, the U.S., and other industrializing countries developed their industries behind protective tariffs, whereas Britain, with its early lead, shifted toward a free trade policy in mid-century, a process completed in 1860. In Germany, cartels were not just permitted but given legal protection and encouragement; the law was less friendly to collusion in Britain, where agreements to restrain trade were not legally enforceable, and became illegal in the U.S. when the Sherman Anti-Trust Act was adopted in 1890.

Prodigious economic changes surpassing those of earlier ages occurred from the mid-nineteenth century to 1914 measured by growth rates, improved technology, development of new industries, and increased trade. Technological innovations transformed the steel industry into a mighty supplier of many kinds of structural materials, equipment, and tools. World fuel oil output surged from virtually zero to over 400 million barrels per year. Following the invention of the dynamo in 1867, electricity came to provide power and illumination. Railroads spanned the continents. These developments along with many other new and improved products demonstrated the creative power of capitalism in the decades leading up to World War I. It was also an era when the European powers, notably Britain, Germany, and France, added to and further secured their colonial territories.

On the eve of World War I, capitalism was the only economic system employed by nations in the Western world although it was not generally described by that name. There were differences in its form from country to country, but capitalism, in generic terms, was the whole show. The notion that there might be one or more viable alternatives to capitalism was heretical. Socialists had succeeded in provoking some responses to their concerns, but socialism had not been embraced anywhere in a major way.

The most influential economics textbook in English at the time was Principles of Economics by Alfred Marshall of Cambridge University, published in eight editions from 1890 to 1920. Marshall did not specify that his subject was capitalism—it was simply political economy or economics, "a study of mankind in the ordinary business of life" that "examines that part of individual and social action which is most closely connected with the attainment and with the use of the material requisites of wellbeing." He explained that capital is the result of saving (not spending on consumption) a portion of income, and that in return the saver/lender earns interest. An increase in material capital will increase the national output and add to the demand for and reward to labor. Capital is demanded chiefly for its productiveness and it is supplied by those willing to sacrifice the present for the future. Capital was one of the necessary agents of production and whoever provided it was performing an essential function; Marshall eschewed the term capitalist which might suggest an economic class.

Nor did American academic economists use the term capitalism early in the twentieth century, although Frank A. Fetter (Cornell) wrote of a "capitalistic age" and of a "class of money-lenders" who transfer wealth between those who own it and those who wish to use it. Charles Bullock (Harvard) took his subject to be how mankind goes about getting material commodities and personal services—the science of economics. Irving Fisher (Yale) defined economics, or political economy, simply: the science of wealth. After considering many definitions of political economy, Herbert Davenport (Missouri) favored the "science that treats phenomena from the standpoint of price." He asked, How much of economics would be valid for a socialist system? The answer, It is difficult to formulate a theoretical economics of socialism, although all economic systems would have some common features. These authors of course considered capital vital but not so dominant that the whole of economic life should be named for it. Essentially the view was that economics was to be approached scientifically. There were a few laws that could be relied upon—demand, supply, supply and demand, and diminishing returns; from these logical deductions could be drawn about the way the economy worked. It was a matter of observing, hypothesizing, and testing, with the physical sciences as models. Of course, the idea that economics was a science did not rule out modification of its institutions. While socialism had not been adopted anywhere as an economic system, various forms of public participation in economic life were used to address problems. It seems surprising, looking back, that in 1905 Professor Fetter observed, quite complacently, that over the previous twenty-five years and from every direction there was "evidence of the increase of state socialism." He looked upon this as part of a cyclical swing historically, and he clearly did not believe that it portended the coming of systemic socialism.[38]

Although the term "capital" had been in use since the twelfth century, and "capitalist" since the seventeenth, "capitalism" was seldom employed before the twentieth. Sources differ concerning the time when the term capitalism was coined. It may have been late in the eighteenth century, or perhaps was introduced by the French socialist Louis Blanc early in the nineteenth. "Father" Adam Smith did not call his conceptual offspring by that name. While Karl Marx titled his magnum opus Capital, the great prophet of capitalism's doom did not directly attach the label of capitalism to the institutional arrangement he dissected. Yet Marx, by freely using the adjective "capitalistic" and by focusing attention on the central role of the capitalist, was largely responsible for the label's adoption. "Capitalism" became a popular descriptive noun following the publication of Modern Capitalism, a three-volume work by Werner Sombart in Germany in 1902. Sombart was an economic historian hostile to classical economics; he described the evolution of capitalism in a way that shocked professional historians "by its often unsubstantial brilliance" as, according to Schumpeter, he threw aside "all qualms about the limits of professional competence."[39] Thus, it was that the term capitalism came into common usage due in part to a Marxist-leaning socialist who later in life, when an ardent Nazi, was antipathetic to both socialism and capitalism.

During the century that ended with World War I, several movements/ institutions emerged in response to the appalling social conditions and environmental devastation that resulted from industrial growth. These counter forces to industrial capitalism will be treated briefly to identify them and indicate something of the roles they played.

Trade unions came into existence as a means by which workers might, by threatening to withhold their labor, bargain over their pay and conditions of employment. They had much difficulty establishing themselves but gradually gained acceptance and influence. Union organizations of course were composed of the workers at specific places of employment.

Two other developments, socialism and middle-class reform movements, evolved that appealed to a broad section of the population to modify or even try to replace capitalism. They utilized the political process to employ public policy to control the power of employers who were generally free under the prevailing laissez faire philosophy to make unilateral decisions concerning production policies that often had a detrimental effect on the lives of other members of society.

Socialism appeared in the late 1820s and early 1830s to protest the harsh conditions of the working classes and to offer an alternative form of social organization. By the middle of the nineteenth century, Karl Marx claimed to have understood the working of historical forces and asserted that such forces, impersonal and inexorable, would eventually bring capitalism to an end to be succeeded by socialism. His interpretation of future developments proved to be faulty, but there is no doubt that he had enormous influence as a prophet who influenced millions of people with hope of a new life, and that his melding of history and economic theory was intellectually important. During the four decades leading up to 1914, socialist parties in Europe grew and became politically potent.

The earliest government welfare programs were adopted in Imperial Germany under Prince Otto von Bismarck, a staunch opponent of the socialist movement. During the 1880s, Germany instituted a comprehensive welfare system that included accident and sickness insurance, and old-age/disability pensions. What was called state socialism was intended to inoculate the working class against radical socialism and it worked.

The British Labour party was born in 1906, but it was not until after World War I that the socialist movement became firmly rooted in Britain. The first stage of the modern welfare state in Britain was adopted during the decade before the war. The Liberal government of 1906-1914 firmly supported capitalism but sought to temper its harshness and viewed its welfare program as providing an alternative to socialism.

In the U.S., the Socialist party was formed in 1901 under the leadership of Eugene V. Debs. It enjoyed strong early growth, electing numerous state and municipal officials. But by the time the U.S. entered World War I in 1917 it was in disarray largely due to its opposition to the war, but also because the reformist government of Woodrow Wilson instituted legislation that appropriated a number of policies on the socialists' agenda including a child-labor law and a graduated income tax.

Middle class reform movements were another response to the problems of the new industrial age. Public awareness of social ills was raised by literature rich in vivid description by writers such as William Blake, Elizabeth Gaskell, Benjamin Disraeli, Emile Zola, Upton Sinclair, and, especially, Charles Dickens.

In England a variety of charitable organizations provided services including churches, friendly societies (mutual associations that provide benefits to members in times of need), and many others. The national government in the 1870s was brought to introduce reforms regarding such matters as workers' housing, public health, and river pollution. The Fabian Society, formed in 1884, was a major influence on both the political process and on non-governmental organizations. It was a middle- and upper-class organization led by intellectuals who provided thorough research and produced a wealth of publications.

In the later years of the nineteenth century and from 1900-1914, the capitalist system in the U.S. was modified in response to deep dissatisfaction with abuses by financial and industrial power concentrations. Resistance took shape in the movement known as Progressivism, a term that sums up a reformist attitude that looked upon the powerful corporations and corrupt machine politicians as destroyers of economic individualism and civic morality. Its support came primarily from the broad middle class—smaller merchants and manufacturers, lawyers, journalists, college professors, and so forth.

Progressivism resulted in legislation at both the federal and state levels. In 1913 two fundamental reforms were adopted, the Sixteenth Amendment to the Constitution and the Federal Reserve Act. The amendment opened the way to a progressive income tax. The Federal Reserve Act gave the country a central banking system designed to end banking panics and provide an appropriate stock of money for economic stability and growth. The banking community contained many skeptics of the new Federal Reserve System calling it socialistic and unworkable. Most of the Progressive reforms were made at the state level. Government requirements, regulations, and oversight introduced micro-socialist elements into the economic system. Despite these changes, capitalism seemed impregnable.

Notes

1.   Claude Levi-Strauss, "The Principle of Reciprocity," in Lewis A. Coser and Bernard Rosenberg, *Sociological Theory*, 4th edition (New York: Macmillan, 1976), pp. 61-63.
2.   Marvin Harris, *Cannibals and Kings: The Origins of Cultures* (New York: Random House, 1977), pp. 155-159.
3.   Shepard B. Clough, *The Economic Development of Western Civilization* (New York: McGraw-Hill, 1959), p. 31.
4.   *The King James Bible*, "Revelation," Chap. 18.
5.   Joseph A. Schumpeter, *History of Economic Analysis* (New York: Oxford University Press, 1954), p. 55.

6.   George M. Calhoun, *The Ancient Greeks and the Evolution of Standards in Business* (Boston and New York: Houghton Mifflin, 1926), pp. 53, 55, 73, 84.
7.   Helen Jefferson Loane, *Industry and Commerce of the City of Rome* (New York: Arno Press, 1979), pp. 123, 156.
8.   M. I. Finley, *The Ancient Economy* (Berkeley and Los Angeles: University of California Press, 1973), pp. 22, 29, 144, 145, 147.
9.   Robert L. Heilbroner, *The Making of Economic Society* (Englewood Cliffs, N.J.: Prentice-Hall, 1968), pp. 20-24.
10.   Clough, *op. cit.*, p.47.
11.   J. M. Roberts, *The Pelican History of the World*, revised (Harmondsworth, England: Penguin, 1980), p. 492.
12.   Warren C. Scoville and J. Clayburn La Force, "Introduction," The Middle Ages and the Renaissance (Lexington, Mass.: D. C. Heath, 1969), passim; Lynn T. White, Jr., "The Medieval Roots of Modern Technology and Science" in Katherine Fischer Drew and Floyd Seyward Lear (eds.), *Perspectives in Medieval History*, a Rice University Semi-centennial Publication (Chicago: University of Chicago Press, 1963), passim.
13.   E. M. Carus-Wilson, "An Industrial Revolution of the Thirteenth Century," *The Economic History Review*, Vol. XI (1941), passim.
14.   Novak summarized the findings of historians Randall Collins, Jean Gimpel, and David Landes on this topic in *The Wall Street Journal*, December 23, 1999, p. A18.
15.   Eileen E. Power, "English Craft Gilds in the Middle Ages," *History*, New Ser., Vol. IV (1919-20), passim.
16.   Henri Pirenne, "The Place of the Netherlands in the Economic History of Medieval Europe," *The Economic History Review*, Vol II. (1929-30), passim.
17.   Daniel J. Boorstin, *The Discoverers* (New York: Vintage Books, 1985, orig. 1983), p. 16.
18.   Kenneth E. Boulding, *Evolutionary Economics* (Beverly Hills: Sage Publications, 1981), p. 138.
19.   R. H. Tawney, *Religion and the Rise of Capitalism* (New York: Mentor Books, The New American Library, 1947, orig. 1926), pp. 188, 194, 199.
20.   Frank Kermode, "Art Among the Ruins," *The New York Review of Books*, July 5, 2001, p. 63.
21.   Barbara W. Tuchman, *The First Salute* (New York: Alfred A. Knopf, 1988), p. 27.
22.   Alexander Hamilton, in Jacob E. Cooke, ed., *The Federalist*, No. 6 (Middletown, Conn.: Wesleyan University Press, 1961).
23.   Albert O. Hirschman, *The Passions and the Interests* (Princeton: Princeton University Press, 1977), pp. 9, 26, 41, 66, 85, 110-111, 123.
24.   Adam Smith, *An Inquiry Into the Nature and Causes of the Wealth of Nations* (New York: The Modern Library, Random House, 1937), pp. 594-595.
25.   Simon Schama, *Citizens* (New York: Vintage Books, Random House, 1989), pp. 73-74.
26.   Quoted by Sylvia Nasar, *The New York Times*, January 23, 1994, Sec. 4, p. 6.
27.   Jacob Viner, "Adam Smith and Laissez Faire," *The Journal of Political Economy*, Vol. XXXV (April 1927), p. 232.
28.   Smith, *op. cit.*, pp. 14, 128, 423, 595, 625.
29.   William O. Thweatt, "Origins of the Phrase 'Supply & Demand'," Working Paper 82-W14, Department of Economics and Business Administration, Vanderbilt University (Undated).

30. Gordon S. Wood, "Inventing American Capitalism," *The New York Review of Books*, June 9, 1994, pp. 44-49. This article is the principal source of the discussion of the American colonial period that follows.
31. Henry Fielding, *The History of Tom Jones* (London: MacDonald, 1953, orig. 1749), p. 482.
32. Paul Krugman, "Seeking the Rule of the Waves," *Foreign Affairs*, July/August, 1997, p. 139.
33. Peter L. Berger, *The Capitalist Revolution* (New York: Basic Books, 1986), p. 18.
34. Karl Marx and Friedrich Engels, *The Communist Manifesto* (Baltimore: Penguin Books, 1967, orig. 1848), p. 85.
35. G. D. H. Cole, *Introduction to Economic History 1750-1950* (London: Macmillan & Co., 1952), pp. 47, 49.
36. *Ibid.*, p. 57.
37. Roberts, *op. cit.*, p. 730.
38. Alfred Marshall, *Principles of Economics*, eighth edition (London: Macmillan, 1947, orig. 1920), p. 1; Frank A. Fetter, *The Principles of Economics* (New York: Century, 1905), pp. 114, 552, 554; Charles J. Bullock, *The Elements of Economics*, revised (Boston: Silver, Burdett, 1923), p. 4; Irving Fisher, *Elementary Principles of Economics* (New York: Macmillan, 1915), p. 1; Herbert J. Davenport, *The Economics of Enterprise* (New York: Macmillan, 1936, orig. 1913), pp. 25, 31.
39. Schumpeter, *op. cit.*, pp. 816-817.

2

Capitalism Becomes an Endangered Species

Post-World War I to the Early Thirties

Following World War I, capitalism was to a very considerable extent displaced, modified, and for a time, seemed in danger of extinction. In the Soviet Union, Communism replaced the market system almost entirely, and although the fascist countries preserved much of its forms, they deprived capitalism of its substance. In the democratic societies, the intention after World War I was to return to prewar capitalist policies and behavior—except that trade barriers were stronger. Nationalist economic policies were certainly not a new development. From the 1870s to 1914 big power rivalry led to a surge of imperialist policies: colonial expansion accompanied by higher tariffs. The Great War of 1914-1918 further inflamed national passions, and new industries that had emerged, as well as older ones that had expanded to replace the flow of goods cut off by war, demanded protection. Thus, resurgent economic nationalism brought a still higher level of trade barriers.

If economic systems could be said to have personality disorders, an apt description of capitalism's state of being between the two world wars is bi-polar (manic-depressive)—as high spirits and enthusiasm in the 1920s were followed by deep depression, anxiety, and sometimes despair in the 1930s. This characterization is especially true of the U.S. which had become the world's foremost capitalist country.

When it became involved as a belligerent in World War I, the U.S. government was poorly prepared for the burden of mobilization. War required quickly shifting one-fifth of national production to military purposes. To direct this effort, various agencies were created including the War Industries Board, the Food Administration, the Railway War Board, the War Labor Board, and a selective service system to draft military personnel. During the war years when government intervened in the economy to an unprecedented extent, output increased to an unexpectedly high level.

37

This war-induced intervention stimulated thinking about the role of government and, in the early postwar period, resulted in the establishment of new planning agencies. These included the National Defense Act of 1920 for industrial mobilization planning purposes and a 1921 act creating the Bureau of the Budget and the General Accounting Office.

The prevailing mood during the twelve years of conservative Republican administrations from 1921 to 1933 under Presidents Harding, Coolidge, and Hoover was strongly in favor of small government and free market philosophy. In the glow of victory, the country wanted to get on with raising its living standards as it turned its attention (for the most part) inward, away from the messy and costly problems of world affairs. The mood was summed up in President Warren Harding's slogan, "return to normalcy." Instead of the progressivism of the prewar era, the spirit of the immediate postwar years was to reembrace the doctrine of laissez faire. Yet it was also true that a doctrine emerged as a counterpoint to the traditional belief that the private market economy should be left to function without government intervention. We shall return to this component of postwar thinking following some comments on economic performance.

The twenties began with a sharp depression in 1920-1921 from which the economy rebounded quickly. From 1922 to the end of the decade the country enjoyed the unusual combination of vigorous economic growth and stable prices. The Roaring Twenties was a time of such optimism and vitality that for the first time anywhere it seemed possible that high productivity would be able to bring an end to poverty. High wages, low costs, and dynamic growth made the American economy a model that foreigners admired and sought to emulate. It should be noted, however, that there were important exceptions to the general prosperity. Agriculture suffered from a sharp fall in crop prices while farm costs remained high, and the coal mining industry had serious problems. Poverty-stricken segments of the population, notably African-Americans in the South and Appalachian mountaineers, remained poor and largely forgotten.

Henry Ford had introduced his inexpensive Model T automobile in 1908, and in 1913 brought in mass production with the moving assembly line. During the twenties the value of auto production in the Unites States increased substantially. The economic and social ramifications of the passenger automobile associated with this era are profound and continued for decades. Another major industry, road construction, was set on a rapid growth path. The federal government had become involved in this industry beginning in 1916 during the Wilson administration, by providing some financial support to the states for building highways and by requiring the establishment of state highway departments. By the end of the twenties, expenditures for highways reached $1 billion a year, financed mainly at the state level. Many other major industries were linked with automobiles: rubber, petroleum, a variety of services for the maintenance and repair of vehicles, and eating and sleeping accommodations for travelers. A vast boom occurred in construction of all types: commercial, industrial, governmental, and residential, including the development of suburbs now accessible to the expanding middle class.

For most of the nation, economic progress was clearly impressive. Electrical power capacity doubled from 1920 to 1930, and the industry's value of plant and equipment increased from $3.2 billion to $7 billion over those years. Great central stations were built, and transmission lines extended electric service to the suburbs and rural areas. Economies of scale were achieved as new technology, improved management, and creative but risky financing reduced the price of power, which in turn resulted in greater use of electricity in production and household consumption. Among the "liberating" aspects of the 1920s were home appliances, notably refrigerators, washing machines, and radios.

During the 1920s, "consumerism" developed rapidly spurred by advertising that was much more creative and heavily financed than before the war and was now linked to buying on credit. The new and popular motion pictures of the day often featured stars who lived lavish lives replete with luxury items that served as models for viewers to emulate and to some extent achieve. Consumer installment debt took off in 1923 and rose rapidly for the next six years. An innovative advertising executive named Bruce Barton saw the great potential for sales and profits stemming from this combination of factors and injected a moral element into the mix. He wrote the best seller of 1924, *The Man Nobody Knows*, extolling Jesus as the founder of business. It was God's will, according to Barton, that we enjoy ourselves; he even claimed that selling goods was an activity similar to prayer.[1]

A quite different interpretation of the "new capitalism" of the twenties has been given by the sociologist Daniel Bell. Bell observed a "disjunction" between the old Protestant ethic of work and saving on one hand and, on the other, encouragement to lavish expenditure on consumption. In early capitalism, work was a calling involving a personal obligation and responsibility to community; but the introduction of the installment plan and easy credit caused capitalism to undercut itself by reducing the need to save. By promoting instant gratification, capitalism's "transcendental ethic" was lost. "American capitalism changed its nature in the 1920s by heavily encouraging the consumer to go into debt, and to live with debt as a way of life."[2]

A classic capitalist malady, the speculative bubble, appeared in two versions in the twenties. Real estate in Florida was a glitteringly attractive investment opportunity given the combination of a climate that made it the Riviera of America, rising incomes, and improved transportation. Its value was parlayed to fantasy-world levels by speculators eager for quick profits and by promotional hype—only to collapse completely by 1928. The widespread mood of great expectations of easy riches was undeterred by the example of Florida, for the much greater stock market boom which was under way by 1925 roared on until its climax and crash in October of 1929. Some of the most respected and influential leaders of the world of business and finance, who supposedly understood what was happening, radiated optimism. Professor Irving Fisher of Yale combined a reputation as the most prestigious American economist of the time, notably in the areas of money and index numbers, with success in business and investment. Yet, in the very month that the stock market crashed, Fisher reassuringly stated that stock prices appeared to have reached a permanently high plateau. The previous June, Bernard Baruch, a financier of towering reputation who advised every president from Wilson to Eisenhower, foresaw a great forward movement of world economic conditions. Millions of ordinary people, many of modest means, joined in the stock market frenzy as "hot tips" on stocks were eagerly sought, and the example of success by many in the market made ever more people anxious not to be left out. Within each stratum of the middle and working classes, many were captivated by the prospect of advancing a notch or two on the social/economic ladder via rising stock prices. Even to those at the foot of life's totem pole, hope for quick riches was raised by prominent men thought to be gifted with financial genius. One such elite Wall Streeter was John J. Raskob, whose credentials included both a General Motors directorship and the chairmanship of the Democratic National Committee. His empathy with ordinary folks took practical form in an article titled "Everybody Ought to be Rich" in the *Ladies' Home Journal*. By investing fifteen dollars in common stocks monthly, a small but thrifty man could expect to accumulate eighty thousand dollars after twenty years. But Raskob proposed a much faster method of acquiring riches, an investment trust to collect the many small contributions of the masses. These would be used to buy stocks of a much larger amount by means of leverage, that is, by borrowing on margin using the stocks as collateral. Buying stock on margin had become common and its effects were marvelous to behold. The magic of margin is seen by the example of someone, say a salesman earning $75 per week, buying 100 shares of RCA at 32 in 1926 on a 10 percent margin, so that he could acquire shares valued at $3,200 for $320 plus commission, borrowing the rest of the purchase price from his broker. The shares could have been sold in 1928 for $42,000, giving our speculator a profit, after repaying his loan, of over $38,000.[3] Stock market players had to pay interest of 8 percent or more to finance their loans, whereas yields on stocks were no more than 1 or 2 percent, but the prospect of a large capital gain overcame this disadvantage. It is not surprising that celebrated major speculators were viewed by small investors as worthy to be emulated, "and that investment bankers and market raiders became folk heroes before the crash."[4]

The charm of buying stock on margin turned to fear when the price of the stock fell, reducing the value of the collateral, and when the price dropped to the level of the loan the broker would demand more "margin." When the crash came, calls for more margin rose rapidly. Stockholders sold some stock to try to save others, and brokers sold stock held as collateral when more margin was not forthcoming. An avalanche of selling was set in motion causing stock prices to plummet. In the aftermath of the stock market debacle, the Securities Exchange Act of 1934 gave the Federal Reserve Board of Governors the authority to set margin requirements on stock purchases. This power has been available ever since and is an exception to the tradition of avoiding interference with the pricing process. In his vivid tale of the crash, John Kenneth Galbraith considers the mood of the times rather than the easy availability of credit to account for the speculative orgy of the late twenties. Individuals by the hundreds of thousands made free choices, impelled to the slaughter "by the seminal lunacy which has always seized people who are seized in turn with the notion that they can become very rich."[5]

Holding companies were used to control the electric power companies basic to industrial expansion, the largest combination being that of Chicago-based Samuel Insull whose plants provided power in thirty-two states. A financial pyramid was built with one holding company owning a controlling interest in a larger company, which in turn controlled another, until a highly complex organization resulted. Ownership of one-fifth of a $5 million company was typically sufficient to control that company which in turn owned one-fifth of a $25 million company. By extending this process, a small ownership at the base of the financial structure could control billions of dollars of corporate assets. The income of the holding companies depended on the dividends received by them from ownership of the operating companies that produced electric power. Insull's utility company pyramid was thought to be too complex to be understood even by its creator; sixty-five chairmanships and eighty-five directorships were concentrated in his hands! Such pyramids were highly profitable during the boom, but the earnings of the operating companies faltered when the economy slumped and the structures collapsed. The bonds of the holding companies could not be paid and bankruptcy resulted. Operating plant investment was reduced to try to maintain dividends, thus adding to the general depression of the economy.

A slightly modified version of the free market philosophy was developed in the 1920s that took a more positive attitude toward the role of government than orthodoxy required. In his insightful study *From New Era to New Deal*, William J. Barber identifies it as the second main component of the Zeitgeist of post-World War I America—a doctrine that resulted from the outstanding record of production achieved under the pressure of strong wartime aggregate demand for goods and services when the leaders of the private sector acted in collaboration with government. This viewpoint took the position that the U.S. should pursue "a fresh and uniquely American course toward human betterment." Although not formalized into an economic theory, there developed an implicit view that a "new era" had arrived. Instead of belief in immutable economic laws, this outlook sought to improve economic performance by adopting policies to influence the economy. It was grounded firmly in empiricism, rejecting the deductive theory of perfect competition that came from the intellectual tradition of Europe in favor of an approach built squarely on facts. The man looked upon preeminently as the leader of the new approach was Herbert Clark Hoover, whose reputation as a humanitarian and administrator had been forged by directing relief supplies to Europe and heading the War Food Administration during the Wilson administration. In 1920 Hoover was considered prominently as a presidential candidate by Democrats as well as Republicans. In the light of what was to come in the early thirties, it is interesting that Franklin D. Roosevelt, while Assistant Secretary of the Navy in the Wilson administration, considered no one better qualified for the presidency than Hoover. But Hoover chose not to run in 1920 and instead served as Secretary of Commerce during the Harding and Coolidge presidencies.

Secretary Hoover expanded the role of government as a provider of statistical data to help markets perform more effectively. Better economic intelligence would contribute to stability as firms used it to avoid excessive speculation, expansion, and inventory accumulation. Under his direction, the Department of Commerce established a Division of Simplified Practice that worked with industry groups to reduce waste. This involved technical details such as the standardization of electrical fittings and couplings of fire hoses and ascertaining what radio frequencies would be optimal—steps that contributed unspectacularly to the dynamism of the economy. By reducing the number of standard tire sizes to sixteen from twenty-four, substantial savings were achieved in the burgeoning tire industry. There were objections to standardizations by firms reluctant to give up advantages of product differentiation, but Hoover was willing to use the power of government purchasing to gain compliance.

To bring the business cycle under control, Hoover advocated a policy of countercyclical capital spending. In response to the steep economic contraction in 1921, a President's Conference on Unemployment convened under his chairmanship explicitly called for the federal government to influence the timing of public works expenditures. Although the federal government had little direct power in this area, for it accounted for only one-tenth of public sector construction spending, it might be able to guide the state and local governments in timing their projects. Furthermore, the conference report found it desirable for the national government to assume an educational role vis-à-vis the private sector by teaching the leaders of American businesses how they could contribute to a sounder national economy by countercyclical capital spending. The report even provided a calculation of the amount of financial reserves to be retained during prosperous times to be released during economic downturns, not only to abolish acute unemployment but also to nearly eliminate fluctuations in employment. The business and labor leaders who comprised the President's Conference on Unemployment, and who were aided by an advisory committee appointed by Secretary Hoover, called for what became known after World War II as indicative planning. The federal government would not force the private sector or the state and local governments to follow any edicts but, like a choirmaster, would lead them to act in harmony for the greater good. The report was in fact followed by a great expansion of bond issues for public works, and in 1923 when the pace of economic activity seemed too rapid, Hoover urged an easing of public works expenditures. As the twenties proceeded, support for the concept of a compensatory fiscal policy grew. Another facet of the new thinking was that rising wages were needed to absorb the increased output resulting from increasing productivity. Higher wages were advocated also to encourage efficiency and to reduce class distinctions. In addition, Secretary Hoover favored a shorter workday, most notably in the notorious case of the steel industry where the twelve-hour day prevailed. When the steel magnates refused to budge on acceptance of the eight-hour day, he forced their hand by rallying public opinion to the cause.

Barber encapsulated the spirit of the distinctive new approach: "The champions of a new economics in the 1920s were in accord about their aspirations to build a new Jerusalem in America and in their willingness to invoke powers of government in this task."[6] To view the ideas of Herbert Hoover as parallel to those of John Maynard Keynes in England seems surprising, but in the 1920s they were actually very similar. In "The End of Laissez-faire," Keynes's essay published in 1926, he advocated a reformation of capitalism by increasing the role of government on the grounds that the profit motive was no guarantee of social well-being. There was a need to guide private interest; while the state should not assume control of the economy, semiautonomous entities could provide "directive intelligence" to business decision making. An abundance of economic data would be needed to illuminate the economic environment and so provide the basis for more intelligent management of economic resources. Keynes also called for the creation of an institution capable of supplying "intelligent judgment" to the determination of the amount of national savings and investment, and the distribution of that investment among alternative types of production both foreign and domestic. In the U.S. the supporters of Hoover's new vision called for the federal government "to perform as a catalyst, as a coordinator, and as a stabilizer of economic activity."[7]

One of Hoover's early actions after assuming the presidency in 1929 was to urge Congress to create the Federal Farm Board. This federally funded agency was authorized to make loans to privately organized and controlled agricultural cooperatives totaling as much as $500 million. The intention was to enable the nation's farmers, through marketing cooperatives, to stockpile commodities in times of surplus production thereby stabilizing prices and incomes. Government was thus sent to the rescue of the beleaguered agricultural sector in which the many individual farmers had, for a decade, been unable to overcome their problem of low income. The government undertook to help farmers to help themselves, not only by loans, but also by providing technical advice.

As the economy began to slide into the Great Depression in 1929, Hoover employed the ideas he had espoused earlier as Secretary of Commerce. He urged accelerated spending on construction projects by all levels of government and by private enterprise, and he expressed confidence in the usefulness of information as a source of stability. From a later perspective, there is a naive, melancholy quality to the following quotation from the *Survey of Current Business* published by the Department of Commerce in December 1929. "While it may be too early to say that the utilization of business data has entirely eliminated the business cycle, there is agreement today among business leaders everywhere that the wider use of facts will mitigate in a large degree many of the disastrous effects of the one-time recurrent business cycle."[8] The president also strongly urged business leaders not to cut wages, and for a brief period his advice seems to have been largely followed. In the early thirties the banking system came under great stress with many bank failures. To meet the mounting financial emergency the Reconstruction Finance Corporation was created at Hoover's request in January 1931 to funnel federal money to the financial sector and to railroads in the form of loans. As time passed it became increasingly clear that the various efforts to hold back the forces of contraction were inadequate.

Later judgments of President Hoover's policies have been harsh. A poll of historians taken by Professor Arthur M. Schlesinger, Jr. in 1996 placed Hoover among seven American presidents considered to be failures. Yet it is not true "that he had presided over the greatest depression in the nation's history and had done nothing."[9] From 1922 to 1929 the economy had performed generally very well. The policy-makers of the time had reason to think that they understood how to achieve growth and stability using government in an enlightened although modest way. But when their policies were applied in the early thirties they failed; the bright hopes for what seemed to be a new era of progress were suddenly dashed.

By the autumn of 1931 the policy of the government changed to an emphasis on raising bond prices in order to save the financial system from collapse. But because this new effort would be undercut if the treasury's debt were increased, Hoover recommended higher taxes and spending cuts to achieve a balanced budget. The need to stimulate demand for economic recovery was recognized, yet a tight fiscal program was thought to be essential. Furthermore the president shared the still widespread belief that free convertibility of dollars into gold at the existing exchange rate by the government was a commitment that must be honored, and so ruled out any policy that would cast doubt on the treasury's ability in that regard. Thus, while Hoover understood that economic recovery required increased aggregate demand, he was trapped by the inherited orthodoxy that permeated the intellectual, business, and political life of the nation. Belief in a balanced budget, in the gold standard, and in a limited role for government was broadly and strongly held, and therefore inhibited the adoption of an expansionary policy despite the growing national crisis. Hoover had acted to modify traditional ideology within limits, but he was unable or unwilling to challenge orthodox thinking and to win over a critical mass of converts for a fundamental policy change.

A picture of the American work force in the 1920s shows great contrast of light and dark, of progress and of severe difficulty in a capitalist system with few restraints on the power of employers to set the terms and conditions of employment. The working population experienced a rising standard of living that included an expanded variety of goods and services, and was particularly impressive to the large number of recent immigrants and the children of immigrants. The "muckraker" author, lecturer, and reformer Lincoln Steffens observed at the end of the decade that the socialist goal of food, clothing, and shelter for all was being provided by American big business. Other favorable developments were the sharp decline in the employment of children and a rise in high school enrollment. The rapid mechanization of industry that made possible a dramatic increase in productivity made for monotonous semiskilled jobs, but also permitted a shift from manual to non-manual, or blue- to white-collar employment. Yet, for a decade of prosperity, the twenties had surprisingly high unemployment. The unemployment rate between 1924 and 1929 is estimated to have averaged about 12 percent, largely due to technological change. In 1928 the National Federation of Settlements "found that unemployment was the prime enemy of the American family."[10]

Business leaders who favored a high wage policy as part of a reformed American economic system were well aware that it could be used to diminish workers' interest in trade union membership. For various reasons, union membership was repressed—falling from 5 million in 1920 to about 3.6 million in 1923, and then to 3.4 million in 1929. By then only about 10 percent of nonagricultural employees were unionized. Some previously strong unions, such as the United Mine Workers and the International Ladies Garment Workers Union, were casualties. A major reason for the weakness of the union movement was the fierce opposition of the leaders of industry. The years immediately following World War I were a time of social unrest marked by a series of strikes within the United States and an increase in radicalism in various countries following the devastation of war and the example of the Russian Revolution. American industry responded by devising an anti-union strategy composed of a collection of weapons packaged as patriotic under the label of the "American Plan." Officials of the National Association of Manufacturers described the open shop as the essence of Americanism. Union members were discriminated against and fired. Employers' associations provided a blacklist of workers; known union members were not hired. Court injunctions were obtained to break strikes. Unions were deterred, weakened, and broken by industrial espionage as spies were engaged by corporations directly or more commonly by detective agencies or employers' associations. There were company towns in which the workers, insulated from outside contacts, lived in a sort of industrial peonage dependent on the company for housing and utilities and were kept under surveillance by company police. One of the most significant developments of the era in labor-management relations was the establishment of company unions or employee-representation plans. Fear of independent unions was the main, but not the exclusive, motive for these plans; they were sometimes used in ways that were of considerable benefit to employees. Company unionism was the key element in the broader concept of welfare capitalism, for it promised a shift away from autocratic to constitutional government in the workplace. Practices used in collective bargaining such as negotiation, arbitration, shop chairman, and grievance procedure were "borrowed" from the union movement including even the watchword "industrial democracy." Employees were given "citizenship" in shop governance instead of being treated as a commodity without any rights deserving of respect by management. Members of company unions experienced benefits, particularly in health and safety matters. But as the tame creations of management to fend off independent unions, the company unions lacked bargaining power. Unarmed (for they were not empowered to strike), lacking financial resources, and unable to coordinate their tactics with other labor groups they could not exert meaningful pressure to get concessions from management. Management was paternalistic and open to some persuasion by the company unions when it chose to be, but bargaining by the unions on wages and hours was ineffective and the grievance procedures were weak. Company unions did serve as a "bridge" to genuine collective bargaining later on, for they acted to acquaint workers and managers with the concept of industrial democracy.

Another feature of welfare capitalism in the twenties was the adoption of personnel management as a professional managerial function. Personnel departments were created to deal with the recruitment, testing, training, promotion and demotion, discipline, and discharge of workers. They also were responsible for matters of employee health in the immediate areas of sanitation and safety, and for providing benefits to meet problems of illness, accidents, old age, and death, as well as a humane work environment with rest periods, recreation programs, and vacations. Personnel management brought a distinct improvement by replacing the haphazard and often corrupt hiring practices of foremen.

When the country came to experience the pain and suffering of depression in the thirties followed by war in the forties, the relatively prosperous and peacetime twenties took on an aura of bliss and contentment for many. But this view tends to ignore significant divisions, conflicts, and hardships that accompanied the general progress. The ambivalent attitude of the employer toward the employee in the U.S. was captured nicely by Irving Bernstein. "He was not sure whether to crush organized labor under the American Plan or to woo the worker with welfare capitalism. He did not know whether it was better to seek discord or concord. More than anything else, he preferred not to think about the worker at all. The outward calm characteristic of the era—the apparent peace and prosperity—encouraged him to ignore the large and critical labor problems that bubbled beneath the surface."[11]

While the 1920s were lean years for the union movement, they were devastating for the Socialist party. The socialists had taken a bold stand against American participation in the war on the grounds that it was a struggle between two sets of imperialistic powers. In doing so, they stood against the rising tide of nationalism in an attempt to lessen the terrible loss of life and human suffering; the price they paid was to be branded by the government and the public as unpatriotic and disloyal. In 1919 a great wave of strikes occurred in an attempt to obtain union recognition and improved working conditions. The most impressive was in the steel industry where the conditions were described as "inhuman" by prominent church leaders. Labor unrest took place in the context of anti-Red hysteria resulting from the Russian Revolution. Attorney General A. Mitchell Palmer conducted a "Red hunt" in January 1920 based on his view that a revolution was spreading through American life like a prairie fire. Over 6,000 persons were arrested and their property confiscated. Friends who visited them in jail were themselves put behind bars for showing sympathy for revolutionaries. Socialists who had been legally elected to Congress and to the legislature of New York State were barred from office. Paradoxically, many traditional socialists who were as fully anti-Communist as the leaders of industry and government were attacked. In calmer times "the Palmer raids" were recognized as farcical, but they were taken seriously in 1920. Repression was extended to many people in education, journalism, and the arts for allegedly fostering "subversive" ideas. The mood is illustrated by the condemnation of women's colleges by Vice-President Thomas R. Marshall during the Wilson administration for the reason that debaters at Radcliffe argued in favor of the proposition "that the recognition of labor unions by employers is essential to successful bargaining." Incidentally, the same Mr. Marshall gave us the memorable comment: "What this country needs is a good five-cent cigar." Many new recruits to the Socialist party at this time were foreign-born and foreign-speaking people who had become enthusiastic about the revolution in Russia, but who knew little about life in America and had little respect for leading American socialists. They provided activists whose eagerness to form a Communist party split the Socialist party. Irving Howe summed up the situation: "What now remained of the socialist movement was a pitiful remnant. Not only had a large minority of the party quit to begin the Katzenjammer intrigues of the communist factions, but thousands of the faithful dropped out in weariness and disgust."[12] The Socialist party in the U.S. had become moribund with only small islands of vitality in New York and Wisconsin.

The United Kingdom, the center of the prewar gold standard, decided that a return to the gold standard after the war was imperative; this was a decision that required a deflationary policy. The pound was made convertible into gold in 1925 at its prewar parity, thereby necessitating continuous deflationary pressure until the country was forced to abandon gold in 1931 during the international financial crisis of that year. Britain endured chronic high unemployment during the twenties causing labor unrest that reached a peak in the General Strike of 1926. The sluggish performance of the British economy hastened the growth of the Labour Party. Labour, in 1918, was still far from being a major political party, but by 1929 it had pushed aside the Liberals, the great nineteenth-century party of individualism and free enterprise. The first Labour government in British political history was formed in 1923 in coalition with the Liberals, but was in office for only one year and could not carry out a socialist program because of its dependence on Liberal support. In the 1929 election, Labour secured 288 seats to 260 for the conservatives and 59 for the Liberals; Labour, with Liberal support, formed a government. In its campaign the Labour Party promised to deal with unemployment through a moderate social reform program, primarily by house building, slum clearance, roads, and other public works. In office, this second Labour government met with disaster as the downward spiral of employment, output, and trade that followed the American stock market crash overwhelmed the socialist government in Britain just as it did the Hoover administration in the U.S.

In mid-1931, in response to a political crisis brought on by the worsening of the Great Depression, the leader of the Labour government, Ramsay MacDonald, abandoned that government, but he continued as prime minister until 1935 in a national coalition government of Conservative, Liberal, and Labour members. Most of the Labour members of Parliament disapproved of this move, and new leaders of the party were chosen. In the October 1931 election, Labour received a mere 51 seats, temporarily removing it as a political force; the conservatives held an overwhelming majority in the government.

Defeated in World War I, Germany had an extremely difficult time in the postwar period. The Weimar Republic, established in 1919, lasted fourteen years until 1933 when Adolf Hitler established the National Socialist (Nazi) dictatorship. In 1923 the monetary system broke down, hyperinflation wiped out the middle class, and there were outbreaks of disorder all over the country. A newspaper that cost 35,000 marks one day cost 60,000 the next. Decisive steps were taken to stabilize the currency on November 15, 1923, but the painful disruption to the payments system and to social cohesion left a bitter memory of the evils of inflation that has remained in the German psyche. The period from 1923 to 1929 saw the Weimar Republic prosper economically and politically as reparations burdens were eased and world economic conditions became more prosperous. With better economic conditions came a more benign political atmosphere so that the new democracy gave the appearance of being secure. But the years 1930-1933 brought economic and political crisis as the world economy plunged into deep depression. Germany was heavily dependent on American investment; when numerous short-term loans were called in, major bank failures followed. German exports fell sharply and unemployment shot up to over 6 million early in 1932. The young German republic was unable to sustain a democratic regime under these circumstances.

The socialists were numerically strong in the Reichstag, but sounded an uncertain trumpet under unimaginative trade unionist leadership. They were reformers, staunchly anti-Communist, but still spoke in the worn phrases of revolutionary Marxism. The American socialist scholar Michael Harrington later lamented that socialists did not know what to do when capitalism began collapsing in 1929; in Germany this failure permitted the emergence of the monstrous regime of Nazism. Sociologist Daniel Bell observed that "when socialists were in office during the Depression in Germany . . . (including the redoubtable Austro-German socialist economist Rudolf Hilferding, the author of the socialist classic *Das Finanzkapital*) . . . no steps to manage the crisis (other than the classic capitalist response of deflation, which deepened the crisis) . . ." were taken. In 1932, just prior to Hitler's rise to power, Hilferding responded to demands for relief from unemployment by saying that it is the anarchy of the capitalist system that causes depressions and they will either come to an end or the system will collapse. Such politics, observed Harrington, "reduced a mass workers' movement to impotence." No solution was offered to deal with the unemployment problem or for some ultimate socialism to come, so that socialism "remained, after more than a century, a concept rather than a program." Calvin Hoover, a Duke University economist who went to Germany in 1932 to study the fascist movement, relates what he learned by interviewing both Hilferding, who had been a finance minister, and Breitscheidt, the leader of the Social Democratic bloc in the Reichstag.

> They still clung to a formal Marxism which was without any reality. Breitscheidt stated quite calmly that the Social Democrats had had no intention of taking over the government at a time when capitalism was in a state of collapse . . . It is no wonder that the Social Democrats had little electoral appeal at a time of deep economic depression when the great majority of the German people were demanding drastic action "to prevent starvation in the midst of plenty."[13]

Deep Depression, World War II, and Recovery

The collapse of the world economy seriously threatened the survival of the capitalist system. The Western democracies, struggling against the powerful and unexpected vortex of falling production, trade, employment, and prices turned desperately to nationalistic policies. Marx had predicted that capitalism would inevitably end in a convulsive depression. Now Marxists were sure that its end was at hand, and many non-Marxists recognized that the system was seriously endangered.

A striking feature of the Great Depression is the remarkable speed of the fall from grace in 1929, to disgrace in 1933. Just where the downturn started is debatable, but clearly the U.S. was among the first casualties. The American investment boom of the twenties reached the saturation point at the end of the decade; U.S. industrial activity turned down in July 1929, and the stock market crashed in October. Over the next four years, 1930-1933, the failure of more than 9,000 banks had a demoralizing effect on economic life. The large size and strength of the American economy had supported much of the postwar world economy via trade and investment. The sudden withdrawal of this support was felt virtually everywhere apart from the self-isolated Soviet Union. Total dollars pumped abroad by American spending and investing fell by two-thirds from the 1927-1929 level to that of 1932-1933 as U.S. imports closely followed declining industrial production, payments for services were nearly halved, and long-term capital lending was actually reversed as funds were repatriated. By 1933 the unemployment rate in the U.S. was 25 percent. There were some 13 million unemployed in the U.S.; worldwide unemployment is estimated to have been 30 million or more.

The depression further reduced the already weak American labor movement; total union membership fell below 3 million in 1933. Unions were concentrated in a few fields: the building trades, mining, and several skilled crafts. Companies used a powerful instrument, the "yellow-dog contract," to deter workers from joining unions by requiring them as a condition of employment to sign a contract stating that they would not do so. Employers were able to obtain court injunctions to enforce such contracts to protect company unions from competing with independent unions and to limit union activities in other ways, especially during strikes. Legal relief was obtained by unions under the Norris-LaGuardia Anti-Injunction Act of 1932 making yellow-dog contracts unenforceable in the courts and by placing limits on the use of injunctions to block certain other actions by unions. But the unions were emasculated by the depression. Few strikes were called in the early thirties. Those that were called were often acts of desperation in resisting wage reductions.

Until this time a hallmark of the American Federation of Labor (AFL), going back to its founding in the 1880s under the leadership of Samuel

Gompers, was voluntarism. This was a policy of self-reliance, of not depending on the government. A heated debate that took place within the Executive Council of the AFL over the principle of voluntarism ended on November 10, 1932 when the federation rejected the old doctrine by endorsing unemployment insurance. "Voluntarism was eclipsed by a new mood—militancy."[14]

From 1933 until the outbreak of World War II in 1939, the shock of the Great Depression resulted in countries generally pursuing economic policies to protect and defend their separate interests at the expense of adherence to the rules of behavior required for relatively free trade based on specialization and stable currencies. The gold standard was abandoned, currencies were depreciated to stimulate exports and restrain imports, and quantitative controls were adopted. By insulating themselves against outside forces, countries were better able to adopt expansionary measures internally.

The conflict between domestic and international economic policies was obvious in the U.S. when President Franklin Roosevelt assumed office in March 1933. Almost immediately he took the nation off the gold standard, after which the dollar was deliberately depreciated as this country joined the overall pattern of competitive exchange depreciation. The New Deal's definitive gold policy was embodied in the Gold Reserve Act of 1934, a watered-down version of the gold standard. All gold within the country was nationalized, domestically held currency could no longer be redeemed in gold on demand, and gold would no longer be coined for domestic use. Domestically held gold could be held or dealt in only for "legitimate" commercial, industrial, artistic, and scientific purposes. The U.S. dollar was still defined in terms of gold however, and dollars were convertible into gold for international purposes. Instead of a full gold-coin standard, the country was now on a limited or international gold-bullion standard.

The U.S. made its final break with the gold standard almost forty years later, in 1971. The actions taken in 1933 and 1934 were major steps, for the U.S. had in effect pledged allegiance to the gold standard by law in 1900 and had been wholeheartedly, even passionately, faithful to that commitment. Adherence to the gold standard was high on the agenda of leaders in the financial world and was a pillar of orthodox economic theory. But, however "sacred," the gold link was now broken to open the way for a policy of economic expansion.

By 1933 it was clear that the traditional, mainly laissez faire, American approach to the social and economic crisis was utterly inadequate. Acting pragmatically, Roosevelt undertook a range of programs intended to have an immediate impact on the economy. He brought a "brain trust" of intellectuals into his New Deal administration to design innovative measures by which the federal government entered the economic life of the nation on a scale greater than ever before. The New Deal comprised some twenty or more major legislative acts plus a plethora of administrative agencies to carry out their provisions. Taken collectively, these measures nudged the country in the direction of a planned economy. But rather than comprehensive plan, they were a patchwork of financial assistance, public projects, regulations, and supervision. A list of major features of this burst of interventionist activity follows.

- Agricultural legislation supported farm incomes by establishing "parity prices" and quotas for agricultural commodities. Surplus commodities were purchased by government. Loans were made to farmers to end foreclosures.
- Financial reforms included the insurance of bank deposits, federal supervision of the securities industry and commodity exchanges, and the separation of investment from commercial banking. The Federal Deposit Insurance Corporation (FDIC) was established in 1934 to end the curse of bank failures that averaged about six hundred per year during the 1920s and over two thousand annually from 1930 through 1933. Companion legislation covered savings and loan associations and federally chartered credit unions. Almost all depositors became fully insured up to a stated amount that was later raised during inflationary periods. This insurance program is generally considered very valuable, perhaps indispensable. The Banking Act of 1933 (Glass-Steagall Act) divorced commercial banking from investment banking. Investment banking consists of issuing, underwriting, and selling new corporate stocks and bonds. This separation of functions was considered necessary to prevent banks from placing new offerings of securities into trust funds under their management when unable to sell them to others. The Securities and Exchange Act of 1934 gave birth to the Securities and Exchange Commission (SEC). This agency is responsible for the oversight of securities markets to make trading fair and to avoid fraud. Its regulations are designed to require that information relevant to the pricing of securities be disclosed to market participants.
- The money stock increased rapidly from 1933 to 1937 following changes in the structure of the Federal Reserve System and in the monetary laws.
- A compensatory fiscal policy of quite modest size was adopted after the recovering economy suffered a recessionary relapse in 1937.
- River-basin regions were developed involving the construction of great multiple-purpose dams.

- Public utilities were put under regulation as to rates and business practices, and the use of holding companies was restricted.
- Employment was provided by the Civilian Conservation Corps which involved projects such as reforestation and flood control. A Public Works Administration and a Works Projects Administration were used to carry out construction projects, and also to provide work for people in education and the arts.
- Workers were guaranteed the "right to organize and bargain collectively through representatives of their own choosing." Maximum working hours and minimum wages were set by law.
- Systems of old-age pensions and survivors' insurance (social security) and unemployment insurance were created, and a provision was made for needy dependent children and for crippled children and blind persons.
- An early New Deal measure, the National Industrial Recovery Act, sought to sanction the self-regulation of industry, allowing corporations to agree to codes of conduct that would limit what was considered to be "cutthroat" competition. It was soon seen as so restrictive of competition as to breach anti-trust laws, and the Supreme Court ruled it unconstitutional in 1935.

For many Americans Franklin Roosevelt was the personification of the state as citizens' protector. He expanded the role of the president vis-à-vis Congress, and he greatly influenced Congress. There can be no doubt that a substantial infusion of socialism occurred in the American socioeconomic system as a result of the New Deal. Not that Roosevelt was at all attracted to socialist ideology. His purpose was to save the capitalist system, and he may well have been its savior. The right wing of American business rejected Roosevelt's economic intervention, came to detest him with a visceral hatred, and charged him with betraying his class. His most vociferous critic was Robert R. McCormick, editor and publisher of the influential mass-circulation newspaper, *The Chicago Tribune*. McCormick considered the New Deal to be an abomination, and his editorials accused Roosevelt of being a Communist. American socialist leaders also scorned Roosevelt's policies, for his numerous reforms directed at specific problems were not at all what their ideology called for, namely, community ownership and control of capital and land. The fundamental nature of capitalism was kept intact; private ownership of the means of production and the legitimacy of profits were not questioned. Indeed, the piecemeal reforms had a leavening effect on capitalism by providing greater personal security, and by purging the system of some of its exploitative aspects, thereby shoring up public support for it. Biographer James MacGregor Burns captured the situation in the following quotation.

> Roosevelt, like major party leaders before him, had no compunction about plucking popular planks from the Socialist party platform--planks such as unemployment compensation and public housing. But he spurned the central concept of socialization. Even more, his aversion had been tested in the crucible; in 1933 he probably could have won congressional assent to the socialization of both banking and railroads, but he never tried. He wanted to reform capitalism, not destroy it. And in this sense he was a conservative. It was precisely because the Socialists had a coherent economic and social doctrine rooted in a systematic philosophy that they recognized Roosevelt's true conservatism.[15]

With capitalism faltering so badly, the time seemed propitious for socialism to come into greater prominence and perhaps supersede capitalism. But the moment was not, and probably could not have been, seized. The socialists were largely unable—if one may so put it—to capitalize on what might conceivably have been the death throes of the old order.

For a short time in the early thirties American socialism appeared to be gaining traction as a political movement, but the party soon slipped into virtual irrelevance. Norman Thomas, the Socialist party presidential candidate in 1932, was an inspirational and appealing leader, but many who heard and approved of his message considered it necessary to vote for Roosevelt to ensure that Hoover be defeated. The prospect of Roosevelt now was more appealing than the possibility of socialism in the future. The political scene in Europe and in America was in flux, and in trying to understand it and devise a viable strategy, the Socialist party in the U.S. fell into self-destructive internal disputes. Veterans of the party, tired from many years of effort without success, had lost much of their zeal and opted for moderation. A younger militant faction disdained caution in the hope of achieving a new socialist world without further delay. By the early thirties the older American socialist leaders realized that the Soviet Union was not bringing a bright new era but was an oppressive state. The left wing of the party was for a time favorably impressed by Soviet economic planning, although critical of its suppression of civil liberties. But according to Irving Howe, who was himself a participant, within a few years even the party's left wing lost its innocence concerning Stalinism and realized that when the economy of a country is state-owned the economic and political systems cannot be separated. The socialists were unable to resolve their internal disputes over whether to work to reform the system or to replace it. Lacking a coherent vision of their own, they did not appreciate the great appeal to American workers of the reforms being made by Roosevelt's New Deal. By the latter 1930s the Socialist party had disintegrated, partly from its internal weaknesses but also from the awful example of the Soviet Union which claimed to be socialism on the road to Communism. The inability or refusal of many people to distinguish between democratic socialism and the regime under Stalin effectively tarred the former with the latter's brush. In the U.S. the terrible force and horror of Stalinism that became evident in the thirties "led to a perhaps fatal besmirching of the socialist idea" which "itself came to be in a state of deep crisis."[16] This point is not limited to the U.S. It helps account for the failure of the socialist movement to have had a more favorable reception in world polity over the long run.

Communism defiled and despoiled the radical heritage. If today we face a world in which there is no grand narrative of social progress, no politically plausible project of social justice, it is in large measure because Lenin and his heirs poisoned the well.[17]

Unionism in the U.S. experienced a boom between 1933 and 1945 when World War II ended. A modern American labor movement had grown up and become established between 1880 and 1920, but then languished until the political tide changed in the national elections of 1932. By then the depressed economic conditions had already begun to create a more accepting attitude by the public and the courts toward unions. Still, the labor movement's imminent rebirth was unexpected. The reduced importance of trade unionism in America after World War I was considered a fundamental change in the organization of the economy. According to an eminent economist of the day, "Little reason appears to exist for the expectation that a weak labor movement will be replaced soon by one which is strong."[18] The movement's rapid expansion during the New Deal period and the war years made it a powerful force in American life. Union membership almost doubled between 1933 and 1937 when it was 5.8 million. By 1940 it was close to 9 million and in 1945, nearly 15 million. Legal protection of the right to organize, essential for unionization to spread rapidly, was provided by Section 7 of the National Labor Relations (Wagner) Act of 1935, acclaimed by labor as its Magna Charta.

The traditional craft unions that comprised the AFL lacked the leadership necessary for a major membership drive. In 1935 a group of dynamic organizers formed a new federation, the Congress of Industrial Organizations (CIO). The moment for a vigorous campaign was seized by organizing mass-production industries, including steel, automobiles, and oil, into new industrial unions. The campaign involved considerable violence; union organizers had to overcome the determined resistance of corporate leaders to a challenge to their "right" to make decisions concerning wages and working conditions unilaterally.

The output of the American economy during the war was enormous, more than doubling in manufacturing, mining, and construction. Durable goods production rose by 260 percent over 5 years as new workers entered the labor force to replace the 14 million men and women who entered the armed forces.

Socialists in Europe were able to achieve political power in the thirties, but as noted earlier, British and German socialist governments failed to adopt successful policies and were soon removed from office. In Austria the Social Democrats had strong support from the working class and served as a shining example to the socialist movements of other countries. They resisted when reactionary forces under dictatorial Chancellor Engelbert Dollfuss moved to suppress them in 1934, but were overcome after several days of fighting. For a time in the mid-1930s France had a socialist government that instituted social reforms similar to those taking place in the U.S., but it was short-lived. It was in Sweden that socialists demonstrated the ability to govern effectively. A socialist government that came to office in 1932 rejected the orthodoxy to which their British and German counterparts had clung and chose an expansionist economic policy. It jettisoned the ideal of an annually balanced budget. By boldly financing new public works with borrowed funds it succeeded in eliminating unemployment by 1938. In *Sweden; The Middle Way,* Marquis W. Childs, an American journalist, called attention to the "middle way" chosen by Sweden between uncontrolled capitalism and the totalitarian systems then waxing strong in Germany and the Soviet Union. At the time, the Swedish model relied heavily on cooperatives to avoid the defects of capitalism without succumbing to Communism or Fascism. The developments in Sweden attracted considerable attention; the U.S. government of the day sent a commission to Europe to study the cooperative movement. Sweden soon moved beyond that movement to embrace a broader planning approach involving collaboration between government and private enterprise. Keynes's *The General Theory of Employment Interest and Money* was published in 1936, and it took years for its influence to be felt among policy-makers, yet the Swedes were using Keynesian policies well in advance of its publication. Michael Harrington saw them as uniquely effective innovators: "With the Swedish exception, the thirties seemed to be a time when socialists wandered in a political and ideological wilderness"[19]

Although socialists were generally unable to establish themselves in positions of power for long in the thirties, the ideological ground was shifting toward collective action. In various advanced countries including the U.S., as private investment fell, public activity rose in an effort to deal with high unemployment. In 1938, the last peacetime year before World War II, in both Britain and Canada government spending rose to approximately one-fourth of national income, "and there was a world-wide tendency for the proportion of public to private expenditure to increase."[20]

When World War II started in 1939 there were still over nine million unemployed workers in the U.S., and national output was only about 5 percent higher in real terms than in 1929. The rapid increase in government expenditures for armaments that followed the outbreak of war drove national output up and unemployment down; for two years during the height of the war effort unemployment in the U.S. was no more than one million.

World War II (1939-1945; 1941-1945 for the U.S.) was "total" war—meaning comprehensive mobilization of resources and nearly total control of economic life by government. In this period of struggle for national survival, the free market was suspended as resources were used according to government fiat and controls contained inflation. The U.S. imposed the following types of direct controls.[21]

1. Price ceilings on goods and services
2. Wage ceilings
3. Subsidies to restrain price increases
4. Rationing of consumer goods
5. Control over goods and services at producer and dealer levels including production directives and prohibitions as well as priorities for the use of materials
6. Export and import controls
7. Government purchases and sales of goods

World War II was the most destructive war in history with the number of deaths, military and civilian, estimated to be 22 million and with over 34 million wounded. It ended with millions of refugees, as cities and communications systems had been devastated by bombing. International assistance was provided by the United Nations Relief and Recovery Administration (UNRRA) and from other, mainly U.S., sources to ward off starvation and disease and to avoid economic collapse in the immediate postwar years.

When the extent of the breakdown in the European economy became clear, the U.S. undertook the Marshall Plan, formally the European Recovery Program, in 1947. By then the Cold War between the Soviet Bloc and the West had begun to bring added urgency to the recovery of the countries outside the Soviet orbit. The Marshall Plan was remarkably successful and when nearly complete at the end of 1951 was phased in with a military assistance program. Industrial production had risen to 35 percent above 1938 levels in the countries that had come together in the Organization for European Economic Cooperation (OEEC) to work out policies for making use of the plan's assistance. To provide for longer-term international cooperation, rules of conduct, and assistance the International Monetary Fund (IMF), the International Bank for Reconstruction and Development (World Bank), and the General Agreement on Tariffs and Trade (GATT) were adopted for the postwar world. Nations were more willing than before the war to act cooperatively under permanent institutional arrangements. The roles of government were greater both domestically and internationally, reflecting the loss of faith in capitalism after World War II. Over the next half century, confidence in free markets was gradually restored and then grew to reach new heights of acceptance.

In 1945, in the first postwar general election in the U.K., the Labour Party scored a resounding victory. Four decades after sending its first small contingent to Parliament in 1906, Labour achieved its first majority and took control of government for the next six years. The British people had endured the hardships of depression followed by a long, bitter, and extremely costly war. Looking for a fresh start that would bring economic recovery and a lessening of the great social and economic inequalities of the past, they entrusted government to the socialists.

In addition to rebuilding the severely damaged stock of housing and infrastructure, the Labour government's chief objectives included full employment, increased social services, and a remodeling of the educational system to provide greater opportunity for the many whose prospects in life were limited. The ethos of British socialism was devotion to greater equality and social justice. The new government under Prime Minister Clement Attlee pursued a gradualist course to partially socialize and plan the economy. The problems of reconversion and recovery from war were particularly difficult due to the loss of income from foreign investments that had been sold to pay for the war effort, but by 1951 economic recovery had been completed.

As recovery from the war painstakingly proceeded, the Labour government carried out some of the socialistic programs it had long advocated, including a moderate amount of national economic planning. Annual assessments were made of the nation's resources and needs, national economic budgets were constructed, and an Economic Planning Board was established, but no long-term planning was attempted. The plans were not strict or detailed, but designed to provide guidance in economic decision making as a result of collaboration between government and groups representing different sectors of the economy. The primacy of the private sector was not questioned. Intended to strengthen Britain's productive capacity by emphasizing gross domestic fixed investment, the planning exercises required restraining consumption. Results were quite disappointing. Actual private consumption spending exceeded planned levels, while domestic investment fell considerably short of planned investment spending. In retrospect, the government may have tried to do more than the nation's resources would allow. Criticism was made of the planning techniques for lack of sophistication and poor organization. National economic planning seems inherently difficult for a free society to implement in peacetime, and Britain's experience during these years failed to generate confidence in it.

Early in the twentieth century, British socialist thought called for nationalizing all major industries, but between the end of World War I and 1945 the Labour Party pared its list of candidates to selected basic or "key" industries considered vital to the success of the economy. Nationalization was intended to avoid the concentration of economic power under private ownership and control that could exploit consumers by restrictions on output and higher prices. Another objective was to eliminate inefficiencies in some major industries, in particular coal mining and railroads, considered to be "sick" and unable to restructure themselves to attract needed capital investment. The postwar Labour government effected nationalization in electricity, gas, communications, transportation, coal, steel, and the Bank of England. The last was clearly ripe for nationalization: the Old Lady of Threadneedle Street had evolved into a central bank; it was an anomaly for it to be in private hands. The financial sector was otherwise left alone, so although the socialist government stressed the importance of capital investment through its national economic plans and in its newly nationalized industries, the British capital market was left to the private sector. The British Broadcasting Corporation (BBC) had been established as a state monopoly in 1927 by a conservative government.

By 1951, when Labour was replaced by a conservative government, the high hopes that nationalization would solve the problems of inefficiency and stimulate economic growth had not been realized. It would take another forty-five years before Clause Four of the party's constitution, which pledged it to nationalization of industry, would be officially abandoned, but faith in nationalization diminished during the 1950s and it came to have a stale aspect. Further attention will be given to this topic at a later point.

The Labour government undertook major changes to broaden and strengthen the system of social services that had gradually been put in place before World War II, but which were seen as inadequate. It reformed secondary education by creating comprehensive schools intended to end class distinctions, by raising the school-leaving age and by devoting more resources to education. A program of new low-rent housing was adopted. A Town and Country Planning Act was passed to control land use in a way that would be beneficial for the environment and enhance the amenities of communities—a matter deemed vital for such a densely populated country.

Of all the welfare measures adopted by the socialist government of 1945-1951, the National Health Service, which began operation in July 1948, is the most impressive and successful. It provided a system of comprehensive health services as recommended in 1942 by a report (the Beveridge Report) written primarily by Sir William Beveridge, the chairman of a committee on social insurance set up by the Ministry of Health. The British Medical Association strongly resisted the new system and was successful in modifying the original proposal. Demands upon the National Health Service were great, and there were problems of providing adequate supplies of medical personnel and facilities. Over time, despite periodic problems of financing and organization and complaints about delays in treatment, the system has been generally popular. Socialized medicine in Britain has become politically secure with no major constituency for its abolition. It is the crown jewel of the British welfare state.

The Beveridge Report covered much more than a proposal for a national health service. It drew up a scheme of comprehensive social security covering maternity benefits and child allowances, unemployment insurance, old age pensions, and death benefits. Its provisions were described as "from the cradle to the grave." The enthusiastic response of the public made social policy a priority of the postwar government. During the war a mood of unity developed out of the sacrifices required of all classes in time of national peril. A sense of determination emerged that the opportunity for a more just, humane, egalitarian society should not be missed at the end of hostilities as it had been after 1918.

The German people were in wretched condition at the end of World War II. Hitler's Reich had been conquered and occupied, leaving the territory stateless. Ten percent of the population had been killed, and the survivors were in desperate need of the necessities of life. The occupying Allies were united in one respect: to punish Germany for the havoc it had caused and to keep it from ever again having the power to assault other peoples. At first it seemed likely that the Morganthau Plan, named for Roosevelt's Secretary of the Treasury, would be imposed to prevent the country from reindustrializing, but this idea was abandoned as too harsh and too costly in terms of economic aid needed from the occupying powers. In the early postwar years, the shortage of goods was accompanied by a huge money supply resulting, as after World War I, in hyperinflation. A black market became rampant; with money useless as either a standard or a store of value, cigarettes served as a medium of exchange. Then, some three years after the end of hostilities, currency reform was carried out in the three Western zones under American, British, and French control, in which the old currency was exchanged for new deutsche marks in much smaller amounts. Soon thereafter, the comprehensive system of price controls and rationing was largely scrapped in favor of free markets. In response, almost like magic, confidence in money was restored, goods appeared in stores, and production increased. Industrial production rose by 50 percent from the first to the second half of 1948 thus beginning a powerful upward surge in the economy that came to be called the "German economic miracle." The recovery was strongly assisted by Marshall Plan aid. Within a decade of the monetary reform, Germany was transformed from virtual prostration to glowing prosperity. Now a pariah nation, a spent force diplomatically and militarily, Germany's strength lay in a skilled, hard-working labor force and a willingness to save and invest. The population saw work as their salvation, and the "German work ethic" combined with investments of over 20 percent of total national production, succeeded in dramatically raising living standards and restoring a large measure of self-respect to a nation which in 1945 had fallen into an abyss "deeper than the one of 1918."[22]

In 1949 the Federal Republic of Germany (West Germany) came into existence in the territory under U.S., British, and French control. This new entity, in contrast to Nazi centralization and dictatorship, was based on devolution of political power and free elections. West Germany drew on prewar free market ideas in adopting a "neo-liberal" approach for its economic policy. This policy carried the label of "social market economy," suggesting balance between free market forces and government intervention. The concept of national economic planning was rejected. Economic and political freedom were seen as necessary to each other, but economic freedom was not absolute by any means. Some areas, such as housing and agriculture, were protected from competitive forces.

Immediately after the end of the war, there was a general belief that public ownership of the means of production was needed to forestall a resurgence of "fascistic capitalism." Support for it came from both major political parties. But under Konrad Adenauer, the first federal Chancellor, the Christian Democratic Union shifted its position so that by 1949 public ownership had been dropped from its platform. The Social Democrats took a little longer to change position for they continued to favor nationalizing heavy industry until the mid-1950s. Then, stung by very poor electoral results, they threw off their Marxist philosophy. Their party leader, Erich Ollenhauer, cited the British experience with nationalized coal and steel as evidence that state ownership was not feasible.

Although West Germany eschewed planning, other West European countries opted for it, including France. French commitment to planning took root in the context of a long history of state intervention; measures protective of domestic industry had been retained in France to a greater extent than in Anglo-Saxon countries since the eighteenth century. Following World War II, it was believed that economic reconstruction would require state leadership to deal with shortages of the means of production. France also had a relatively large nationalized sector, and industry depended heavily on the state for credit.

In 1946 a Plan of Modernization was adopted in France under the leadership of Jean Monnet, whose career as an advisor and government agency director began during World War I. A planning commission was created that met with leaders of industry and government agencies to expedite economic reconstruction, in particular, by concentrating on selected heavy industries. Broad targets were set for investment and production; individual firms were not assigned targets but were encouraged to collaborate through favorable regulatory treatment and financial incentives. Thus, the market system was supplemented by planning to light the way to greater efficiency through improved information and guidance. By examining the economy as a whole, the planning process provided firms with a greater awareness of the "big picture" to assist them in making sound decisions, and it sought to anticipate potential production bottlenecks in time to prevent shortages. The results of this plan were heartening, for over the years of its life (1947-1953) the economy took off from its immediate postwar stagnation into a mode of steady growth.

In the post-World War II adjustment era of 1945-1951, the U.S. basically returned to its prewar economic system but with greater belief that enlightened government intervention would keep the economy on a stable growth path or at least avoid a return to depression. Predictions of massive unemployment following the end of hostilities were not realized, as the pent-up demand for consumer goods fueled with the purchasing power of vast individual savings of the war years kept the economy running at a high rate. Reconversion from wartime to peacetime production was unexpectedly swift.

The influence of the "Keynesian revolution" in economic thought that appeared in the mid-thirties was now taking hold in the policy arena. It is true that the general pattern of prewar New Deal policy was consistent with Keynes's prescriptions, but clear evidence that Roosevelt's policies were influenced significantly by Keynes is lacking. It was a likely case of "getting Hamlet without reading it."[23] The power of deficit spending to overcome unemployment was unambiguously demonstrated by the financing of the war. What Keynes had presented in 1936 was a new paradigm of economic theory with profound policy implications. Over the next ten years a critical mass of economists and then policy-makers were converted to the new approach. Traditional economic theory held that the economy, left to itself, would automatically tend to reach equilibrium at full employment through market adjustments in wages and interest rates. Keynes refuted this comforting classical (neoclassical) theory, which had been severely shaken by the events of the early 1930s. He focused on the need to maintain aggregate demand, the total spending for goods and services. Without sufficient aggregate demand, the economy could well settle at an equilibrium below the full employment level with investment spending equal to saving at this level. To correct a deficiency in aggregate demand, public expenditures financed by borrowing might be needed to supplement privately generated expenditures, thus legitimizing deficit spending. It followed that the opposite fiscal policy would be appropriate if the private sector were to "overheat" through excessive spending. "Keynesian policies became central to what was called postwar planning and designs for preventing the re-emergence of massive unemployment."[24]

That Keynes's contributions to economic theory and policy have been of preeminent importance to capitalism is now well understood. By inventing modern macroeconomics, he is responsible for half of modern economic analysis. For many years, conservative business leaders and politicians considered him to be too "left wing" for justifying a prominent role by government, but gradually his ideas became orthodox doctrine. In 2004 a leading business publication honored him as one of "the greatest innovators of the past 75 years" and hailed him as "capitalism's savior."[25]

The postwar American economic scene was also much influenced by organized labor, and by inflationary forces. In little more than a decade labor unions had been transformed from puny to powerful organizations with about 36 percent of all non-farm workers unionized by 1945. The cost of the war had involved huge deficit financing by government, adding greatly to the amount of money and near-money in the economy, but prices had been held in check largely by direct controls. Most of the wage and price controls were allowed to expire in June 1946, after which the smoldering inflation flared up. Prices rose relatively rapidly for the next two years; over 60 percent of the rise in consumer prices between 1939 and 1948 occurred after the end of the war. Prices fell slightly during a recession in 1948-1949, but after the Korean War began in 1950 the danger of excessive demand became palpable. The Federal Reserve System responded in March 1951 by terminating its policy of supporting the government securities market at pegged prices, a policy begun nine years earlier to assist the treasury in financing the war. By taking this step, the Fed no longer allowed the monetization of the national debt at the will of holders of treasury securities and was therefore able to reassert control of the money stock, the crucial role of a central bank.

While the U.S. did not at this time firmly commit itself to the maintenance of "full employment" and certainly did not adopt a central planning mechanism, by enacting the Employment Act of 1946 Congress declared:

> that it is the continuing policy and responsibility of the Federal Government ... to coordinate and utilize all its plans, functions, and resources for the purpose of creating and maintaining, in a manner calculated to foster and promote free competitive enterprise

. . . conditions under which there will be afforded useful employment opportunities
. . . and to promote maximum employment, production, and purchasing power.

New structures were created for monitoring, analyzing, and reporting
on economic conditions to facilitate policy-making appropriate to changing circumstances. Further attention will be paid to this legislation in the
next chapter when the subject of economic planning will be discussed
in a broader context of postwar developments.

The major social reforms of the New Deal were retained. Government
spending was greater relative to GDP than before the war mainly due to
the tense international situation that evoked Marshall Plan aid, military
readiness in response to the developing Cold War, and participation in
the Korean War beginning in June 1950.

By the middle of the twentieth century, it was clear that socialist policies had very significantly infiltrated and transformed capitalism as it had
existed fifty years earlier. Begun slowly late in the previous century, the
movement away from laissez faire gained ground following World War
I and then accelerated rapidly as a result of the Great Depression and
World War II. At the century's mid-point, Professor Joseph A. Schumpeter addressed the American Economic Association on "The March
Into Socialism."[26] Far from advocating socialism, Schumpeter viewed
capitalism as highly successful and, if not interfered with, capable of
virtually unlimited expansion. Yet the trends he observed led him to
expect socialism, by which he simply meant "the migration of people's
economic affairs from the private into the public sphere," gradually to
replace capitalism.

A brilliant economist originally of the highly abstract Austrian school
of economics, Schumpeter was the Austrian Minister of Finance briefly
after World War I. He then taught at the University of Bonn followed by
a professorship at Harvard from 1932 to 1950.

For Schumpeter, the central feature of capitalism is its ability to
revolutionize the economic structure from within, what he called the
"process of creative destruction." New production techniques, products,
organizational forms—indeed, all manner of new and better ways of
producing and selling—are developed bringing progress and at the same
time making existing products, technology, processes, and so forth obso-
lete. The role of undertaking these innovations is a distinct function that
requires energy and aptitudes possessed by only a small fraction of the
population, the entrepreneurial elite. But Schumpeter thought that heroic
individual entrepreneurs were being displaced by dull managers of large

corporations, business leaders with little charisma. Public esteem for the leaders of business and industry was declining. Respect for capitalism was also being undermined by criticism from newly powerful workers' unions and by hostile intellectuals with great influence over written and spoken communication. Schumpeter believed that there was a lack of sustaining faith in capitalist institutions and values that makes the system vulnerable when things go wrong.

The view that business leaders were losing their élan as public confidence in business fell in the thirties was noted by historian Arthur M. Schlesinger, Jr. in his study of the New Deal. "For the first time American businessmen were questioning their own judgment, methods, and goals. Never had the business community felt such a sense of its own fallibility . . ."[27]

From its beginning in 1933 the Roosevelt administration pursued a policy of decreasing the degree of inequality of income and wealth. The Revenue Act of 1935 called "The Wealth Tax Act" was justified by Roosevelt on the grounds that the laws had given an unfair advantage to the few, resulting in an "unjust concentration of wealth and economic power." Individual surtax rates were as high as 73 percent on very large incomes, various taxes were placed on corporations, and the inheritance and gift taxes were raised. Further tax increases followed. In 1936 Roosevelt castigated his right-wing business opponents by calling them "economic royalists" who considered economic slavery to be nobody's business.[28]

Antipathy to capitalism was almost certainly longer and deeper in England than in the U.S. Why capitalism had lost public esteem in Britain is seen through the eyes of the American columnist/author Russell Baker, who drove from London to Scotland in 1953. "Along the way, looking at the grim urban ruins created by an industry harnessed to greed, I learned why the socialist faith was so much stronger than the Church of England."[29]

The business community, of course, defended capitalist values and practices, and there was strong support for them from some intellectuals. One of the most prominent of the latter was the Russian-born American social philosopher and novelist Ayn Rand. Her work inspired conservatives and infuriated liberals, and it is easy to understand why. In presenting her philosophy of objectivism that combined capitalism, reason, and individualism, she repudiated altruism and praised selfishness. Rand used novels as a means of popularizing her philosophy. *The Fountainhead* (1943) became a film in 1949. Her influence continued for decades with annual book sales of some 300,000 in the 1990s.

Following World War II and for the next half century, the most influential American exponent of capitalism in its pre-New Deal version was Professor Milton Friedman. Working as an economist in the treasury department during the early 1940s, he developed a strong antipathy for the federal legislative process and for the use of direct controls. Shortly after the end of the war, Friedman joined the Department of Economics of the University of Chicago where he became the dominant figure in a department almost completely staffed by economic and political conservatives. It was a time when the economics profession generally had lost much of its traditional faith in the pricing mechanism of the market to allocate resources efficiently, and the "Chicago School" took on an evangelizing role to restore the faith.

The economic journalist Leonard Silk called Friedman the "most distinguished spiritual son" of Adam Smith.[30] Adam Smith's work on economics was part of a broad approach reflecting the fact that he was a moral philosopher. Friedman, however, insisted on "positive economics," an approach that in principle does not allow ethical or normative judgments to trespass on its territory.

In addition to Friedman and Schumpeter, capitalism had another very eminent academic advocate, Professor Friedrich Hayek, who taught at the London School of Economics and the University of Chicago. Possibly the most influential conservative economist of the twentieth century Hayek, in his *Road to Serfdom* (1944), maintained that instead of saving the capitalist system from collapse the New Deal approach would eventually lead to totalitarianism. Thirty years later he admitted that "if his view that the welfare state would lead to totalitarianism is taken to have been a prediction he was wrong." He chose to think of his early work as a warning rather than a forecast.[31]

The topics of economic planning, public ownership, regulation, and the welfare state will be discussed further in Chapter 3 to show how they developed over a considerably longer period of time.

Notes

1. Robert Sobel, *The Great Bull Market: Wall Street in the 1920s* (New York: W. W. Norton, 1968), pp. 41-44.
2. Daniel Bell, *The Cultural Contradictions of Capitalism* (New York: Basic Books, 1976), pp. 21-22, 75, 242.
3. Illustration from Sobel, *op. cit.*, p. 75.
4. *Ibid.*, p. 76.
5. John Kenneth Galbraith, *The Great Crash* (Boston: Houghton Mifflin, 1955), p.

4.

6. William J. Barber, *From New Era to New Deal* (Cambridge: Cambridge University Press, 1985), p. 31.

7. *Ibid.*, p. 41.

8. Quoted in *Ibid.*, p. 82.

9. *Ibid.*, p. 188.

10. Irving Bernstein, *The Lean Years: A History of the American Worker 1920-1933* (Boston: Houghton Mifflin, 1960), p. 60.

11. *Ibid.*, p. 188.

12. Irving Howe, *Socialism and America* (New York: Harcourt Brace Jovanovich, 1985), p. 48.

13. Bell, *op. cit.*, p. 230; Michael Harrington, *Socialism: Past and Future* (New York: Arcade Publishing, 1989), pp. 58-59; Calvin Hoover, *Memoirs of Capitalism, Communism, and Nazism* (Durham, N.C.: Duke University Press, 1965), p. 129.

14. Bernstein, *op. cit.*, p. 354.

15. James MacGregor Burns, *Roosevelt: The Lion and the Fox* (New York: Harcourt Brace, 1956), p. 243.

16. Howe, *op. cit.*, p. 86.

17. Tony Judt, "The Last Romantic," *The New York Review of Books*, November 20, 2003, p. 45.

18. Lyle Cooper, "The American Labor Movement in Prosperity and Depression," *American Economic Review* (December, 1932), p. 641.

19. Harrington, *op. cit.*, p. 92.

20. William Ashworth, *A Short History of the International Economy Since 1850*, 3rd edition (London: Longman, 1975), p. 167.

21. List adapted from Lester V. Chandler, *Inflation in the United States 1940-1948* (New York: Harper, 1951), p. 203.

22. Gustav Stolper, Karl Hauser and Knut Borchardt, *The German Economy, 1870 to the Present* (New York: Harcourt Brace, 1967), p. 222.

23. Seymour E. Harris, *The New Economics* (New York: Knopf, 1948), p. 18.

24. John Kenneth Galbraith, *Economics Peace & Laughter* (New York: Signet, New American Library, 1972, orig. 1971), p. 51.

25. *Business Week*, April 12, 2004, p. 20.

26. Joseph A. Schumpeter, *Capitalism, Socialism, and Democracy*, third edition (New York: Harper, 1950), pp. 415-425.

27. Arthur M. Schlesinger, Jr., *The Coming of the New Deal* (Boston: Houghton Mifflin, 1959), p. 424.

28. Louis M. Hacker, *The Course of American Economic Growth and Development* (New York: John Wiley & Sons, 1970), p. 319.

29. Russell Baker, *The Good Times* (New York: William Morrow, 1989), p. 203.

30. Leonard Silk, *The Economists* (New York: Basic Books, 1976), p. 47.

31. Leonard Silk, *Economics in the Real World* (New York: Simon and Schuster, 1984), p. 111.

3

Economic Cohabitation—
A Thirty-Year Paradigm

It is a truism that pure capitalism and pure socialism are not found in the real world. When an economy is called capitalist, what is meant is that it is predominantly capitalist in its institutions, values, and practices, despite the presence of some degree of socialism. The socialist component may be so small that it can be considered of little consequence. But the socialist component may over time become large enough so that it cannot realistically be ignored. If we think of a continuum running from pure capitalism to pure socialism, each point on the line represents a different mixture of disparate elements. And whereas in 1925 an economy might have had 95 percent capitalist and 5 percent socialist components, perhaps by 1950 the socialist components had risen to 20 percent or 35 percent, making the term capitalism less descriptive. By the middle of the twentieth century, historically capitalist countries had become sufficiently modified by socialist elements that they were in fact recognized as "mixed economies." The composition of the mixture varied considerably with, for example, Sweden and the U.K. more "socialist" than the U.S. or Canada, but as a group the predominantly capitalist countries had moved farther from the capitalist end of the spectrum than before the world wars, Great Depression, and Keynesian economics had affected them. They were generally still in the capitalist "camp," but some commentators might consider one or more of them as having crossed into predominantly socialist territory. The term mixed economy, like mixed race, hardly provides a precise description. Yet, it has the virtue of admitting the reality that the economies of the West had changed significantly. Socialist forms and practices had entered into the inherited corpus of capitalism to a considerable extent. The new mélange did not fulfill any theoretical ideal, but was an ideological hotchpotch reached by increments and experiments in response to urgent and sometimes desperate circumstances. Beginning soon after World War II and continuing for a period of about thirty years, this mixture, while varying somewhat, was relatively stable. The idea that capitalism and socialism could cohabit successfully in modern liberal democratic systems was generally implicitly accepted, although of course there were those who yearned for a more clearly defined capitalism or socialism. A review of these decades follows with attention to public ownership, planning, regulation, the welfare state, and other features of the time. We are concerned here primarily, but not solely, with the years 1950-1980.

Public Ownership

Originally socialism, as it emerged in the nineteenth century, was synonymous with public ownership, and it still is today in narrow dictionary definitions. Socialism, according to *The New Shorter Oxford English Dictionary*, is "a political and economic theory or policy of social organization which advocates that the community as a whole should own and control the means of production, capital, land, property, etc." Such a definition is archaic for it deals with only one facet of a set of ideas and practices that constitute modern socialism. Certainly it was the core idea of those intent on evicting capitalism in the early days of socialist thought when capitalism was condemned in toto. According to Marxist doctrine, it is private ownership of capital and land that enables the capitalist class to exercise political control over society. Once social ownership of these resources is achieved, the working class majority of the population would have the means to control the state.

Public ownership increased to a very limited extent before World War I in capitalist Britain. Nationalization was carried out by the conservative government of Prime Minister Disraeli in 1868 when the Post Office (a government monopoly since the seventeenth century) was authorized to purchase the country's telegraph companies.[1] In 1903, after decades of very unsatisfactory service by London water companies that included water famines, the companies were municipalized.

The major twentieth century drive for public ownership in Britain culminated in the nationalization of "key" industries by the Labour government of 1945-1951. Created by Parliament, the ultimate authority over them, the public corporations were structured to be run by largely independent boards under the supervision of government ministers. The three levels of control and oversight resulted in uncertainty and occasional conflict, a problem inherent in the fact that both social and commercial objectives were involved. If the results that followed had been more successful, other industries would likely have been added to the roster, but Labour did not again form a government until 1964 and by then much of the luster had worn off nationalization. As early as 1953, a proposal at a party conference to commit the party to additional nationalization was scotched when the general secretary of the Transport and General Workers Union threw its great weight of votes against the resolution. Following its election defeat in 1959, the Labour Party, while still advocating additional state ownership, toned down this goal in practice. Nationalization of the means of production, distribution, and exchange was still a principle to which the Labour Party was committed when it held office from 1964 to 1970, but it ceased to rank as a major objective in its legislative program. It simply did not have strong electoral appeal. While in opposition in the early 1970s, Labour did take an interventionist posture that included more nationalization to improve the country's weak economic performance, but when the party was in office from 1974 to 1979, additional nationalization was not pursued.

Neither nationalization nor denationalization was carried out, except minimally, during the fifties, sixties, and seventies. The steel industry had been nationalized in 1951, the last year of the first postwar Labour government. In a political tug-of-war, it was denationalized by the Tories just two years later, but then nationalized again in 1967 by Labour. The latter step was taken to reorganize and modernize what had become a stagnant industry unable successfully to compete internationally; however, some 250 small firms making up one-tenth of total production were left in the private sector. Some unprofitable companies in other industries, British Leyland and Rolls Royce being prime examples, were nationalized on the grounds of employment, trade, or strategic reasons. Britain did not want to be excluded from technologically advanced and defense related industries.

By 1979 the U.K.'s nationalized industries had had, for the most part, three decades in which to reorganize and experience whatever advantages they might possess or devise. They were a significant part of the economy although overshadowed in size by the private sector. They accounted for 10 percent of GDP and 15 percent of aggregate investment, and they had 1.5 million employees. But employment costs per employee had outpaced the national average. Collectively their bottom line—return to investment—had registered just about zero.

In May 1979 the conservatives won the national election, thereby setting the stage for a rollback of nationalization. But if Prime Minister James Callahan's Labour government had won, it is unlikely that nationalization would have been extended. During the seventies, one of the methods used to deal with the persistent problem of inflation was to restrain the prices that nationalized industries charged, notably for the basics of fuel and transportation. As a result, nationalized industries failed to cover costs and had to make up the difference by borrowing or by government subsidies. The cost of the British welfare state, which has to be supported by the output of its private and public sectors, had grown substantially. Parts of the nationalized sector were not contributing to its support but had themselves become recipients of "welfare," for example, by paying unnecessary steelworkers because unions would not agree to a more efficient use of manpower. By injecting considerable new investment into nationalized corporations to modernize them, it was hoped they would experience cost reductions, but the results were disappointing.

Post-World War II West Germany began its new national life strongly free market oriented, but after twenty years, by the 1960s, its position became similar to that of the Western mixed economies and less strongly market oriented in fact than in reputation. Reacting against the dictatorship of the Nazis, the West Germans sought to provide "capitalism with a human face" by adopting their self-styled "social-market economy." A significant publicly-owned sector has been part of the system. Some of Germany's government-owned enterprises compete against private competitors.

About 7.5 percent of employment and 10 percent of value added came from the government sector in the seventies. The public utility sector is largely a government monopoly that includes electricity, gas, water, urban passenger transportation, railroads, airlines, and communications. Hard coal mining is, in practice, a nationalized and protected industry. There is a close similarity between these industries and those that were nationalized in Britain. Of course, East Germany had a very much larger government sector prior to its reunification with West Germany in 1990.

Government enterprises are prominent in German banking and housing construction, as well as in manufacturing. In general, public industrial firms were acquired or established before 1945 as legacies from government rescue operations of the depression era, Third Reich ventures to help make the country less dependent on foreign sources, or for rearmament in the run-up to World War II, although some were created to provide production and employment after the war. The federal government has a major stake in many manufacturing enterprises, mainly in heavy industry, through several holding companies in some cases with a controlling interest. The sectors run by state and local governments are almost entirely non-manufacturing.

Nationalization is of particular importance in France where it has long been accepted. State industry goes back to Jean Baptiste Colbert, Louis XIV's finance minister in the seventeenth century. Such enterprises are compatible with the French tradition of active participation by the state in economic life and with that country's largely centralized governmental system.

Like Britain and Germany, France's nationalized sector included gas, electricity, coal, railroads, air transportation, and communications. In addition, four leading commercial banks as well as the aircraft industry and most of the insurance industry were state-owned in the post-World War II period. A searching out of industrial collaborators in wartime resulted in nationalizing the Renault automobile firm. After nationalizations shortly after the war, the extent of the nationalized sector held steady until the 1980s. It was responsible for 25 percent of gross fixed investment. The French government also held a third or more of the shares of close to 500 industrial and commercial enterprises.

Government has played a smaller role in providing goods and services in the U.S. than in other developed countries. In this country municipalities typically provide water, sewer systems, garbage collection, and local public transportation, less often electricity and gas. The role of government expanded during the administrations of Franklin Roosevelt but seldom took the form of ownership of productive facilities except for the Tennessee Valley Authority, Bonneville Dam, and other projects for the production and distribution of electric power and related water resource control and development. In the post-World War II era the federal government has provided major agencies for special tasks of great national importance, notably the Atomic Energy Commission which created national laboratories whose work is managed by universities or private corporations under contract, and the National Aeronautics and Space Agency which has technical capacity of its own as well as contracts with private industry. It has also subsidized some publicly desired but financially weak rail services via Amtrak and Conrail, but generally railroads are on their own and little passenger rail service is available. Highway construction is financed by federal and state governments.

A historical flashback provides perspective on the topic of government's role in the transportation sector. A vast and efficient transportation system was essential to develop the nation's economy. Early in the nineteenth century, the federal government built the National Road linking the East with the Midwest. For the same purpose, New York State constructed the Erie Canal between 1817 and 1825. Constitutional restraints on the ability of the federal government directly to finance internal improvements led it to convey public lands to the states starting in 1823 mainly to finance canals and roads. Both state and municipal governments were important organizers and financial backers for improvement projects during the nineteenth century. From 1850 through 1871 generous federal land grants totaling 131 million acres were used to encourage railroad construction, added to which were 49 million acres of public lands contributed by the states. In the second half of the nineteenth century the railroad industry was foremost among American enterprises and "public help, in its many and various ways, was the key factor."[2] In addition to financing the transcontinental railroad system, the federal government brought major public universities into existence and greatly strengthened the productive capabilities of farmers through research and the dissemination of improved practices via agricultural extension services. These nineteenth-century endeavors fall under the rubric "industrial policy," a twentieth-century term, since they involve state promotion and support but not nationalization.

One theme that emerges from a careful examination of American economic development is the "incorrigible insistence of private citizens that government encourage or entirely provide those services and utilities either too costly or too risky to attract unaided private capital."[3] Thus, while it is true that the American economy has throughout its history developed primarily as a result of private decision making through the market, an important supporting role has been played by the public sector even when belief in self-help and the "self-made man" was virtually universally accepted and celebrated.

Planning

Economic planning had much greater appeal in Western democracies after World War II than before, although the degree to which they chose to adopt planning varied greatly. France enthusiastically embraced it, modified it repeatedly, and continued it through many changes of government. Britain adopted it rather half-heartedly, created a formal structure for it, then failed to use it effectively. There was some interest in planning in the U.S. but the temptation to try it was resisted. Germany shunned it.

The type of planning that was implemented was a supplement to the market system; the intention was to remedy deficiencies in the market process, not to eliminate or negate it. It was a response to perceived failures of the market. In particular, it addressed the lack of information to market participants by pooling information and disseminating it to improve the basis on which long-term decisions are made. In contrast, the original Marxist conception called for comprehensive planning to replace the market after the demise of capitalism. Marx himself did not attempt to explain how a planned economic system would work, but he anticipated that an appropriate democratic procedure would be forthcoming when the time was ripe, and that a rational, scientifically designed planning structure would fulfill the new classless society's goals.

National economic planning was first implemented as an emergency measure during World War I. Germany adopted "war socialism," under the direction of General Erich von Ludendorff, to mobilize the entire society for war production through a single powerful agency. In 1918 when Lenin imposed a centrally planned economy on Soviet Russia, Germany was his model. From 1918 to 1921, the years of civil war, the Bolshevik regime attempted to achieve full communism through War Communism, by which agricultural surpluses were forcibly requisitioned, industry nationalized, private trade banned, workers mobilized, and money largely eliminated. A big step back toward the market system followed during the New Economic Policy (NEP) era, 1921-1928. In the latter year the Soviet Union, under Joseph Stalin, abolished the NEP and adopted comprehensive five-year plans that centralized decision making for the remainder of the Soviet era. Stalin used command planning to transform the backward economy of the Soviet Union quickly by a forced march into the modern era. In little over a decade, at enormous human cost, an industrial sector was built that enabled the country, with the help of its Western wartime allies, successfully to resist Hitler's invasion. It also provided the means by which the USSR became a military superpower rival to the U.S. for nearly half a century. In addition, Soviet planning was a model that inspired underdeveloped countries in various parts of the world. It promised a shortcut to economic modernization. But, as the second half of the twentieth century unfolded, it gradually became clear that the Soviet economic system lagged farther and farther behind the West in technology and in the development of sophisticated new products. By the eighties it was obvious that it was hopelessly rigid and inefficient. Highly insular and pretending to be more productive than it was, the USSR, while still maintaining tremendous military strength, had economically become one huge Potemkin village. The attitude of workers was cynically expressed: "They pretend to pay us, and we pretend to work."

The U.S. and Britain also considered it necessary to adopt a large measure of central planning during World War I. Those chosen to administer the state economic bureaucracy in the U.S. were leaders of major industries. A by-product of the resulting regulatory structure by the corporate elite was protection from market forces. Although national economic planning was not continued into the postwar era in the West, experience with it was viewed as successful. It has been argued that the 1914-1918 wartime planning experiences of Germany, Britain, and the U.S. had considerable influence over ensuing decades for they became "the practical model for later schemes for planning all over the world"[4]

As noted earlier, France undertook a Plan of Modernization (1947-1953) designed for transition to a primarily market system by the economist Jean Monnet. Monnet is best known for leading the movement to economic unity after World War II that eventually resulted in the European Union. The initial plan was followed by six others, the final one ending in 1980. They were "indicative" in that growth targets were set for economic sectors indicating the availability of finance, investment, labor supply, productivity improvements, and output/factor input relationships. Firms could then use the projections to supplement the usual market signals in making their strategic management decisions. Essentially the planners indicated what was possible and what policies were needed, whereas planners in a centrally planned economy not only form the plans but also try to carry them through. The French plans were formed by a small organization, the General Planning Commissariat, after consultation with business, union, and regional groups and with advice from civil servants and university faculty. In practice, at least during the 1950s, planning was a sort of elitist conspiracy in the hands of senior civil servants and leaders of big business, "a rather clandestine affair."[5]

The Second Plan (1954-1957) encouraged businessmen to invest heavily thereby giving planning "in the French style" favorable recognition. The adoption of planning by General de Gaulle, who was President of France from 1959 to 1969 and who embraced it as contributing to national pride and unity, provided political legitimacy. Planning was given full acceptance as establishment doctrine.

French economic growth was impressive during the first two postwar decades. As an example of improved efficiency, manufacturing productivity increased by 8 percent per year from 1955 to 1958, a faster pace than in any other country in Western Europe. The French experience certainly impressed the British author Andrew Shonfield who wrote the following in his early 1960s study of postwar capitalism for the Royal Institute of International Affairs: "In the form in which it has developed today the French method is probably the most interesting and influential expression of capitalism in its new guise."[6] In 1962 President Kennedy, looking for ways to accelerate American economic growth, asked his Council of Economic Advisers to pay attention to what the French were doing, and British planners looked to France for a model to imitate. The main function of French planning was to overcome the absence of a good capital market by having the government raise and allocate funds for investment. Setting target rates of economic growth was practiced by many countries at the time and was not peculiarly French.

The high marks for French planning did not last, and indeed, at the end of the sixties the French lost much of their enthusiasm for it. Planning forecasts became less reliable in an increasingly open international economy. Instead of a comprehensive industrial strategy, attention became limited to the encouragement of a few key sectors. In 1968 France was shaken by student unrest. Under the Fifth Plan (1966-1970), while the rate of economic growth was high as business investment and private consumption rose, social investment faltered seriously. University students protested violently against poor facilities and overcrowding. The logic of the Fifth Plan came under severe criticism.

By the last half of the seventies, government policy was clearly market oriented; a Seventh Plan was adopted to assist the movement of resources toward rising industries but it was largely ignored. Planning that had successfully focused on the problems of postwar recovery and revitalization lost its effectiveness as its role became diffuse in a rapidly changing environment.

For a third of a century beginning in 1947 France carried out a socialist concept, peacetime economic planning, although it was not the work of a socialist government. During the sixties and seventies the country was under conservative rule; an all-left government was not elected until 1981, the first of its kind since the 1930s.

The British government took a stab at national economic planning in the sixties, but it had little effect and was more rhetoric and administrative structure than substance. The circumstances are nevertheless of interest in revealing attitudes and responses to economic problems.

It is striking that planning was instituted by a conservative chancellor of the exchequer, Selwyn Lloyd, who in July 1961, called for an organization consisting of management, trade union, and government members to study the economic outlook of the country over a five-year period or longer. In 1962 the National Economic Development Council (NEDC), a quasi-independent body, began to consider the nation's production potential and distribution of resources with the objective of identifying specifically how a faster rate of economic growth could be achieved. Britain's growth rate had lagged behind that of other developed countries. The NEDC examined the implications for a 4 percent annual growth rate of national output for the years 1961-1966. In effect, a growth plan was presented as a basis for policy and was accompanied by guidelines and monitoring systems for industrial groups.

The question arises, Why was planning not adopted during the sixteen years between the end of the war in 1945 and 1961? The Labour government of 1945-1951 undertook major changes in the role of government in the economy by nationalizing industries and expanding the welfare state, yet its broad economic policy decisions were confined to short-term objectives. There was much discussion of long-term planning that led to expectations that it would be implemented, but no long-term planning mechanism was forthcoming. It seems that the traditional British view of the limited role of the state kept the Labour Party from "too much" interference in the market economy. As Shonfield put it, "the ethos of the Labour Government during its period of rule in the immediately postwar period was curiously antipathetic to this type of activity."[7] From 1951 to 1964 the conservatives held sway and until 1961 continued the use of short-term economic management techniques in an effort to maintain full employment while, as expected, holding to their anti-planning free market philosophy. Then, quite suddenly and dramatically, the Tories embraced long-term planning under the leadership of Prime Minister Harold Macmillan. During the 1950s and the 1960s as well, governments swung back and forth from an obsession with the balance of payments to an obsession with unemployment. "Hence, the usual sequence, known as 'stop-go' policy, would be sharp deflation to bring the balance of payments back into equilibrium at the old exchange rate, followed by rapid expansion designed to eliminate the unemployment caused by the preceding policy stance."[8] As the economy expanded, inflation would accelerate, and a serious balance of payments deficit would endanger the value of the pound in the foreign exchange market. Strong union pressure would contribute to higher production costs and prices. To deal with the pressure of demand on imports and the emerging crisis of confidence in the pound, interest rates would be raised, the economy would slow down, and real investment would be choked off. It had become apparent that the economy could not gain momentum, and by its slower growth over the long run, Britain was gradually slipping in the league standings of per capita national product. With their minds concentrated by this un-nerving trend and with encouragement from expansionist critics outside the government, policy-makers opted for what seemed a promising, bold new course but, in fact, it was far from a panacea and had a short life. The NEDC, lacking any real power, was soon viewed as ineffective.

A Labour government under Harold Wilson ruled Britain from 1964 to 1970. It created a new ministry, the Department of Economic Affairs (DEA) that took over the work of indicative planning from the NEDC, with the intention of implementing technically sophisticated planning methods. But immediate pressing problems of inflation, a balance of payments deficit, and slow growth again took precedence over planning. In 1967 the struggle to maintain the value of the pound was abandoned, and when that line of defense fell, the planning process was also aban-doned.

The inflationary problem was attributed to reciprocal action by trade unions and corporations; wage increases brought price increases and vice versa in a vicious upward spiral. In response, the Wilson govern-ment adopted wage and price controls that were voluntary 1964-1966; mandatory 1966-1967; voluntary 1967-1970. The 1970-1974 conserva-tive government of Edward Heath at first continued voluntary wage and price controls but soon made them mandatory. It also created a Price Commission and Pay Board that paralleled the income policy of the Nixon administration in the U.S. from 1971 to 1974. Then a new La-bour government of Wilson, followed by James Callaghan from 1974 to 1979, ended wage controls while controlling prices and profit margins. In return, the unions agreed to restrain their wage demands, but early in 1979, they rejected a new "social contract" and rampant industrial unrest disrupted the economy.

Over the thirty-four years from 1945 to 1979, the socialist Labour Party and the "capitalist" conservative party each governed for seven-teen years. The welfare state and nationalization policies introduced in the early years were essentially continued thereafter, and the economic programs carried out by each of the successive alternative governments were much the same. Their demand management policies differed mainly with respect to timing and extent. The distribution of income held steady as they tinkered with fiscal policy. It was a period when "the two parties differed more in their rhetoric than in the implementation of policies."[9]

After the searing experience of the Great Depression and World War II, the U.S. was receptive to a policy of some degree of government intervention to achieve economic stability. The fear of mass unemployment was sufficiently great that for the first time in our national history the federal government was declared by Congress to have responsibility for managing the economy with particular emphasis on the maintenance of employment. The Employment Act of 1946 gave Congress its own Joint Economic Committee and provided the president with a Council of Economic Advisers. These new institutions were designed to monitor, analyze, and report on the economy with the expectation that in response the executive and legislative branches would devise policies appropriate to changing needs and circumstances as they become apparent. Forewarned by professional economic advice of any trouble on the horizon, or of more imminent danger, the government would be prompted to take steps to keep the economy from veering off course. When the bill for this act was introduced in the Senate, it called upon the president to present a production and employment "budget" regularly at the start of congressional sessions—on the basis of which a program of fiscal action was to be proposed as needed. Congress would be required to respond by a certain date with appropriate legislation. This was an attempt to commit the federal government to a Keynesian fiscal policy. Although far short of national economic planning, it was more than Congress would swallow, and the legislation was watered down to requiring the president to submit a report that the Congress had only to consider.

John Kenneth Galbraith developed a comprehensive interpretation of the American economy that included a somewhat idiosyncratic concept of planning and which led him to espouse a "new socialism." Galbraith divided the private sector into two roughly equal parts in terms of amount of output. One, the market system, had some 12 million firms in a highly competitive environment in which they had little or no market power, so that the result of their exertions was reasonably consistent with the expectations of the neoclassical model. The other half of the private sector of the economy, dubbed the planning system, consisted of one thousand giant corporations in such areas as manufacturing, transportation, energy, and finance. These large corporations had much power, not only in markets, but also in shaping community attitudes and in dealing with government. To exercise this power, companies utilized executives, managers, and a corps of various specialists including scientists and engineers to design and produce output, as well as a large supporting cast of lawyers and lobbyists and marketing, advertising, public relations, and other personnel. The term technostructure was coined to apply to this collection of people with specialized knowledge who constituted the corporation's power center.

Giant corporations spend vast amounts of money on investments to produce products with long gestation periods. To eliminate as much uncertainty as possible they replace the market to a large extent by determining price and quantities to be bought and sold. To do this they supersede the market through vertical integration; they control markets by virtue of their size in relation to their suppliers and customers; and they suspend the market for substantial periods of time through long-term contracts. The big corporation has influence over the state. In dealing with public regulatory bodies, the corporations tend to dominate the relationship. It is in the interest of both the technostructure and the regulatory agencies to avoid conflict. The legislature has also become supportive of the planning system, most notably in the area of the armed services where the military bureaucracies and defense contractors are symbiotically linked. It was about this relationship that President Eisenhower warned in 1961 at the end of his second term of office when he spoke of the "military-industrial complex." At the time Galbraith was writing, the Cold War was in full progress and the military budget was enormous and sacrosanct.

Overall, Galbraith saw the planning system as dominating the state and causing major societal problems including greater inequality, unbalanced social development, environmental degradation, and a distorted foreign policy. The concentration of power in the corporate technostructure required radical change. His cure was not to eviscerate the planning system but to extend its organization and protection to the market system to the benefit of people relying on it. This required a new form of socialism.

> The older socialism allowed of ideology. There could be capitalism with its advantages and disadvantages; there could be public ownership of the means of production with its possibilities and disabilities. There could be a choice between the two. . . . The new socialism allows of no acceptable alternatives; it cannot be escaped except at the price of grave discomfort, considerable social disorder and, on occasion, lethal damage to health and well-being. The new socialism is not ideological; it is compelled by circumstance.[10]

Galbraith had a large readership because he dealt with major economic questions in a broad social/political context and because of his witty, graceful prose. His writing style is probably the most felicitous of any economist since Adam Smith. But he did not convert the economics profession to his views on planning and the public policy prescriptions related to them. His call for a democratic reformation that would redistribute power in society via a greater role for government went unheeded.

The post-World War II economy of the U.S. was fundamentally market oriented. Government did not ignore the market system; it engaged in short-term management of aggregate demand, and it intervened through regulatory means to modify the way the market worked to nudge it toward politically preferred results. But proposals to adopt economic planning were contrary to the prevailing ideology and had no real chance of adoption.

With respect to market structure, an unusual wave of mergers took place in the sixties and seventies in the U.S. Earlier and later takeover surges occurred around 1900, at the end of the twenties, and again in the eighties, in each case combining companies in similar types of production. This time, however, combinations were formed of firms in entirely different businesses, such as food production, telephone service, hotels, and electronics. Such aggregates were presumed to benefit from centralized management under the strategic leadership of outstanding chief executives. Called conglomerates, they were promoted as a means by which synergy would bring greater efficiency and profitability. The results were generally well below expectations and did not merit a passing grade, an outcome attributable in large part to inexperienced senior management in swollen bureaucracies dealing with dissimilar enterprises. A disappointing performance by the American economy followed with low productivity growth and a loss of competitiveness in the world economy. During the 1980s, many of the conglomerates that had been formed in the previous two decades were disassembled as poorly performing components were detached from them. The businesses sold off were frequently merged by their new owners with other units in the same type of production. Much of this rearranging or restructuring was carried out with the use of junk bond financing, a topic to which further reference will be made.

For the period from the late 1940s to the late 1970s economic planning, as a way of rationalizing and guiding whole national economies, was a concept with considerable theoretical support that was embraced politically in varying degrees in some Western countries but, with the passage of time, gradually lost its appeal. At the same time, a less comprehensive approach known as industrial policy was used to encourage some industries that governments identified as particularly important, often because they appeared to be capable of making great contributions to national productivity growth, or because of their strategic or prestige value. In the U.S. a major debate took place over industrial policy in the early eighties, a topic pursued in the next chapter.

Industrial policy is a rather wide-ranging term that targets certain industries or firms for loans, grants, selective planning, and various degrees of public ownership. Business activities may be influenced by measures such as laws regarding competition, government purchases, support for research and development, and for education and training. Such policies were used by all European countries following World War II. As time passed their emphasis changed. In the first decade, emphasis was on basic infrastructure of coal, steel, and transportation and on education, health, and housing. After reconstruction was achieved, emphasis turned to competition policy. For example, France and the U.K. encouraged grouping of firms to achieve size in competing with the U.S. Belgium focused on getting multinationals with their technology and capital. West Germany aided research and development and created a program in the field of data processing. During the mid-1970s, following the 1973 oil crisis that brought a halt to the relatively strong growth in the developed countries, policies were adopted to resist changes called for by market signals in order to cushion the impact of slower growth on employment and output. Certain industries that were adversely affected were somewhat shielded from the winds of competition.

To conclude, by the end of the 1970s all of the major countries of Europe as well as Japan had adopted policies for the purpose of restructuring industry and promoting the competitiveness of selected sectors and firms. The U.S. did not have a deliberate industrial policy, although it did have bits and pieces of one.

Regulation

After World War II the U.S. resisted the trend to nationalization and planning. Government direction of the economy during the war, mainly by the War Production Board and the Office of Price Administration, was far greater in its bureaucratic reach than had been the case during World War I. This resulted in a wary attitude toward government intervention when the war ended. In contrast to the period after World War I when the aftertaste of federal direction of the economy was pleasant, in 1945 it was tart despite the success of industrial mobilization. The troubling fear of a postwar return to depression evaporated as the recession of 1948-1949 proved mild, and American capitalism entered a growth period for several decades that restored its luster. Generous amounts of government spending helped quite a bit; the level of aggregate demand was strengthened from 1950 over the next forty years by huge military spending on the wars in Korea and Vietnam, and on the Cold War between the West and the Soviet Union.

It is particularly noteworthy that the regulatory framework adopted under the New Deal was not dismantled. There was criticism of regulation for rigidity and delay, yet "the postwar years were a time of a regulatory equilibrium."[11] With the economy prosperous, regulatory reform was not considered an urgent item on the national agenda except by those most directly affected by the controlling agencies.

By the 1960s, at least until the Vietnam War led to inflationary financing, an active role for government in economic stabilization through the use of discretionary macroeconomic policy reached a high level of acceptance. It was a time when the economics profession was viewed as having mastered the techniques necessary for maintaining stable economic growth by skillfully applying the lessons Keynes had taught a quarter century earlier. President Richard Nixon assumed office in 1969 bearing moderately conservative credentials and thus predisposed to a reduction in the role of government in the economy. Yet within two years, with unemployment on the rise and the 1972 presidential election on the horizon, in January 1971 he declared himself to be a Keynesian, a somewhat startling comment at the time that irked many of his ardent supporters. While this volte-face hardly ranks with Constantine's conversion to Christianity, it does indicate that practical circumstances had led the president to soften his ideological opposition to government management of the economy. Much more intrusive intervention came in August 1971 when Nixon attempted to halt inflation by imposing a ninety-day freeze on wages and prices. Controls limiting wage and price increases followed for nearly three years until they were abolished as failures. But, as Daniel Yergin and Joseph Stanislaw point out, the Nixon administration "also carried out a great expansion of regulation into new areas, launching affirmative action and establishing the Environmental Protection Agency, the Occupational Safety and Health Administration, and the Equal Employment Opportunity Commission." Indeed, the Nixon presidency probably outstripped all other administrations since the New Deal in imposing new economic regulations.[12]

. A major change soon took place in attitude and policy direction. By the late 1970s confidence in the ability of government to deal effectively with the economy was eroded by an accumulation of persistent problems. Rising cynicism resulted in "the appearance of a fundamental questioning about the system of regulatory capitalism that had emerged out of the New Deal."[13] Criticism of regulation began to bring action to dismantle much of the structure established forty years earlier. Because of its strong opposition to government intervention, the Reagan administration that began in 1981 might be thought to have initiated the regulation rollback, but the regulatory walls began falling earlier. In 1975 the Securities and Exchange Commission ended the uniform setting of stockbrokers' commissions; Congress acted to deregulate airlines in 1978 followed by railroads and trucking in 1980, and in the latter year it allowed a phase-out of deposit interest rate ceilings.

> Much of the impetus for . . . deregulation was built up in the 1970s . . . and as a result many of the legislative, administrative, and legal changes were made in the years shortly before President Reagan took office; other recent ones were the result of court action initiated before 1981. The Reagan administration has had only a minor role of continuing the momentum for deregulation.[14]

Welfare State

According to a leading Swedish authority, the term "welfare state":

> can be taken to mean a state that accepts collective responsibility for its citizens and . conceivably also for other residents within its territory. It strives to abolish poverty and give to all concerned reasonable security against falling unwillingly into destitution, which is more or less arbitrarily defined from time to time as a level significantly below average prosperity. Also the welfare state attempts to create equality of op-portunities for advancement.[15]

Clearly the programs that are provided through or by government to promote the well-being or welfare of the population are socialist in nature since they are by definition outside of or supplementary to the privately functioning capitalist market system. The welfare state has been grafted onto the tree of capitalism. But the welfare state has generally not been presented by its proponents as "socialistic." It was adopted primarily as a pragmatic way of meeting widely felt needs rather than for ideological reasons. Bismarck, as observed earlier, introduced it to counteract the rise of socialism. The liberal government in Britain adopted a welfare program before World War I in response to recognition of a growing need for some amelioration of social distress. It did have the support of socialist reformers, one of the most prominent being Philip Snowden who emphasized that the Sermon on the Mount inspired him more than did Karl Marx. The Scandinavian social reformers also advanced their cause on the basis of a sense of responsibility apart from any ideology.

The welfare state concept spread through the Western world during the twenty years between the two world wars (1919-1939). Denmark was the first of the Nordic countries to adopt an ambitious system of social insurance, and Sweden became famous for its comprehensive welfare programs. Indeed, all of the Scandinavian countries gave welfare a key role in their societies. The labor movement was the prime, but certainly not the only, mover in developing a national ethos of solidarity. During the 1930s, when faith in laissez faire was sinking, Keynesian economics and the welfare state were the life rafts that were grasped.

As noted earlier, some American industrialists introduced paternalistic employee benefits early in the twentieth century that were described as welfare capitalism, a sort of private embryonic precursor to a welfare state. Over time elaborate programs were developed. Government assistance in the U.S. prior to the 1930s was meager—most of the states provided some "mother's aid" payments to destitute single mothers who met certain legitimacy qualifications. When the Great Depression hit and it became obvious that people of all walks of life and social status might fall into despair due to forces beyond their control, the New Deal administration responded to the emergency with a variety of relief and reform measures. These largely experimental initiatives were advanced by their supporters under the logo "liberal" rather than the politically incorrect labels of socialism or social democracy. The fundamental purpose was to use the state to create the conditions in which people could effectively use their democratic freedom to make the most of life according to their abilities and choices. In the phrase of Herbert Croly, a very early influential American progressive or liberal intellectual, the objective was to pursue "Jeffersonian ends by Hamiltonian means." Thus, the U.S. was brought into the family of welfare states that had emerged earlier in European countries.

The welfare capitalism of well-established corporations has of course been limited to giving their own workers a privileged status in the work force. Such corporate welfarism, a prime means of developing employee loyalty, did not die out with the arrival of the welfare state. Corporate pension and health plans, and recreational programs continued to be important to company recruitment, morale, and productivity. A satisfied employee might enthusiastically say, for example, when Sears, Roebuck was a strong and much-admired company, "Sears has been good to me." But critics have noted that corporations may exploit the ties that bind their employees to them. Employer-employee relations tend to deteriorate sharply when corporations wriggle out of their commitments to pay pensions, as some did in the 1980s by tapping into pension funds as a way of raising cash for leveraged buyouts, and again in the 1990s by unilaterally converting existing conventional pension plans to cash-balance pension plans that can result in major pension reductions.

Corporate programs have been a significant part of modern capitalism but they don't benefit the population as a whole and they lack the greater stability and continuity that government can provide via the welfare state. The transformation of the relationship between welfare and capitalism since the New Deal has been viewed as the coming of a new phase of welfare capitalism. There is, of course, a clear change in meaning between the earlier and the later use of the term welfare capitalism.

The widespread acceptance of the welfare state in the middle of the twentieth century is evident from its continuation in the 1950s when leading countries had conservative heads of government: Eisenhower in the U.S., Churchill and Macmillan in the U.K., Adenauer in West Germany, and de Gaulle in France. The economies of the West were thriving and continued to do so for another decade. Capitalism had broken free of Marxist criticism that it was flawed beyond redemption because of its periodic depressions and the hopeless deprivation of its working masses. Keynes and Beveridge had together provided the means of giving capitalism greater legitimacy, i.e., reasons for considering its institutional arrangements morally just. Significant problems remained, high on the list of which were the disenfranchised and poverty-stricken minorities in the U.S., but contrasted with the 1930s, the times were remarkably good. Keynesian economic policies provided for government intervention on the demand side to maintain high and growing levels of output and employment, while Beveridge-type social insurance systems gave protection against the hazards inherent in a market economy. Society, through the collective agency of government, was seen as capable of keeping the economic engine running much more smoothly than in the past, while simultaneously directing some of the fruits of production to those who would otherwise be unable to maintain a reasonable minimum standard of living. The two types of government intervention were considered by Keynes and Beveridge to be complementary to capitalism, improving the way it worked, perhaps even saving it from weaknesses that otherwise might have caused its overthrow as a failed socioeconomic order. It was widely believed that the inherited market system had been made more humane and more secure.

Belief in the welfare state as an essential part of modern life continued—reaching a peak of acceptance in the sixties. New programs were developed in the U.S. in the middle of that decade as a result of the adoption of the Community Mental Health Centers Act of 1963, the Food Stamp and Economic Opportunity Acts of 1964, the laws creating Medicare and Medicaid in 1965, and other legislation. A welfare scholar made the following assessment of welfare programs at this time.

> On the whole, the period from the mid to the late 1960s represents the high watermark of the welfare state idea. . . . Overall, the blend of affluence and welfare appeared as a triumphant vindication of the western social system. And social welfare looked like an eminently successful way of tempering freedom with security, enterprise with stability, economic growth with a measure of social concern and amelioration. No wonder all western industrial societies seemed to be moving, willy-nilly, in the same direction. Who but the diehard ideologue (of the Right or Left) could doubt that the welfare state was at once the correct and righteous path for the West?[16]

But the pinnacle of acceptance was now followed by a sharp attack on the post-World War II economic/social paradigm. The American consensus in favor of the policies developed from the New Deal of the 1930s to the Great Society of the 1960s lost much of its support in the 1970s. Steady economic growth gave way to economic stagnation accompanied by high rates of inflation—a painful combination that came as a shock. Keynesian economics was believed by many to have lost its magic, and confidence in the ability of the state to manage a mixed economy came under serious questioning. Critics blamed "stagflation" on the growth of government and forcefully called for reducing its role and cutting taxes to revitalize the private sector. Furthermore, studies suggested that welfare programs were ineffective, abused, or counterproductive. By the early 1980s, a small library of books and articles appeared with titles such as "The Welfare State in Crisis," and the belief spread that indeed a crisis had been reached. This view was by no means limited to the U.S., but was evident in various countries with well-developed welfare states, among which Britain and Sweden were prominent. There was no consensus about what to do about it however.

That the welfare state was inherently unstable and would reach a crisis was not a new thesis, but at this time it gained greater force and intellectual support. "With astonishing speed, the warnings of a looming crisis (particularly those of the New Right) seemed to replace the benign assumptions of social democracy as a privileged discourse among governing and 'opinion-forming' elites."[17]

From the end of World War II until the early seventies, the American economy enjoyed substantial economic growth as labor productivity steadily improved. Median family income increased by an impressive 2.7 percent annually between 1947 and 1973. These decades were also a time when income inequality was generally fairly stable with a slight downward trend.[18]

The U.S. Bureau of the Census provides data showing trends in family and household income inequality. Families are defined as two or more persons related by blood, marriage, or adoption and living in a unit. A household is a broader concept combining families and persons living alone or with unrelated roommates. Income data are arranged to show what percentage of all income goes to the poorest 1 percent of income receivers, and then for succeedingly larger percentages of income receivers until all have been covered. From the data, a standard statistical measure of inequality, the Gini coefficient, is derived that describes the whole distribution of income. The measure lies between two hypothetical extremes: if income were distributed completely equally, the Gini coefficient would be zero; if income were completely unequal—one income unit receiving all income—the coefficient would be 1. In 1947 the Gini index for family income distribution was .376 after which it fluctuated along a downward trend to a post-World War II low of .348 in 1968, so "it could be said that between 1947 and 1968, inequality in America had dropped by almost 8.0 percent."[19]

While the 1960s were years when income inequality was relatively low, it was during this decade that President Lyndon Johnson launched his War on Poverty. In *The Other America*, published in 1962, Michael Harrington, whose ethos was fully in the socialist tradition, succeeded in calling national attention to the millions of poor in the U.S. who were largely "invisible." Recalling Disraeli's "two nations" of rich and poor in mid-nineteenth-century Britain, Harrington wrote that while tens of millions of Americans enjoyed an affluent lifestyle, the U.S. contained "an underdeveloped nation" whose inhabitants are "sunk in a paralyzing routine."[20] *The Other America* was recognized as important at the time for awakening the conscience of the country and contributing to Johnson's new drive to eliminate poverty. A Harrington biographer notes that some historians have compared its significance to that of *Uncle Tom's Cabin* a century earlier, and that as the twentieth century neared its end "*Time* magazine described *The Other America* as one of the ten most influential books of the 20th century to be published anywhere in the world."[21]

A legislative declaration of war on poverty was embodied in the multifaceted Economic Opportunity Act of 1964. Programs included Head Start, for preschool children of poor families; Volunteers in Service to America (VISTA), a domestic version of the already established Peace Corps; Neighborhood Youth Corps for part-time teenage employment; Job Opportunities in the Business Sector (JOBS) to aid the hard-core unemployed to find jobs; the Community Action Program (CAP) to co-ordinate health, housing, and employment at the local level; and agencies to address the problems of children without homes, migrants, seasonal workers, and Indians.

Four decades after publication of *The Other America*, poverty remained a serious social blot. Of 15 million people living in poverty, most of the adults were employed, many full-time. The problem is not neglected by writers, but the necessary will and resources to overcome it have been lacking. In 2004 David Shipler published *The Working Poor: Invisible in America* designed to provide an understanding that the working poor are all around us and really no different from most of society. Like Harrington, Shipler hoped his book would make the people he studied and empathized with known well enough to bring the needed improvement in their lives. He points out that the health and strength of a society are reflected in how its various public and private institutions are used to correct endemic suffering and how they respond to injustice and the denial of opportunity.[22]

Government Expenditures

An important measurement of the relative roles of the public and private sectors in a country is government expenditures as a percentage of gross domestic product. A first approximation of the degree of socialism in a country is suggested by this figure. The data reveal a powerful trend toward reliance on government in the twentieth century. For a group of 14 industrial countries, the average percentage of government spending as a share of GDP was about 10 percent before World War I, 15 percent in 1920, and 21 percent in 1937. The high cost of World War II and reconstruction drove the rate up further, and it did not return to the prewar level as the century progressed; in 1960, a decade and a half after the war ended, it was 29 percent. Then over the next twenty years came the most striking development, a further surge to 43 percent in 1980, or double the pre-World War II level. All of the countries shared, to different degrees, in the climb. A list of ten of the countries shows them falling into three ranges in 1980 (see Table 3.1).

Table 3.1
Government Spending as Percentage of GDP

	1960	1980
Sweden	31.0	60.1
Belgium	30.3	58.6
Netherlands	33.7	55.2
West Germany	32.4	47.9
France	34.6	46.1
Britain	32.2	43.0
Italy	30.1	41.9
Switzerland	17.2	32.8
Japan	17.5	32.0
U.S.	27.0	31.8

Adapted from "A Survey of the World Economy," *The Economist*, September 20, 1997, p.8

The Great Depression and World War II are obvious causes of the expansion of government spending in the second quarter of the twentieth century. Some countries adopted major health and education programs after the end of the war. But the great surge in spending after 1960 took place in a prosperous and (generally) peaceful era. Instead of raising expenditures in response to crises, countries did so to fulfill aspirations of a better, more secure life for their populations. After 1960, transfer and benefit payments were the chief reason for the rise. This holds true even for the U.S. despite heavy spending on the war in Vietnam and the Cold War. Clearly the expansion of government spending in the world's most advanced economies is a prime characteristic of the history of the twentieth century.[23]

It was stated above that government spending is a barometer of sorts indicating the degree of socialism present in a society. It is important to bear in mind, however, that this rule of thumb needs to be adjusted for the difference between government spending for public consumption—in which the state procures (or itself produces) goods and services—and transfer and benefit payments, by which money is put into the hands of retirees and others who decide themselves how to spend it. Obviously, in the latter case individuals are influential in determining what is produced and by whom. Thus the rise in government spending after 1960 is socialistic mainly as to income distribution and not so with respect to the important functions of resource allocation and production.

Role of Debt

It was noted earlier that consumer debt as a "way of life" became a feature of the American economy in the twenties; it became intensified in the second half of the century, notably by the aggressive promotion of credit cards with less and less attention to the creditworthiness of consumers. The use of debt is an old, familiar, and basic feature of business finance that traditionally has been excessive during boom periods. In the sixties, the use of "leverage," or the raising of the debt/equity ratio of corporations, was high as firms relied relatively less on the slower process of retained earnings or the issuance of new stock to obtain funds for investment. Obviously the greater the role of debt, the greater the vulnerability of the economy becomes when money becomes tight.

These developments sharpen the distinction made by Daniel Bell between the values and behavior of early modern capitalism and today's prevailing ethos. Instead of an ethic of duty to work and responsibility, hedonism and impulse characterize much of present conduct, and this he sees as "the cultural contradiction of capitalism."[24]

Labor Relations

The American labor movement, a ninety-seven-pound weakling in 1933, had become quite formidable by the late forties. National unions (roughly two hundred) varied greatly as to size, extent of democratic procedures, degree of honesty versus corruption, political party orientation, and bargaining power. At the end of World War II, a rash of strikes coupled with the pressure of higher wages on the price level was widely interpreted to mean that the union movement had become too powerful, and this perception led to passage of the Labor-Management Relations

(Taft-Hartley) Act of 1947 which placed restraints on unions. Unions, like employers, were now required to avoid specified unfair practices, and the rights of individual workers were given protection against abuse by unions.

Communist influence in unions was present to some small extent in the 1920s; it became more widespread in the 1930s and continued in some organizations through the 1940s. While relatively few union members were involved, committed Communist organizers and other activists acquired influence due to perseverance and dedication to their political cause. In 1949 the CIO expelled a small group of unions found to be beyond the pale in terms of Communist infiltration, and the problem gradually faded away, "for in a relatively short period, a number of the Communist dominated unions ceased to exist." A few of the expelled unions survived but most of their members left them and joined alternative organizations.[25]

Some unions were plagued by gangsters and corruption. When it became evident that the labor movement's own efforts to prevent improper practices were not adequate, the Labor-Management Reporting (Landrum-Griffin) Act was adopted in 1959. The law requires unions to provide financial statements, prohibits certain practices, and authorizes the Secretary of Labor to seek court remedies to protect members' rights and to end financial malpractices. This law added considerably to the intervention by government into union affairs, but the results of the reporting and disclosures provided some degree of assurance concerning the extent of wrongdoing. According to the labor historian Philip Taft, "One of the great contributions of the Landrum-Griffin law is . . . to show that for probity and integrity the labor movement compares favorably with other American institutions."[26]

The AFL and CIO federations, both loose organizations of national unions, played political and public relations roles, and served to foster the common interests of the nationals. A serious problem arises when two unions claim the right to organize some particular group of workers, the result often being a bitter and costly jurisdictional dispute in which the union movement harms itself. In 1955 the AFL and CIO merged into one federation, the AFL-CIO, healing the twenty-year-old breach between them and, as one important result, substantially reducing the number of jurisdictional disputes.

By the mid-1940s the growing strength of American unions was impressive enough to suggest that the balance of power between business and labor might move steadily toward labor. An eminent labor economist, Professor Sumner H. Slichter, took the view in 1946 that our society was shifting from capitalistic to "laboristic," i.e., employees would succeed management in terms of primacy of influence. But union membership over the next third of a century did not meet this expectation. It grew in absolute terms from roughly 15 million in 1945 to 20 million in 1980, but the work force grew at a faster rate, so in relative terms union membership declined. After peaking at 35 percent when World War II ended in 1945, union membership as a percentage of working men and women fell to 22 percent in 1980. Multiple reasons have been given for the slippage. Heavy industry, where unions were strong, no longer needed as many workers. The rapid growth of service industries, increased employment in the South and of women and white-collar workers were factors that made union organizing difficult. Increased opposition by employers, including alleged firing of union activists, contributed to the unions' difficulties. When unions made determined efforts to organize in areas and industries where they have been viewed with suspicion, their success rate in winning representation elections was disappointing to them.

A major change in the composition of American unions occurred during the sixties and seventies as public sector workers, notably postal workers and teachers, joined unions. The expansion of public sector members between 1960 and 1980 more than offset an absolute decline of membership in the private sector.

While the strength of unions ebbed, the federal government during the sixties and seventies enacted a number of new laws offering various types of protection to workers in general, both union and nonunion. The postwar era inherited the National Labor Relations Act of 1935 that limits the ability of companies to either discharge or discipline employees for engaging in union activity, as well as the Fair Labor Standards Act of 1938 setting a national minimum wage and a forty-hour normal work week, plus other provisions. Adding to these holdovers from the New Deal, the following laws were adopted.[27]

1. Equal Pay Act of 1963—to prohibit sex discrimination in pay
2. Civil Rights Act of 1964 and Age Discrimination in Employment Act of 1967 (amended to disallow mandatory retirement before age seventy in 1978)—to protect against discrimination in hiring, promotion, and discharge
3. Occupational Safety & Health Act of 1970 and Federal Mine Safety & Health Act of 1977—for a safe and healthful workplace

4. Employee Retirement Income Security Act of 1974—to protect employee pensions and other benefit plans by setting standards for funding, vesting, etc.
5. Federal Privacy Act of 1974—to protect employee privacy

In addition, many states enacted laws on behalf of employee rights. This development added to the protection of whistleblowers who report violations of law or who refuse to violate a public policy as part of their job. It also enacted laws to require that workers be informed concerning hazardous substances, to protect worker privacy, and to prohibit companies from forcing workers to retire because of age. Thus, the states acted to reinforce the thrust of the federal government to make the workplace safer and more secure and to reduce discrimination. The ability of employers to decide as they please about hiring, promotion, discharge, and behavior of employees was significantly limited.

In Britain, union membership as a proportion of the labor force declined very gradually for about two decades following World War II. In this respect, the U.S. and the U.K. were similar. Indeed, until the late 1960s the two countries experienced the same general growth pattern of unionization throughout the twentieth century, although the share of the work force unionized was much higher in the U.K. throughout. But the trends in the two countries diverged sharply from 1968 through 1979, for union membership in Britain grew rapidly in both absolute and relative terms during those years. This sudden climb in membership occurred despite an ongoing redistribution of the pattern of employment toward sectors in which unionization was historically weak. Employment was shifting away from the highly organized sectors including coal mining, textiles, and railways.

The increased influence of British unions grew out of the deeply troubled economic conditions. To restrain inflation without seriously dampening the economy, it was deemed necessary to adopt an incomes policy which, to be accepted and effective, required the cooperation of the trade unions. Thus, governments in the late sixties and most of the seventies, whether conservative or Labour, reached out to unions as well as to management to forge a national policy by which unions would restrain their wage demands in return for business restraint in product pricing, while government provided a macroeconomic policy to fuel the economy sufficiently to reach its growth potential. This approach worked to some degree but only temporarily.

In early 1974, a conservative government was brought down as the result of hardship due to a severe energy shortage brought on by an international oil shortage compounded by a coal miners' strike that became violent. There followed a determined attempt by a Labour government to solve the problem of economic sluggishness through a "social contract" between the government and the unions. The unions pledged to moderate wage demands in return for government policies acceptable to them. The basis for true cooperation existed in the close links between the union movement and the Labour Party ever since the latter's founding. Progress in taming inflation followed; the rate of inflation, close to 25 percent at the end of 1975, fell to about 10 percent at the end of 1978. But the degree of wage restraint required by this policy proved too great a strain on the independently structured union movement with its traditional attitudes and practices. A horrendous crisis developed as strikes spread, causing a "winter of discontent." The entire nation seemed on the verge of grinding to a halt as transportation by rail and truck was disrupted. But probably most shocking to the public were the stringent rationing of medical care, mounds of uncollected garbage, and unburied dead as public-sector employees stayed out. The use of "industrial action," injurious to the sick, as well as picketing that was seen as intimidation, caused public disgust. The Labour Prime Minister, James Callaghan, said that "free collective vandalism" rather than free collective bargaining was taking place. At the end of March 1979 the government fell from power and in May a new era began with the formation of a conservative government led by Prime Minister Margaret Thatcher.

The close ties between the labor movement and governments during the pre-Thatcher years increased the size of union membership. Employees had an incentive to be represented in the determination of incomes policies that would largely determine wage increases. A careful analysis concluded that "the demand for collective bargaining services rose during this period of economic instability, particularly because of largely unanticipated changes in the rate of inflation."[28]

Britain's relatively poor economic performance in the years 1950-1980 has been attributed to many causes, some of them rooted in historical and cultural forces. Managerial ineffectiveness and stubborn resistance on the part of the unions to technical progress were recognized as prominent causal factors. The unions, like the Luddites of the early years of the Industrial Revolution, were a prime obstacle to innovation. Even a Marxist interpretation attributed the country's low productivity growth to the restrictive practices of unions that blocked the introduction of new, laborsaving equipment.[29] Labor relations, traditionally carried out in a climate of class divisiveness, had deteriorated into a chaotic state of constant warfare.

Following World War II, several Western European countries, notably West Germany and Sweden, adopted legal requirements known as codetermination, industrial democracy, or worker participation in management. Procedures were created by which workers in private sector enterprises participate with management in decision making on a wide range of issues. These take place at the low level of the shop floor and at the high level of the boardroom. Codetermination in Germany at this time was a sort of reincarnation of mandatory workers' councils created by the Weimar assembly in 1920 in response to a revolutionary working-class climate. Their development was subsequently limited by union leaders who saw the councils as an encroachment on their power, and when the Nazi regime came to power in the 1930s the councils were suppressed.

Germany has dual sets of labor relations. There is the collective bargaining system by which unions and employers' associations negotiate wages and related matters regionally or nationally. The works councils are not part of the collective bargaining process but are independent bodies of workers to whom management must furnish information concerning the affairs of the company. Management must have council consent prior to making changes in the hours of work, safety matters, hiring and transferring employees, and many other aspects of the job situation. Management must even have prior approval from the works council on such major decisions as plant closings, layoffs, and related matters. Furthermore, the councils must be informed and consulted on broad company policies involving investment plans, mergers, production processes, and other matters that affect employees. While the unions and works councils are separate organizations, they are indirectly related through union influence in the election of council members.

Workers have benefited from "substantial improvements in working conditions, plant safety, paid leisure, and training" to complement gains made through collective bargaining agreements. On the negative side, they tend to reduce efficiency and raise costs; in particular, decision making is slower and more cumbersome so that management loses the flexibility to act quickly to changing conditions.[30] As the twentieth century progressed and was succeeded by the twenty-first, intensified global competition increased the importance of the negative aspects.

Notes

1.   Robert Blake, *Disraeli* (New York: St. Martin's Press, 1967), pp. 495, 704.
2.   Hacker, *op. cit.*, p. 185.
3.   Stuart Bruchy, *Enterprise: The Dynamic Economy of a Free People* (Cambridge, MA: Harvard University Press, 1990), p. 208.
4.   Don Lavoie, *National Economic Planning: What is Left?* (Cambridge, MA: Ballinger, 1985), p. 226.
5.   Andrew Shonfield, *Modern Capitalism* (New York: Oxford University Press, 1965), p. 131.
6.   *Ibid.*, p. 73.
7.   *Ibid.*, p. 90.
8.   Wilfred Beckerman, "Economic Policy and Performance in Britain since World War II," in Arnold C. Harberger, ed. *World Economic Growth* (San Francisco: ICS Press, 1984), p. 21.
9.   *Ibid.*, p. 15.
10. John Kenneth Galbraith, *Economics and the Public Purpose* (Boston: Houghton Mifflin, 1973), pp. 300-301.
11. Daniel Yergin and Joseph Stanislaw, *The Commanding Heights* (New York: Simon and Schuster, 1998), p. 58.
12. *Ibid.*, p. 64.
13. *Ibid.*, p. 66.
14. Perry D. Quick, "BUSINESSES: Reagan's Industrial Policy," Chapter 9 in John L. Palmer and Isabel V. Sawhill, eds., *The Reagan Record* (Cambridge, MA: an Urban Institute Study, Ballinger, 1984), p. 304.
15. Gunnar Heckscher, *The Welfare State and Beyond* (Minneapolis: University of Minnesota Press, 1984), p. 6.
16. Ramesh Mishra, *The Welfare State in Crisis* (New York: St. Martin's Press, 1984), p. 6.
17. Christopher Pierson, *Beyond the Welfare State?* second edition (University Park, PA: Pennsylvania State University Press, 1998), p. 137.
18. Paul Ryscavage, *Income Inequality in America* (Armonk, NY: M. E. Sharpe, 1999), pp. 46, 55.
19. *Ibid.*, p. 54.
20. Michael Harrington, *The Other America* (Baltimore: Penguin Books, paper, 1963), p. 155.
21. Maurice Isserman, *The Other American* (New York: Public Affairs, 2000), p. viii.
22. David Shipler, *The Working Poor: Invisible in America* (New York: Knopf, 2004), passim.
23. *The Economist*, September 20, 1997, pp. 8, 10.
24. Bell, *op. cit.*, pp. 22, 242.
25. Philip Taft, *Organized Labor in American History* (New York: Harper & Row, 1964), p. 629.
26. *Ibid.*, p. 706.
27. The list of laws and related material has been adapted from "Beyond Unions," *Business Week*, July 8, 1985, pp. 72-75.
28. David C. Smith, "Trade Union Growth and Industrial Disputes," in Richard E. Caves and Lawrence B. Krause, eds., *Britain's Economic Performance* (Washington, D.C.: The Brookings Institution, 1980), p. 103.
29. Beckerman, *op. cit.*, p. 19.
30. Theodore Geiger, "The Movement for Industrial Democracy in Western Europe," *Challenge*, May-June, 1979, p. 16.

4

A New Wave of Capitalism—
And Undertow of Socialism

The economic performance of the Western democracies over the half-century following World War II, especially the third quarter of the century, was generally highly successful. When compared with the dismal record of the years between the two world wars, it was a brilliant demonstration of how errors of the past could be avoided by adopting appropriate new policies. The phrase "mixed economies" aptly describes the intermingling of old and new ideas and practices, the core of which was what Professor Paul Samuelson called "the neoclassical synthesis," i.e., the use of Keynesian monetary and fiscal policies to maintain a high level of resource use together with traditional market forces to allocate them efficiently. To this was added the welfare state and various degrees of government ownership and regulation. So impressive were the results that "golden age" and "glorious years" have sometimes been used to describe this period.

During the course of the 1970s, however, the mixed economies experienced difficulties that grew in intensity and called into question the policies that had given so much satisfaction. Inflation and relative stagnation resisted attempts to deal with them, and, as a result, confidence in the ability of government was gradually eroded until by the latter part of the decade a frontal assault was made on what had become accepted ideology and policy. Margaret Thatcher in Britain and Ronald Reagan in the U.S. led the assault politically with the support of a phalanx of free market economists who provided studies to support the case for drastically reducing the role of government.

The linking of Thatcher and Reagan to the movement toward greater emphasis on market economics in the West is obvious. But capitalist ideology also spread around the world during the last two decades of the twentieth century. In the context of a world "capitalist revolution," Margaret Thatcher and the Chinese Communist leader Deng Xiaoping have been cited as the two principal leaders. On the twentieth anniversary of Mrs. Thatcher's 1979 assumption of power, Daniel Yergen noted that they had a common message. One gave it to change the mixed economy model of the industrial world while the other undertook a basic revision of the Communist economic system. Curiously, only months separated the dates on which they came to power.[1]

In May 1979, Thatcher became the first female prime minister in British history when the conservative party gained an absolute majority in Parliament. The ousted Labour government bore the onus of the disruptive labor disputes of the previous six months. In Mrs. Thatcher's view, "No theory of government was ever given a fairer test or a more prolonged experiment in a democratic country than democratic socialism received in Britain. Yet it was a miserable failure in every respect." She blamed socialism not just for failing to reverse Britain's decline relative to other countries but of actually accelerating it, so that by 1979 Britain was viewed as "the sick man of Europe."[2]

Thatcher defined her government's purpose to be the restoration of a balance between the individual and the state. Central to her program was the belief that collectivism had become excessive, so she decried the "nanny state" and set out to reduce its size and scope. This involved the sale of nationalized industries, the abolition or liberalization of administrative controls, the end of government intervention in industrial disputes and wage fixing in the private sector, and the elimination of budget deficits. The new prime minister identified three chief goals: the restoration of sound money by strictly limiting the growth of the money supply in accordance with the influential monetarist doctrine of Milton Friedman; the reduction of public spending as a proportion of national income; and the reduction of taxes to improve economic incentives. The dragon of inflation was at last to be slain and the conditions created for sustaining growth of output and employment. To prevent powerful unions from dominating labor relations and forcing up wages, the legal position of trade unions would have to be amended. By carrying through on this set of ideas to some considerable extent, a capitalist revolution (or counterrevolution) was set in motion that subsequently spread around the world.

In January 1981 Ronald Reagan, a conservative Republican, became President of the U.S. having soundly defeated incumbent Democratic

President Jimmy Carter in the election of November 1980. The radical economic policy change introduced twenty months earlier in Britain was now followed by a generally similar program in the U.S. Reagan aimed to revitalize the American economy by simultaneously cutting taxes and public spending and by restricting monetary growth. Three desirable results were expected: inflation would fall, output would rise, and the federal budget would move to a balance by 1984 as the stimulus to the supply side of the economy raised government revenues. As the decade proceeded, inflation fell and output rose, but the budget deficit increased enormously and became a major issue extending into the 1990s.

The ideology of the Reagan administration was revolutionary in tone and intention although its results turned out to be evolutionary. The administration drew strength from the public's loss of confidence in the curative power of government. Regulation was considered excessive and had already been addressed by the previous (Carter) administration; taxes were widely viewed as too high; and national security was viewed by many to be in decline, a problem exacerbated by the taking of American hostages in Iran on Carter's watch. The revolutionary tone of President Reagan came from his belief that government was itself the problem, a sharp reversal of the view that government had a duty to identify and solve problems. In addition to tax and spending cuts and less regulation, government would retrench by eliminating much of the welfare state and by federal withdrawal from federal-state responsibilities, shifting control to the states. Overall, domestic spending would be reduced by 25 percent or more. Underlying the embrace of laissez faire was strong faith in American progress when the public sector does not spoil it: "the Reagan vision proclaims an era of boundless private market growth with no worrisome, much less tragic, side effects—a kind of space-age, high technology version of Norman Rockwell's America."[3]

West Germany also joined the right turn toward greater emphasis on capitalism in the early eighties. The center-left coalition of Social Democrats and Free Democrats broke up in 1982 bringing Helmut Kohl, leader of the Christian Democrats, to the chancellorship where he shared the international stage with Thatcher and Reagan. But American-style capitalism was not to be emulated: the welfare state was a success from the 1950s forward, and the institutions of the "social market" economy adopted after World War II retained much support in a society that placed a premium on security. It was true that the postwar economy, celebrated as a miracle in the 1960s and still impressive in the 1970s, had lost momentum. Kohl spoke in favor of more personal freedom and a reduced state, and public opinion in favor of the free market became more apparent in West Germany at this time. Yet no radical transformation of the German economy occurred. Chancellor Kohl remained in office for sixteen years until 1998, and at the end of his tenure, the longest of any chancellor during the twentieth century, his government's achievements fell short of what was necessary to maintain Germany's competitive place in the world economy.

Ironically, a "left-wing" coalition government led by Chancellor Gerhard Schroeder, a Social Democrat, succeeded the Kohl administration and in 2000 adopted policies reminiscent of the Thatcher/Reagan mode of twenty years earlier including substantial cuts in personal and corporate taxes. Perhaps more important from the standpoint of encouraging competition, the 40 percent capital gains tax on sale of corporate assets was eliminated. Large German corporations traditionally have held stock in each other and have been represented on each other's boards of directors, even in the same industry. While there is a German saying that "business is business, and schnapps is schnapps," shared ownership and interlocking directorates make for anticompetitive collegial relationships. As the world economy has grown increasingly competitive, the need to break up the clubby fraternal way of life became apparent, but the cost of doing so by selling off stock holdings was steep given the tax on capital gains. A restructuring of the German economy was encouraged as huge proceeds from the sale of assets became available for reinvestment. The change in times and attitudes is strikingly clear considering that earlier in his political life Herr Schroeder was a firm advocate of putting an end to capitalism. Yet despite the reforms, the German economy did not experience the dynamic effects anticipated.

From the time the constitution of the Fifth Republic, inspired by General Charles de Gaulle, its first president, was adopted in 1958 and until 1981, France was governed by conservative presidents and parliaments. The state played a considerable role during those years as it had traditionally; economic planning was in vogue, although its usefulness was seen as much diminished by the 1970s. During the last half of that decade, under the leadership of Prime Minister Raymond Barre, the hand of the state was relaxed and the economy became freer and more competitive. Price controls on industrial products were largely abolished, and tax incentives were provided to spur investment. The shift clearly had its limits, for even this strong advocate of free markets selected certain areas, including telecommunications, aerospace, and biotechnology, for generous special treatment in an attempt to wean France away from declining heavy industries to those with greater potential in the expanding world economy.

During the early eighties, the pendulum swung sharply toward state ownership and control. At the time when Thatcher, Reagan, and Kohl were moving their countries away from socialism, France did the opposite. After many years as leader of the Socialist party, Francois Mitterrand was elected president, and parties on the left were given a considerable majority in the National Assembly. The new government implemented its campaign promises quickly by nationalizing major banks and other firms to give government the ability decisively to exercise leverage in economic affairs. Industry nationalizations were patterned on the highly successful model of the large automobile manufacturer Renault that had been nationalized in 1946. In the area of social policy, the welfare state was expanded in various ways: full social security benefits became payable at age sixty, down from sixty-five; annual vacations became five weeks, up from four; minimum wages were raised; and family housing allowances were increased. The wealthy were taxed more heavily. Mitterrand came into office, a la de Gaulle, calling on the spirit of the nation to bring about great things by mobilizing all productive forces for renewal and growth. Nationalization plus social reform were to bring reconciliation between industry and labor. A new dynamism would follow resulting in economic expansion and high employment. As banks, industry, and the state worked in close collaboration a synergy would be created that would revitalize the private sector.

When Mitterrand came to power in 1981, France was in recession. As the economy was stimulated to spur growth it quickly experienced pronounced inflation and a severe current account deficit in its balance of payments; in March 1983 the franc was devalued for the third time since the Left assumed control of government. Disillusionment and a sense of failure resulted in a reevaluation of policy. The turning point came that same month when reflation was abandoned and a program of austerity begun. Tough measures followed over the next two years that withdrew considerably the paternalistic hand of government. Nationalized companies were required to modernize and the restructuring that followed resulted in massive job losses. Controls over bank lending were relaxed and exchange controls loosened. Restrictions on Japanese investment in France were removed. Mitterrand stunned supporters by authorizing a private television station, thus ending the state television monopoly. These and other measures to deregulate the economy reflected the rise to dominance of moderates in the Socialist party. By the mid-1980s, France had turned away from the strong socialist rhetoric and policies with which Mitterrand and the party had begun. Ideology had been trumped by realism in a competitive international economy in which other major nations were placing increasing emphasis on market forces.

Privatization

Privatization—the transfer of state-owned companies to private ownership—is the most striking and fundamental way of converting from socialism to capitalism for it reverses the nationalization of industry at the heart of collectivism. The privatization movement began in 1981 when the conservative government of Margaret Thatcher sold off part of British Aerospace, but it was the success of the sale of British Telecom in 1984 that attracted attention throughout Europe and then in many other parts of the world. British Telecom was then the fourth largest telephone company in the world; its sale demonstrated the importance of the government's privatization program. About half of the approximately 2 million people who bought shares had not previously owned stock, so that the well-publicized sale provided a notable fillip to the goal of promoting share-owning popular capitalism.

The privatization movement emerged quite unexpectedly in the 1980s and quickly developed great momentum. The term was little known prior to its use by the Thatcher government. Peter F. Drucker, a seminal thinker about the theory and practice of management, social theorist, and explicator of capitalism, claims to have coined it in 1969.[4] A young Tory politician picked up the word from reading Drucker and used it in a pamphlet that same year. Norman Macrae of *The Economist*, while unsure of its source, noted that the word was used in that journal as early as 1961 and recalled that during the 1960s it "seemed part of a hopeless crusade."[5] As late as 1979 the election manifesto of the Conservative party gave only "a small passing reference" to privatization, for this key element of its social philosophy was still viewed as too radical to put forward with confidence in an election campaign.[6]

Following the landmark sale of British Telecom, many other prominent state enterprises including British Gas, British Steel, British Airways, and Rolls-Royce were privatized as well as the more mundane but vital utilities providing water and electricity. It is remarkable how quickly the

British lead was emulated, for as early as 1991 over seventy countries had adopted privatization policies including some with Labor governments in Scandinavia and Australia, as well as many former Communist countries. Even France began a privatization program in 1986. This was a time of uneasy "cohabitation" between President Mitterrand, the head of state, and right wing Prime Minister Jacques Chirac, the head of government. During 1986-1987, the French government sold thirteen companies, some of which had been nationalized in 1982, and Societe Generale, one of three large banks taken over by the state in 1945. A notably successful sale of shares of the great Credit Lyonnais bank took place in July of 1999 after that venerable institution had been through a rough period requiring state subsidies for survival.

A prime example of the compelling force of privatization comes from Brazil where in 1988 workers struck the state-run National Steel Company, South America's largest steel plant. Violence broke out and the army was used against the workers who took control of the plant. The steelworkers fought to retain their jobs and benefits under state operation. Four years after that bloody battle the workers demanded that the mill be privatized; they had come to view privatization as necessary to keep the company competitive and so protect their jobs. The firm was fully privatized.[7]

Between 1988 and 1993 some 2,700 state-owned enterprises worth $271 billion were privatized in ninety-five countries.[8] Commentators spoke in superlatives such as "the sale of the century," and when Yergin and Stanislaw looked back at the phenomenon in 1998 they referred to "the greatest sale in the history of the world" by which governments divested themselves of assets worth trillions of dollars.[9] However, the quickest act of privatization historically may have been carried out by Peter the Great on a day in 1722 when visiting Kazan. "Inspecting a government-owned textile mill, he observed that it was languidly producing shoddy materials while, not far away, a privately owned mill was flourishing. On the spot, Peter simply gave the government mill to the private owner."[10]

By the mid-1990s, the Labour Party underwent a profound change in its philosophy concerning state ownership of industry so important in its history. The loss of four consecutive general elections was the catalyst for the way the party now presented itself. It distanced itself from its socialist past by embracing the free market, rejecting so-called "tax and spend" policies, and by abandoning the previously almost sacrosanct Clause Four of its constitution adopted in 1918 calling for "common ownership of the means of production, distribution, and exchange," an icon prominently displayed on party membership cards. The transformation from "old" to "new" Labour was inspired and led by a charismatic young member of Parliament, Tony Blair, who became party leader is 1994. He persuaded the party to abandon Clause Four in April 1995 and became prime minister as a result of the election of May 1997 when the new moderate Labour Party defeated the Conservatives after the latter had been in power for eighteen years. The last major industrial sale by the Conservative government before the 1997 election was the breakup of British Rail into many private companies, and it was carried out despite a high level of popular skepticism. In this case, privatized companies were far from being launched on their own resources, for the government provided generous subsidies stretching over many years. Ironically, the railway system now had a reliable stream of income from public funds rather than having to lobby for them annually through a nationalized system, and as a result much-needed long-term capital investment could be made and service improved. Or so it seemed in 1995-1997 when British Rail was split into about one hundred pieces. Over the next four years, the privatized system experienced a combination of enormous profits for some companies, lack of investment in needed basic facilities, incompetent management, and miserable passenger service. In an effort to rescue the rail network, the Labour government created a new Strategic Rail Authority and appointed a new rail regulator in mid-1999.[11]

As experience with privatization proceeded over the years in Britain questions accumulated and resistance gradually strengthened. Substantial increases in prices, profits, and executive salaries among newly privatized companies led to charges of abuse of market power.

When the Labour Party scrapped Clause Four it gave up the goal of nationalization, but it did not embrace further privatization. It was, therefore, unexpected when in June of 1998 the Labour government announced its intention to sell state assets worth about one billion dollars each year for three years, including the air-traffic control system. Labour backbenchers may well have been stunned by this decision of the chancellor of the exchequer, who also urged municipal councils to sell large amounts of property.[12] That policy choices reflect the clash of ideology and pragmatism was strikingly clear.

When the sunshine of democracy dawned in Eastern Europe at the beginning of the 1990s, the various countries of the region transformed themselves into market economies over the next several years with much, some, or little success. Privatization, central to the transformation, was successful in many places but was badly botched in others. Both Russia and Czechoslovakia used vouchers for the purpose of distributing ownership of state enterprises to the general public. Corruption, in the form of manipulation by insiders, allowed the existing managements virtually to steal enterprises. Having passed into the hands of "oligarchs," the companies often failed to convert themselves into efficient competitive entities. Lacking the foundation of an effective government based on the rule of law, economic reform was thwarted.

The term privatization is generally used to mean the transfer of facilities from government to private ownership or to private control under franchise. Another form of privatization, widely used in the U.S., refers to the contracting out by government of public services to profit-making private operators. The motivation is to achieve lower cost and higher productivity, and the process relies on competitive bidding. The extent to which desirable results may be achieved tends to vary depending on the type of service. Garbage collection is a prime example of successful outsourcing. The idea of contracting out by government incubated among conservatives, but by the early 1990s it was embraced by both Democrats and Republicans. In Chicago the administration of Mayor Richard M. Daley adopted it for a variety of purposes including towing abandoned cars, tree-trimming, stump removal, and janitorial services. Certain services of a sensitive and emotional nature, for example managing prisons and providing health care, are more controversial than routine tasks such as laundry. In the case of prisons, there is probably little scope for innovation and/or lower labor cost, and there is a danger of lax or inhumane treatment of an incarcerated population. The range of functions that governments in the U.S. have transferred to private management grew substantially during the last years of the twentieth century to include such activities as the running of civic arenas, golf courses, and libraries. Even uranium-enrichment, an operation of national security sensitivity, was privatized in 1998. Basically, the question of the desirability of private management depends on realizing benefits of competition, where they are available, with careful supervision to maintain high standards of safety and reliability. The choice between public and privately contracted services depends on practical considerations.

By 2002 the privatization movement in Europe had slowed to a crawl. Britain had no major state-owned companies left other than the post office, and the public strongly opposed its sale. The huge step of railway privatization had turned out to be of doubtful benefit, and it was in part undone when the Railtrack Company went bankrupt in 2001 and became a ward of the state.

On the continent where privatization was carried out to a lesser degree than in Britain, enthusiasm for it had waned. Private investors who bought shares earlier in German and French telecom giants sold by governments were disappointed by their performance. Also, the state, particularly in France, continued to hold a large proportion of shares in partially privatized firms. Privatization on the continent has been used, to a large extent, to raise revenues of governments rather than for the purpose of letting market forces take control. According to one survey, governments "have rarely forfeited control and have remained inclined to meddle."[13]

Planning Fades Away

In the 1980s, as reliance on the market increased, it followed that indicative planning continued to decline in importance. Even in France, its reputation tarnished as a result of the disappointing experience of the 1970s, planning seemed to have lost its appeal. But upon assuming office in 1981, the Mitterrand administration boldly (or rashly) gave it a central role. Planning was given enhanced administrative standing by the establishment of a new Ministry for Economic Planning and Regional Policy. A fresh start was made by replacing the draft eighth plan for 1981-1985 with a two-year interim plan plus a ninth plan to run through the end of Mitterrand's first presidential term in 1988. Hopes for success were soon dashed. The interim plan (1982-1983) called for monetary and fiscal expansion to reduce unemployment, but with the world economy in recession the result was inflation and a series of devaluations of the franc that soon brought about the austerity program referred to earlier. French planning had lost its bid for a comeback and was demoted to a lower level in the hierarchy of government administration. By 1990 one close observer felt free to dismiss it with a terse observation: "If 'indicative planning' once worked in France it has long been abandoned for de-socialization and free markets."[14] In that same year a conference was held in Washington, D.C., sponsored by the Association for Comparative Economic Studies that brought together academic and other specialists in the field of indicative planning. One paper noted that the French plan had become a think tank with little power, a description applied to the Japanese plan also. Careful examination of the institutions and practices of indicative planning by the experts suggests that a revival of reliance on planning is unlikely in the foreseeable future. The high level of economic interdependence among the nations of the world together with widespread acceptance of the principles of market economics made indicative planning essentially irrelevant as a policy tool at the close of the twentieth century.[15]

Planning as carried out in the Communist countries of Eastern Europe and the Soviet Union was, of course, "hard core" in that the state undertook to implement the plans by direct command so that the market was superseded for the most part. Such planning simply evaporated when Communist government fell in late 1989 in East Germany, Hungary, Czechoslovakia, Poland, Bulgaria, and Romania, and when the Soviet Union disintegrated in December 1991.

Regulatory Crosscurrents

A major policy statement issued at the outset of the Reagan presidency called for "a far-reaching program of regulatory relief." Regulatory reform was undertaken in 1981 by officials zealous for the task. The Office of Management and Budget rejected rule proposals by government agencies, and Vice-President George H. W. Bush headed a deregulatory task force. As a result, there was a decline of 15 percent in the work force of federal regulators over four years. Some deregulation legislation was adopted, although not to the extent advocates had hoped. During the second Reagan term the trend went into reverse. In 1986 a major hazardous waste law was adopted despite a threatened presidential veto, and in 1987 Congress passed a clean-water bill over Reagan's veto. As the Reagan presidency wound down, some government agencies as well as Congress acted to assert regulatory control on a variety of fronts particularly in the sensitive areas of environment, public safety, and consumer protection. On the whole, the Reagan program did not deliver as much as its rhetoric had promised. The failure to build substantially on the economic deregulation momentum begun during the Carter years was "the major missed opportunity of the Reagan program," according to William A. Niskanen who served on Reagan's Council of Economic Advisers during 1981-1985.[16] Also, in response to the Reagan administration's efforts to withdraw federal restrictions on corporate freedom, the states took on a more active regulatory role. States became more aggressive in the areas of the environment, consumer protection, and antitrust. An example is the setting of tougher standards for pesticides. A group of states took the Environmental Protection Agency to court to require a reduction in acid rain, and California brought suit against the Department of Energy to get it to carry out restrictions on coastal drilling. This behavior by the states is instructive, for it demonstrates that government units closer to local communities than the federal government are willing to impose rules of behavior on businesses. It also shows the flexibility of a plural system of government in responding to concerns of the public.

President George H. W. Bush installed a moderate administration staffed by pragmatists rather than anti-government crusaders. By the late 1980s, public support was growing for greater environmental, health, and safety protection, as well as for stricter regulation of business in the financial area. At the end of the Bush presidency in 1993, the number of federal regulatory staff members topped 122,000 surpassing the number so employed at the time Reagan assumed power in 1981.

A major crisis in the savings and loan industry became evident at the end of the 1980s and took several years to resolve with a bailout of some $300 billion in public funds, giving it the distinction of being the most costly financial disaster in our nation's history. This fiasco resulted from removing limits on the interest rates these financial intermediaries could pay to depositors while simultaneously allowing them enhanced freedom to invest their funds in risky investments including junk bonds. In some states savings institutions were permitted to invest in real estate developments. During the 1980s many of the loans and investments soured, and the problem was worsened by the conduct of savings and loan executives who were guilty of mismanagement, embezzlement, and fraud. Insolvency engulfed hundreds of what had traditionally been solid, reliable institutions. The deposits held by the public in the thrifts were guaranteed by the federal government. When the thrifts failed, the Federal Savings and Loan Insurance Corporation reimbursed the insured depositors until its resources were exhausted. Funds were then provided by the treasury from the sale of its bonds, and so ultimately would have to come from taxpayers. This sordid episode sprouted in the soil of a naive attitude that viewed regulation as superfluous. The savings and loan industry failed because regulation and supervision failed, as Paul Volcker, Chairman of the Board of Governors of the Federal Reserve System, pointed out. Careful bank examinations could have stopped the savings and loans from acquiring high-risk assets had not heavy pressure been applied politically. Eventually it became clear that large political contributions by savings and loan executives gave them influence with high elected officials to stay the regulators' hands.

Over the years the case for regulation to meet newly recognized problems has often been made, and major regulatory policies and programs have been adopted. To be more specific, a selection of these developments will now pass briefly in review.

In 1987 an investigative report on the accuracy of Pap-testing revealed that it was frequently done in a slipshod manner with the result that cancer or precancerous cell abnormalities went undetected in about a quarter of the tests performed. Technicians in laboratories referred to as Pap mills analyzed far more specimens than could be done accurately according to recommended standards. Poorly paid technicians were pressured by their employers to perform as many as four times the number of reports that could be done with proper care and in some cases were paid piecework wages. This shocking situation stemmed from the fierce competition of laboratories that sought to underbid their market rivals, and by the gynecologists who used them to pad their charges to patients. It was a case of a malignant market, and of deficient state and federal regulation.[17]

Industrial plants throughout the U.S. began to be subject to new reporting requirements early in 1988 concerning the use and storage of over three hundred substances considered to be extremely hazardous. Such data collection applies to the vast majority of manufacturing plants and constitutes a fundamental change in how society handles the problem of dangerous substances. Local emergency committees are the recipients of the data as are state governments and the Environmental Protection Agency.

Problems that occur in interstate commerce may indicate a need for regulation, as was illustrated by a truck wreck in the Atlanta area in October 1988. The truck's cargo, en route from Wisconsin to Florida, consisted of bees that were infested by a mite capable of destroying a hive. If the Georgia state agriculture authorities had been notified of the shipment, as they are of intrastate cargoes, they could have acted quickly to destroy the infested bees. While this case is relatively minor, it makes the point that local authorities may be unable effectively to cope with matters that extend beyond their legal reach and therefore require a broader set of controls.

In a decision that was unexpected, the California Supreme Court upheld Proposition 103 in May 1989 providing for major reform of the property and casualty insurance business. New regulations require insurers to gain the approval of the state insurance department as a condition of raising rates. Existing rates were cut, and the industry is no longer exempt from California's antitrust laws. The insurance industry is exceptional among major financial services in the U.S. in being the only one regulated by states and not the federal government. A series of huge failures in property casualty has called into question the ability of state regulators to supervise and regulate a market that has become national and international. The spotlight fell on state regulators in the spring of 1999 after a financier named Martin Frankel, operating a brokerage called Liberty National Securities, was found to have bilked insurance companies in six states of hundreds of millions of dollars before fleeing the country.

Even when political power rests with ardent opponents of regulation, they may find a compelling need to support an expansion of regulation to meet a particular problem. The Republican Party swept into control of Congress in the 1994 elections and its congressional members then began a barrage of criticism of regulation by federal agencies, notably the Environmental Protection Agency and the Food and Drug Administration. But, at the same time, serious abuses came to light in the market for derivative investments. Regulators imposed rules for more disclosure by issuers of securities and the monitoring of transactions that might involve fraud. The chairmen of the House and Senate banking committees supported these regulatory measures and began considering legislation. According to Chairman James A. Leach of the House Banking Committee, "Washington can no longer credibly continue to rationalize a laissez-faire approach to derivative oversight."[18]

Major changes in the meat and poultry industry were required by new regulations announced in July 1996 to improve food safety in the U.S.. An amendment to the ninety-year old federal regulatory process called for a scientific system of controls to be placed in every plant where animals are slaughtered, to detect bacterial contamination. Regular testing by inspectors was mandated; plants repeatedly found to have high levels of salmonella were made subject to closure by the federal Department of Agriculture.

An attempt to deregulate American agriculture was made with considerable enthusiasm and fanfare by Congress in 1996 when it adopted the "Freedom to Farm" law. This intended return to market forces was hailed as historic. It set in motion a phasing out of farm subsidies going back more than six decades. But something soon happened on the agricultural freedom road that caused an about-face. Exports to Asia dropped sharply and so did farm prices and incomes. In response Congress, in 1998, passed and the president signed a bill to increase farm subsidies (transition payments) temporarily. While the basic law remains on the statute books, its goal is not being achieved. Indeed, by 2000 federal direct payments of $28 billion, a record, was half of farm income. Instead of phasing out government aid to farmers, the "Freedom to Farm" law brought a tripling of payments between 1996 and 2000. The agricultural sector has largely evolved into an income transfer program with government subsidies used to prop up rural areas that are in decline. Farmers traditionally have cherished their independence and been disdainful of government, but now find themselves in a culture of dependency. It is ironic that there are parts of agrarian America where a welfare state has become the norm. The form of federal farm aid has changed from price supports and acreage restrictions to direct income supports. These are mainly provided to row crop and dairy farmers; beef and pork subsidies are relatively small. The fruit and vegetable sectors are generally unsubsidized.

In June 1997 new Ambient Air Quality Standards were established in the U.S. The new regulations require an extensive monitoring network and citations to be issued for violations.

A Food and Drug Administration regulation was announced in March of 1999 covering some 100,000 nonprescription drugs. It requires uniform labels printed in type large enough to be easily read covering ingredients, uses, warnings, and directions.

The national minimum wage established by the Fair Labor Standards Act of 1938 for most nonfarm workers engaged in interstate commerce in the U.S. has been increased periodically as prices and the general level of wages have risen. While ritualized debate in Congress repeats familiar arguments over the timing and extent of each increase, the amount set lags behind the rising cost of living and is inadequate to maintain a family of four above the poverty line. In the mid-1990s a movement for a "living wage" sprang up in various communities, and by 1999 had succeeded in getting ordinances adopted in over forty cities including Los Angeles, Miami, San Antonio, San Jose, and Detroit. The ordinances require a wage rate sufficient to raise family incomes above the poverty level, which means doubling or almost doubling the national minimum wage. Workers covered are employees of local governments and of firms that hold government contracts. Staunch opposition by private industry has kept such laws from applying to workers generally.

New technology brings not only benefits but disutilities that in turn spawn new regulations. As the Internet expanded in the 1990s it was accompanied by the emergence of bulk e-mailers ("spammers") who, by 2002, dispatched billions of unsolicited commercial messages world-wide daily, about one-third of all e-mail on the Internet. They clog in-boxes with many promotions such as schemes to get rich quick, to lose weight, and to obtain pornography. By mid-2003 some form of prohibition had been adopted in thirty-three states. One state, Virginia, adopted a law in April 2003 under which a sender of more than ten thousand deceptive messages a day can be jailed for up to five years. But enforcement of laws against spamming is exceedingly difficult making them virtually useless. If action to control spam is to become effective, it will likely require strong federal legislation along with technological advances and consumer cooperation.

Government regulation of unsought commercial telephone calls was given an enthusiastic public response in mid-2003. The Federal Trade Commission (FTC) adopted a "do not call" registry to which almost 20 million people signed up in less than two weeks. Telemarketers can be fined as much as $11,000 for each call made to a number on the prohibited list.

While the parade of new regulations has been marching along as time passes, there has also been an enormously important overturning of the regulatory machinery in some areas. Two leviathan industries that affect the entire society, telephones and electric power, stand out.

AT&T had become a great jewel in the crown of American enterprise, recognized for its excellent nationwide service. The largest corporation in the nation, it was long considered a natural monopoly and therefore regulated. But by the 1970s its supposedly impregnable position came under assault by aspiring entrepreneurial rivals armed with rapidly developing new technology. In 1974 an antitrust suit was begun by the Department of Justice, and a trial began in 1981 that resulted in the divestiture of its local telephone companies effective January 1, 1984. The immediate post-breakup scene consisted of eight regional companies under regulation providing "local" service, and AT&T as a long-distance provider in competition with many rivals nationally and internationally. But no fixed pattern has persisted—price and product competition have been increasing throughout a vast communications industry churning with new technology, new firms, and new combinations of firms. A mélange of services, traditional and wireless telephone, cable television, and computer are offered in a rapidly changing and somewhat confusing market.

From the 1930s to the 1970s the electric power industry in the U.S. consisted of many companies all of which were regarded as natural monopolies requiring regulation. Over time costs and prices fell. Then came rapidly rising utility prices as the cost of nuclear plants rose and the utilities experienced high costs for fuel inputs and interest charges. Consumers complained of rate increases while at the same time the utilities' balance sheets became a matter of considerable concern. Striking changes then occurred to provide a means of escape from this double bind. Newly constructed power plants using breakthrough technology produced electricity relatively cheaply and sold it to the utilities. Then the Energy Policy Act of 1992 permitted the dismantling of the regulatory system as the natural monopoly model was replaced with a competitive model. Local utilities were required to make their transmission lines available to buyers and sellers of electric power. Since the mid-1990s it is possible for "a local utility in one part of the country to contract for electric power from a cheap generator in another part of the country." The whole ethos of the industry changed and the regulators became guarantors of a competitive environment.[19]

Like the privatization movement, the deregulation of major industries tended to spread from country to country. At the start of the 1990s, members of the U.S. Federal Energy Regulatory Commission observed the working of the post-privatized British power industry, an example that encouraged them to support the strong deregulatory measures described immediately above. The British and American experiences were then emulated in Germany, a country where regulation has been and remains widespread. In the latter half of the 1990s German telecommunications and electricity were deregulated with the result that costs to consumers fell considerably. Such cost reductions have wider macroeconomic implications by helping to keep inflation under control.

When the administration of President George W. Bush came into office in 2001 it brought a strong commitment to rolling back government regulations. It lost little time in implementing its views in many areas of the economy including health, financial services, natural resources, and telecommunications. For example, the Department of Health and Human Services reduced the frequency of examinations of nursing home practices, the Treasury reduced reporting requirements for corporations, and the Labor Department reduced the number of firms subject to review of compliance with workplace laws. For officials of the administration and leading contributors to the Republican Party, such steps were seen as completing the process of deregulation begun in the 1980s under President Reagan.

An unexpected U-turn away from deregulation occurred in 2001 and 2002 as terrorist attacks on the U.S. and the revelation of stunning corporate wrongdoing led to a resurgence of the regulatory role of government in some areas of the economy.

Starting even before the advent of the George W. Bush administration, electric power deregulation at the state level suddenly and dramatically suffered a severe setback. As a result of action taken by the State of California in 1998, the industry was largely deregulated; rules were set with administrative oversight, but the new limited regulations proved ineffective. When, in 2000, demand for electricity soared and shortages developed, the state experienced rolling blackouts and price spikes hundreds of times above the long-run average. A crisis situation prevailed for a year during which the state government bought power at great expense and eventually found it necessary to negotiate long-term contracts at exorbitant prices. Ironically, instead of withdrawing from the market the government of California became a participant in it.

An end to the crisis came in June 2001 as supplies increased, demand declined as the economy lost momentum, conservation was practiced, and the Federal Energy Regulatory Commission (FERC) adopted price ceilings for the western states. It later became evident that the market had been rigged by the creation of artificial shortages involving the shutting down of power plants, and by energy companies such as Enron Corporation that manipulated the market. Some of the contracts made by the state to buy power at very high prices during the crisis period were renegotiated following investigations by the FERC. The "demonstration effect" of California's experience had a chilling effect on the movement to deregulate public utilities throughout the country. Advocates of deregulation blamed the failure on the way in was done, asserting that it did not create a truly free market. Yet the aggressive, innovative, and greedy behavior of market participants intent on opportunities for quick and enormous short-term profits clearly engendered a climate of concern for the protection of the public interest from instability and exploitation.

Industrial Policy

In 1980 an important and spirited debate began in the U.S. over "industrial policy." It grew out of frustration with the slow rate of American economic growth during the 1970s and lasted for over a decade, although it was most intense during the early eighties. It referred primarily, although not exclusively, to a variety of government measures to promote particular patterns of investment. Pleas for the adoption of such a policy implied that the U.S. did not have one, but this was not strictly true.

Policies to nurture and support certain industries are not as "old as the hills," but they probably are as old as the mills, for nations traditionally have given succor to selected industries and firms for reasons of national defense, development, pride, employment, or because of the political clout of certain persons or groups. As previously noted, the innovation of the moving assembly line in 1913 by the Ford Motor Company brought the revolution of mass-production methods to American industry. Advances in manufacturing techniques that led up to this important development extend back to the early part of the nineteenth century when the U.S. government subsidized gun manufacturers for the purpose of developing precision measuring and machinery techniques necessary for the production of products with genuinely interchangeable parts.

The U.S. government played a vital role in the development of major new industries early in the twentieth century. Shortly before the nation entered World War I, the realization that American aircraft manufacturing was not competitive with more advanced European producers prompted Congress to create an agency, the National Advisory Committee for Aeronautics (NACA), charged with making cutting-edge aerospace technology available to domestic companies. More direct intervention came when orders for naval aircraft set Boeing on its way to leadership in military and commercial aircraft production. Immediately following World War I, President Woodrow Wilson used the resources of the navy to create the Radio Corporation of America (RCA). The results were greater than could have been anticipated. RCA not only enabled the U.S. to take the lead in radio technology as intended, but later repeated its success in television and electronics.

Computer technology emerged from research designed to break enemy codes and for other purposes during World War II. After the war, no private firms were willing to develop a computer industry without major government support. Strong support was forthcoming in the form of funds for R&D expenses and contracts for aircraft guidance systems and air defense systems. The great success of companies such as IBM, Intel, and Microsoft, and the fame and fortune of Bill Gates and other geniuses is now part of the folklore of the second half of the twentieth century. A review of these events has led, however, to the following conclusion that may be surprising because it is not advertised and celebrated: "The point is that the U.S. government created the world's dominant computer industry."[20]

Many government programs were in place by 1980, but because they were not consciously designed to form a national strategy, there did not seem to be an industrial policy at all. The issue was brought vividly to public attention by the federal government's response to the financial plight of the Chrysler Corporation. A law was signed by President Carter in January 1980 that provided a federal loan guarantee of $1.5 billion to save the company from bankruptcy. This extraordinary rescue operation was adopted to protect 200,000 jobs and to avoid the payment of hundreds of millions of dollars for unemployment, welfare, and other expenditures by the government.

Two leading proponents of a new industrial policy for the U.S., Ira C. Magaziner and Robert B. Reich, argued that the existing policy was haphazard and ineffective.

> The United States has an irrational and uncoordinated industrial policy that is comprised of "voluntary" restrictions on imports, occasional bail-outs for major companies near bankruptcy, small sums spent for job training and job relocation, a huge and growing program of defense procurement and defense-related research, and a wide array of subsidies, loan guarantees, and special tax benefits for particular firms or industries. It is an industrial policy by default, in which government and business are inextricably intertwined but in which the goal of international competitiveness has not figured.[21]

It was generally agreed that the American economy had lost its edge. Japan and the countries of Western Europe were utilizing industrial policies put in place over the previous twenty years or so. The performance of the Japanese economy was so impressive that it invited emulation. A central feature of the Japanese approach was to use government to target certain industries identified for their growth prospects, particularly those deemed capable of competing strongly in foreign markets. Government was seen as necessary for the effective use of national resources on the grounds that individual corporations did not have the necessary information and vantage point to make decisions required to maximize the economy's potential. Competition domestically was regarded in Japan as wasteful of national resources. So to guide export-led growth, a prestigious government bureaucracy was created after World War II with the Ministry of International Trade and Industry (MITI) the architect of policy. It played a variety of cards including cooperative research and development backed by government support, subsidies, and legalized cartels. Japanese firms were sheltered from the cold winds of import competition, and investment in Japan by foreign companies was strictly limited.

Many voices were raised in favor of a new American policy of guiding investment into growth areas and away from sectors of declining demand. Help was proposed to encourage high-risk projects that require a long time to bear fruit, to take into account returns to society as a whole as well as to private investors, and to assist workers in making adjustments required as industries are restructured. Broadly speaking, the advocates of a comprehensive industrial policy were liberals, and it appealed to influential members of the Democratic Party. But considerable support also came from business executives traditionally opposed to government influence in decisions determining the direction private enterprise should take. A leading proposal for implementation of an industrial policy called for reincarnation of the depression-era Reconstruction Finance Corporation to serve as a development bank. Oversight would be by a public-private group of business, labor, and government representatives. The agency would be assigned the task of identifying and promoting high-tech industries and assisting older industries in need of rehabilitation. Funds would flow from it in the form of loans and subsidies, and it would provide loan guarantees. In addition, it might be authorized to approve companies for tax breaks and decide which industries should be given protection from import competition. Negotiations might be used to work out agreements to restructure enterprises with the participation of labor. Apart from the proposal of a new RFC, a Democratic Party caucus in November 1983 called for formal cooperation among business, labor, and government through a "council on economic competitiveness and cooperation." This group would examine the competitiveness of U.S. industries. Other recommendations were to loosen antitrust laws, provide permanent tax incentives, and establish so-called "clearinghouses," i.e., government centers that could serve as conduits to pass along technological advances to firms able to apply them.

No major new policy emerged from all the soul-searching concerning the ability of American business to compete in the world economy. A formidable case against a new industrial policy was made by a former chairman of the Council of Economic Advisers and former director of the Bureau of the Budget under a Democratic administration, Charles L. Schultze. Schultze had no doubt that such a policy would be a huge mistake. He did not believe that the American economy was in dire trouble; in particular, his reading of the data indicated that U.S. industry had performed relatively well during the 1970s and he rejected a central tenet of the advocates of an industrial policy, the charge that America was "de-industrializing." Schultze acknowledged that the economy did have certain structural problems, but he argued that an industrial policy could only create new ones. As for Japan, it was a virtue of the Japanese that they could work cooperatively in pursuit of national objectives. MITI very probably deserved praise for guiding Japan's success in the world market for semiconductors, notably with respect to memory chips. But it struck out a number of times too, for example by attempting to keep Honda from producing automobiles. Japan had prospered because its hard-driving business leaders had used the vast savings of their society to take advantage of modern technology, but as early as 1983 Schultze observed the beginning of less exalted performance. As for the U.S., it was beyond the ability of our political system to make hard-headed investment choices among regions, industries, and individual firms. "Not only would it be impossible for the government to pick a winning industrial combination in advance, but its attempt to do so would almost surely inflict much harm."[22] This position supported that of the Reagan administration.

President Reagan shared the widespread concern that U.S. industry had lost vitality and was losing its position of leadership in the world economy. His administration's approach to solving the problem was to rely more fully on Adam Smith's free market ideology, to which end it favored reducing business taxes, reducing regulation, and relying on free trade. It viewed an industrial policy as worse then useless. But the rhetoric of government officials is not always consistent with what is happening. In 1958, following the launching of the first successful satellite, Sputnick, by the Soviet Union, the U.S. established the Defense Advanced Research Projects Agency (DARPA) within the Department of Defense. The agency was assigned the task of exploring advanced technology for the Pentagon, and over the following decades it worked on lasers, helicopters, stealth technology, computers, and other projects. In the 1980s DARPA became involved in industrial policy due to pressure from industrialists for assistance and because it was the agency with the money. For example, it funded a research consortium called Sematech to help American firms compete with Japan in semiconductors, and it took on a collection of other programs with industrial applications. Such involvement would have aroused strong opposition if carried out forthrightly as an industrial policy by a civilian agency of government. But under the banner of national security, it passed muster rather easily. Indeed, DARPA evolved into "the closest thing this nation has to Japan's Ministry of International Trade and Industry."[23] The highly successful electronics and aerospace entrepreneurs in California generally needed government contracts from NASA and the Department of Defense to establish their companies, and they relied on research at California universities that, in turn, depended on federal funding.

The 1990s saw a reversal of fortunes on the part of Japan and the U.S. Success had led to a belief by some policy-makers in Japan that they had devised a new and superior brand of capitalism, so that Japan was in a class by itself. Given the remarkable performance of the Japanese economy and the admiration, if not adulation of foreigners, a surge of national pride is understandable. Inevitably or not, it was followed by a serious fall. Capitalist economies historically have experienced intoxicating speculative booms that ended in bust; in the late 1980s, the Japanese were caught up in a spiral of rising stock market and property values, a "bubble economy" that burst in 1990 and 1991. The value of stocks fell to 40 percent of their peak. Bank solvency was jeopardized as the value of real estate loans reflected the steep fall in property values. Probably what was most unexpected was the depth and length of the slump that began in 1992. For the remainder of the decade Japan's economy could not get traction. Credit was scarce as a result of a weakened banking system. Government attempts to provide fiscal and monetary stimulus failed to achieve the desired results. Soon the élan that had resulted from the success of three decades of rapid economic growth was replaced by a loss of confidence as the country's competitiveness declined. Analysts now searched for what was wrong with the Japanese form of capitalism. As the decade ended there was a need for bailing out financial institutions, and reforming and making more transparent the regulatory system. While some regulations stimulated innovations by setting standards for quality, safety, and energy usage, and by creating a demand for newly designed goods, others had a crippling effect. Probably the main prescription emerging from all the diagnoses was for an end to anticompetitive policies. "Japanese policymakers need to rethink lax antitrust policy, rampant cartels and consortia, government guidance, and regulatory barriers to competition. Enhancing competition, not just deregulation per se, must be the goal of regulatory reform. The same holds true for trade."[24] After years of delay, action was taken in 1998-1999 with respect to Japan's financial markets, making them about as free of regulation as those in the U.S. and Britain. In an extraordinary change of policy, foreign investors have been permitted to acquire Japanese firms. Yet the new emphasis on competitive capital markets was not the whole story, for government retained the ability to bypass market decisions by loan guarantees to firms that otherwise lack the ability to raise funds.

In 1997 Hong Kong reverted to Chinese rule but retained a large measure of autonomy. Over the next two years, its government began to dismantle the banking cartel and the tightly controlled airline and telecommunications sectors that were a legacy of the British era, in this way enhancing the territory's reputation as exemplar of a free market economy. But in response to the financial typhoon that spread over much of Asia soon after the transfer of political control, Hong Kong adopted a multi-form industrial policy. This shift to state interventionism included participation directly in the stock market by the purchase of large amounts of stock, the creation of a fund to assist new businesses in the development of technological innovation, and the extension of funds to small businesses through grants and loans. In view of these developments, Hong Kong lost some of its image as the ultimate example of a laissez faire economy.[25]

Consideration of industrial policy in the U.S., largely put to rest after the debate of the 1980s, has been somewhat revived in the early part of the twenty-first century. The case has been made that American success in scientific and technological competitiveness is greatly enhanced when industry and government are complementary. A good entrepreneurial climate with flexible capital and labor markets is basic but insufficient because industry dedicates over 90 percent of its R&D spending to applied research. Federal spending on basic research is needed to ensure healthy technological progress. In an article warning of a coming challenge to America from Asian countries, Adam Segal, a Senior Fellow in China Studies at the Council on Foreign Relations observed: "Money for basic research, especially in the physical sciences and engineering, and support for the National Science Foundation should . . . be maintained at current levels or increased" to avoid weakening "one of the pillars of the country's future economic and technological health."[26]

The case for a well-balanced, effective American industrial policy has been presented by Clyde Prestowitz. Prestowitz draws on extensive experience in industry and foreign trade policy in both the private and public sectors. His urgent call for an active government role is a response to the "new wave" of globalization that "will challenge all the conventional wisdom as it shifts wealth and power to Asia." Global manufacturing is already locating in China, and India is attracting software development and service.

"Economists have held it as an article of faith that high-tech manufacturing and services are done in advanced countries, while routine low-value work is done in developing countries." Now, however, semiconductor plants are locating in China and high-tech work is being performed in China and India in the fields of mobile phones, software, radiology, major surgery, and pharmaceuticals. High-tech work is often outsourced by companies in the U.S. and Europe because it is performed abroad not only more cheaply but also better. "The view that the uniquely inventive U.S. economy will always maintain economic leadership by doing the next new thing no longer necessarily holds. U.S. spending on research and development has declined in critical areas, and its technology infrastructure is deteriorating."

Significantly, the President's Council of Advisers on Science and Technology (PCAST), in an assessment made in 2004 pointed out that U.S. companies avoid participating in many of the industries that utilize high-tech equipment. The fact that manufacturing is a declining part of the American economy is significant not just for the jobs involved. It is vital because research and manufacturing are part of an ecosystem linking basic R&D, prototyping, and manufacturing, i.e., "there is a link between the factory floor and the research lab."

American firms are competing against foreign countries, not just foreign companies. Overseas governments use an array of incentives consisting of "packages of capital grants, tax holidays, free land, worker training" to attract investments, whereas "the U.S. government proclaims its devotion to laissez faire and retains no mechanism for considering industry structure issues." Prestowitz provides detailed suggestions for devising a competitiveness policy for the American economy.[27]

Satchel Paige's advice, "Don't look back. Something may be gaining on you," is appealing in some contexts, but national economic policy is not one of them.

Globalization

The march to freer markets over the final two decades of the twentieth century was worldwide, cutting across a wide variety of political systems. In a remarkable turnaround, not only did governments sell off nationalized companies, but multinational corporations were lured back by countries that had previously banished them. Capitalism became acceptable to socialists in many parts of the world. Greater economic interdependence among nations created new trading opportunities, intensified competition, and, inevitably, exposed national populations to increased influences and shocks from outside their borders. Of course worldwide trade, now greatly expanded, has been an important feature of modern times going back to the great voyages of discovery of the 1490s and the century that followed. By circumnavigating the globe in 1519-1522, Ferdinand Magellan and Juan-Sebastian Elcano demonstrated that all parts of the earth are linked, and worldwide trade became a major factor in global economic growth.

Much attention was given to trade liberalization during the second half of the twentieth century to reverse the disruptions and barriers created by two world wars, depression, and the autarchic policies of fascist and Communist countries. As a result, during the final years of the century the proportion of world output being traded internationally was about the same as it was when war broke out in 1914. By the late 1990s the U.S. economy was considerably more closely linked to the world economy through trade than it was a generation earlier. At 15 percent of national output, American exports and imports were triple the 1960 proportion and twice that of 1980. But the relative size of trade is only part of the story. The developments of the 1980s and 1990s were of a kind and magnitude that brought the term "globalization" into use; a new phase of capitalism, worldwide in scope, had arrived. When the Cold War ended, the great ideological gulf that it embodied quickly waned and was, to a large extent, replaced by acceptance of world markets by almost all countries. If Karl Marx could rise from his grave in Highgate Cemetary in London, he would hardly be surprised by globalization, for he observed that capitalism constantly revolutionized production, disturbed social conditions, and caused the "universal interdependence of nations."

Globalization has many facets. People in different parts of the world were made more familiar with other cultures through films, and this familiarity increased greatly with the spread of television. Far more profound, the computer has been a great transforming agent. Electronic technology enables services to be readily available internationally. The term information technology (IT) is comprehensive of computers, software, telecommunications, and the Internet. Since services are steadily increasing relative to physical goods as a share of economic output, the ability to trade them worldwide provides a great enlargement of markets. The power of the new technologies to provide large, unanticipated benefits is illustrated by the experience of the oil industry. Daniel Yergin, who won a Pulitzer Prize for his study of the industry, found that "the revolution in information technology . . . when adapted by the oil industry," drove costs down dramatically in the early nineties and brought about a virtual doubling of proven oil reserves between 1970 and 2000.[28]

Globalization means that all over the world countries have "signed up" for free market capitalism. If ideology is a secular form of religion, most nations now have much the same faith, although cultural and historical differences make for a range of acceptance and enthusiasm. Conformity to certain fairly objective standards is required. This means primary reliance on the private sector, acceptance of the principles of monetary and fiscal orthodoxy, relatively free trade in goods and services, and generally free movement of capital in and out of the country. The social arena in which economic activity occurs must be based, in the main, on the rule of law fairly enforced, civil liberties, and reliable sources of information.

It may seem that globalization means returning fully to the system of the nineteenth and early twentieth centuries, but such is not the case. There is now clearly a role for government regulation in the areas of the environment, health, and safety. The welfare state is well established, and the size of government is far larger. Monetary and fiscal policies are fully accepted as necessary to successful governance. In other words, the role of "socialist" institutions in the capitalist world is much greater than during the earlier period of globalization from around 1850 to 1914.

There is a real danger that the supercharged global financial system may spin out of control. Its salient features are the speed, ease, and low cost of transferring capital. Countries that are judged to have strong growth potential and are viewed as conforming to the required standards of conduct, experience abundant capital inflows to their financial markets and their production facilities, but if the outlook for a country becomes dubious for any reason, financial or otherwise, capital can be withdrawn from it almost instantaneously. Weakness in one country may raise suspicions about others, causing instability to spread from one market to another, including from weak to strong.

There is no agency or institution in this new global market system that can be depended on to rescue it from itself in time of trouble. The power to control capital flows is largely held, in the evocative term of *New York Times* columnist Thomas L. Friedman, by the "Electronic Herd," i.e., "all the faceless stock, bond, and currency traders sitting behind computer screens all over the globe, moving their money around with the click of a mouse from mutual funds to pension funds to emerging market funds." The changes in technology, finance, and information that created the globalized system have made capitalism the only ideology acceptable to the market movers and shakers—so that "every government lives under the fear of a no-confidence vote from the herd."[29] The Electronic Herd has become the enforcer of the capitalist code of conduct; governments must conform or risk retribution in the form of capital flight. The institutional nature of the financial markets has shifted toward participants who move quickly in and out of markets using leverage to magnify their effect and with a short-term mind-set. Hedge funds are the most conspicuous, sometimes notorious, players, but the broader financial community—banking, insurance, brokerage, multinational treasurers—are in this high-stakes game as well. The old-fashioned, more staid, and deliberate type of investment activity by banks and insurance companies has been partially displaced by the movement of funds in and out of many different instruments by those placing bets in a global casino.

The global economy experienced painful turmoil beginning in mid-1997 with the forced devaluation of the Thai baht, the result of a burst real estate bubble, excessive foreign debt, unsound banks, and a rigid exchange rate that fostered abundant borrowing and lending. For the next two years financial crises spread like a firestorm through much of Asia (notably Indonesia, South Korea, Malaysia, the Philippines); Russia and Brazil; and, to some extent, most of the world's developing countries. Much more than financial losses occurred as currencies depreciated and stocks plunged: economic recession, soaring unemployment, sudden loss of wealth, and increased poverty. The International Monetary Fund used its resources and laid down financial prescriptions for its client states to observe, but the ability of it and other official institutions to deal effectively with the problems was far from fully satisfactory.

The global stock and bond markets were staggered in 1998 by the near collapse of Long Term Capital Management, a hedge fund that suffered a loss of $4 billion over the course of a few months. It could have been called "Risks-R-Us," given its high leverage ratio—borrowings of thirty times equity. Considered a financial genius before the losses, John Meriwether, partner and chief strategist, later admitted that the approach taken was fundamentally flawed. A crisis atmosphere that threatened to seize up the securities markets was relieved when the Federal Reserve System organized a bailout of $3.6 billion by Wall Street houses. The markets generally recovered well, although the memory of the narrow escape left the bond market less liquid as traders became more cautious.

In response to the perception that there was a serious systemic problem, a reevaluation of the existing institutional structure was deemed necessary and was undertaken by the private-sector Council on Foreign Relations in the form of an Independent Task Force on the Future of the International Financial Architecture. It was composed of eminent experts and leaders in finance and public affairs. A detailed report with specific recommendations was subsequently issued by this group.[30]

In addition to the report cited various other proposals were put forward for consideration, including those of the G-7 group of industrialized countries and the Basel Committee of central banks. Thus, a chorus of voices called for banks to be subject to internationally coordinated supervision and regulation, for regulation of securities, and for disclosure requirements. As Professor Benjamin M. Friedman has pointed out, there is widespread recognition that governments need to act in concert "to restrain economic behavior in the private sector."[31]

Banking history is replete with episodes of lenders taking excessive risks under competitive pressure during economic expansions followed by the harsh aftermath of collapse. A description of bankers in pursuit of borrowers at a World Bank/IMF meeting—which served, in part, as a posh bank salesmen's convention—is suggestive of their eagerness to lend. An investment banker explains that "there are ten hares chasing each fox. When you get to the minister, your rivals have got there before you." A South American prime minister complains that he "can hardly face going back to the hotel; there are six different banks waiting for me."[32] Excessive lending is an occupational disease, a compulsive disorder, that periodically afflicts loan officers. It is a sobering fact that all of the countries that experienced crises during the 1990s had accumulated massive amounts of debt.

High-speed data transmission permits historically revolutionary transfers of labor services worldwide. Traditionally, before the computer age, an employer could obtain labor services from another country in the congealed form of imported goods, including from the firm's own factories abroad, or the labor could emigrate and join the work force of the employer's country. Now, by using computers, firms in one part of the world can directly employ the services of workers located in other parts, however remote geographically and politically they may be. For example, IBM, working with subsidiaries and partners abroad, has produced software across national boundaries in a continuous process. Work begun in Beijing is sent in turn to Seattle, Belarus, Latvia, India, and back to Beijing before culminating in Seattle.[33] American insurance companies use foreign workers to process paperwork, and publishers have books typeset overseas. By 1991, American Airlines reached to Barbados to employ many hundreds of data-entry clerks.

By the early years of the twenty-first century, a software and information technology industry in India had become of major importance to leading international corporations by providing a variety of services such as accounting, billing, tax preparation, computer problem solving, and research that are at the heart of their operations. Well-educated, competent, high technology employees had become vital to the running of numerous high-profile corporations, for example, American Express, Sony, and General Electric. This sophisticated sector of the Indian economy has significant political importance to that country's government for the foreign exchange it earns; and, therefore, it encourages policies to avoid tension or disruptions in international relations that might jeopardize its continued success.

The freeing of markets around the world has brought economic benefits in the form of rapid growth through competition, new technologies, and capital formation. Direct foreign investments by multinational corporations create jobs for workers in poor countries eager to escape the alternatives of working the land or working for inefficient local firms that are part of a rigid, often corrupt, elite. Greater prosperity fosters a rising middle class with better education and higher aspirations. Thus, the groundwork is laid for stable democracy. The wealthy and talented in the advanced countries that provide the capital, technology, and skills to developing countries, of course, are also prime beneficiaries of rising output.

But while globalization raises world output, it has its downside as well. Workers in advanced countries have to compete against the cheaper, often much cheaper, labor of the newly industrializing countries. They feel the competition in lower wages and layoffs.

A combination of developments—in technology, globalization, market power, competitive practices, labor relations—are involved in the remarkable rise of Wal-Mart Stores. Beginning in 1962 as a discount store in a small Arkansas town, Wal-Mart expanded to become the world's largest company with over one million employees. The range and volume of consumer goods that pass through its hands made it a gigantic early twenty-first-century general store that appeals to a great variety of consumers all over the world. It is admired and feared by competitors and suppliers for the intensity with which it focuses on cutting costs and paying attention to small details. Its management capitalizes on advanced technology used in a global market context. As a quintessentially capitalist enterprise, it exemplifies both the positive and negative aspects of capitalism.

By keeping prices low, Wal-Mart contributed to the low level of inflation during the boom years of the nineties in the U.S. It lays claim to raising the standard of living of low- and middle-income workers. Its employment practices include promotion from within and the availability of stock options. As a buyer, it has not been shy in taking on well-established suppliers. When the prices of goods have been kept high by a coterie of dominant companies, Wal-Mart has initiated its own brands to bring prices down, as it did with vitamins. The efficiency with which the company is run has made it an exemplar to be emulated, in particular, by greater reliance on information technology.

But Wal-Mart's competitive practices have had adverse effects on others, some of whom cry "foul." Many retail competitors have been driven from the field, and larger rivals have been forced to seek strength through mergers to continue in business. While such restructuring may be expected, there is much concern about the labor practices used to grow and expand market share. Wal-Mart avers that it requires suppliers to provide appropriate working conditions, yet it has repeatedly been accused of importing goods from factories with very poor conditions. Its own workforce is nonunion, whereas many firms with which it deals or competes are unionized. It has been charged with overworking and underpaying its employees. Unions see their standards to be jeopardized by the market clout of the giant retailer in two realms. Wal-Mart is able to demand very low wholesale prices, so its suppliers must do all they can to pare production costs. As a low-price seller, it forces retailers to meet, or at least come close to, its prices; and this may mean reducing wages and benefits, especially where labor is a major cost component. By 2003 it had some 4,750 stores that were visited by roughly 140 million customers. Its relentless competitive practices in product and labor markets, and its conflict with community groups who oppose its plans to build huge new stores has led to questions concerning its compatibility with major segments of society. Wal-Mart has been described in a business periodical as "a cult masquerading as a company."[34]

Real wage levels in the U.S. for unskilled workers were depressed from the seventies into the nineties in part because of lower cost foreign production. Not surprisingly, organized labor has developed an antipathy to globalized free trade. It prefers an alternative, so-called fair trade, which relies on protectionist policies. In addition, opposition to globalization comes from environmental groups such as Friends of the Earth and the Sierra Club, consumer groups that resist the power of big business, and from advocacy groups for poor countries that are considered to be victims of exploitation. At the end of November 1999, these organizations coalesced in a forceful display of opposition to globalization at a summit meeting of the World Trade Organization (WTO) in Seattle. They share a belief that the rules of the WTO benefit multinational corporations while destroying jobs and damaging the environment. The WTO is criticized as a secretive and unaccountable body.

Despite the general trend of trade liberalization since World War II, much protection remains, partly in the form of tariffs but in a variety of other forms as well. Anti-dumping duties, are used to block imports that are considered in violation of international agreements, and once imposed they tend to persist. To deter importing countries from imposing barriers, exporting countries adopt restraints on exports that are euphemistically described as voluntary. Other ways of discouraging foreign competition involve industry standards. Then there are some economic sectors, notably agriculture, textiles, and shipping, that have been consistently resistant to liberalization.

Trade policy is not something to which the general public has paid much attention. Indeed, the opening of negotiations was, until 1999, held in an atmosphere of public apathy. Corporations on the other hand, with well-paid lobbyists to represent their interests, exert strong influence on government trade policy. When the WTO met in Seattle, demonstrations against it by aroused opposition groups were expected. Reality far exceeded expectations, for it was as if a forecast for a thunderstorm were followed by a tornado. A rally of tens of thousands of union members showed their solidarity and marched in protest. A carnival atmosphere was created by environmental and human-rights activists. The organization of all these protesters was accomplished with the aid of e-mail and websites. The WTO was pilloried and the city virtually immobilized. Although the vast majority of protesters were peaceful, a mass of fierce activists blocked the center of the city, and masked rioters broke store windows. A civil emergency was declared by the mayor, the city police were overwhelmed, and the National Guard was sent to the city by the governor. The violence took attention away from the messages of the peaceful demonstrators, but it certainly made the occasion more memorable than it otherwise would have been to globalization's leaders. Siege tactics aside, the sheer size of the mass of protesters assembled by more than a thousand nongovernmental organizations was impressive.

At the end of January 2000, two months after the Seattle debacle, spokespersons for the anti-globalization forces were given a sympathetic hearing at the annual meeting of the World Economic Forum in Davos, Switzerland. That they were even invited suggests that the global economy's elite had become aware that some of the effects of globalization may have a boomerang effect on them. The forum assembles the crème de la crème of the business, political, and academic worlds—people of wealth, power, and ideas. The corporate chief executives, high government officials, and influential economists on this stage are central figures in the new age of capitalism. Major groups critical of the way globalization has developed, including the AFL-CIO, Greenpeace, the World Wildlife Fund, and Amnesty International, were invited to make their cases for ending child labor, reforming labor laws to set global standards, and protecting the environment. Despite their hostility to aspects of globalization, there was a consensus among the protest groups that it cannot be undone: globalization is recognized as inevitable, so it must be expanded beyond commerce to include the environment and labor. In response, business leaders offered proposals for greater social consciousness. Advocacy groups have demonstrated their ability to cause change in corporate behavior by, for example, pressuring Nike to alter its sources and Royal Dutch/Shell to adopt better environmental policies.

A Seattle-like protest disrupted the Washington, D.C. meetings of the World Bank and the IMF in mid-April 2000. Again the protesters sought to prevent meetings from taking place, and while they did not succeed, downtown Washington was paralyzed and serious inconvenience resulted. Most of the demonstrators were reported to be of college age. Their message was that the World Bank and the IMF, like the WTO, oppress the poor and hold down wages in the U.S. It had become clear that considerable distrust, even loathing, existed on the part of determined activists and others sympathetic to their cause, toward the international business system and international organizations that are viewed as co-conspirators in benefiting the elites of the world to the detriment of the "have-nots." Indeed, the view that globalization would overcome poverty and inequality as world production and trade rose was now questioned even by some who have worked diligently to achieve an open trading/investing world economy. In a report assessing globalization, the World Bank found that the reduction of poverty had been minimal and expressed its determination to bring about better results. It reported that for nations that adopted the most open trade policies, the wealthy were the chief beneficiaries and income inequalities grew larger during the nineties. The belief that the world economy failed the poor had grown by the spring of 2000 to the point that the term globalization was apparently being avoided by high public officials.[35]

The globalization protest movement erupted again in July 2001 at the (now) G-8 summit of national leaders in Genoa, Italy. Nearly ten thousand protesters participated. The messages of the peaceful vast majority were spoiled by a violent small contingent whose rioting brought about one death, hundreds of injuries, and devastation to much of the city; this was the highest toll to date in the series of antiglobalization protests.

At the root of the problem of great inequality among regions of the world—growing abundance for a minority, some improvement for others, and immiseration for the rest—lies a fundamental difference in technical ability. Technological innovations, the key to progress, have come from a limited number of rich countries. According to an estimate by Jeffrey Sachs, about one-third of the world's population is "technologically disconnected," unable to innovate or adapt new technologies. A completely new strategy involving international organizations, governments, industry, and academia seems necessary to address the growing imbalance.[36]

Reshaping the globalized economy to accommodate noncommercial concerns will require a high level of negotiation and cooperation. While free trade is needed for economic efficiency, other values are also vital. The WTO has the potential to evolve into an international regulatory body that combines the now traditional role of establishing rules for trade and investment with new areas of labor and environmental standards. This, however, is a daunting task given that there are thousands of corporations, thousands of nongovernmental organizations, and well over one hundred countries with governments jealous of their sovereignty and subject to powerful pressure groups.

The rise of labor and public interest groups to exert influence sufficient to restrain and to modify the market power of large corporations is an application of what John Kenneth Galbraith described as countervailing power. Galbraith observed how labor unions were developed to cope with the power of corporations in the labor market, and how food, department store, and mail order retailers developed the ability to countervail the market power of strong suppliers. In the 1930s the U.S. government used its power to strengthen the market position of farmers and introduced the Wagner Act and minimum wage legislation to strengthen the position of workers.[37] Countervailing power needs to reach beyond national boundaries to be effective in today's global economy.

On May 24, 2000 the U.S. House of Representatives voted, after bitter debate, in favor of granting Permanent Normal Trade Relations to China. Four months later, on September 19, the Senate overwhelmingly passed companion legislation, thereby opening the way for China's entry into the World Trade Organization. This victory for free trade supporters gave a green light to American corporations to invest in China. It was achieved over the strenuous and passionate objection of organized labor and human rights organizations.

The entry of China into the fold of the WTO, an organization widely considered a world capitalist club, is a mark of capitalism's rout of Communism. The Communist party rulers of China deemed it essential to participate fully in the competitive world economy in order to provide increasingly productive employment and rising incomes for its vast and growing population. Yet, this confirmation and extension of globalization carries with it reasons for doubt about its long-run viability. The trade bill was adopted only after a major political struggle in a time of prosperity and very low unemployment. New jobs have been created, many in export-oriented businesses, but other jobs have been lost. The losses are attributed to globalization whereas the newly created ones are not as readily recognized or appreciated as the result of new and expanding markets abroad. The constant churning of markets makes for a sense of insecurity for workers and business owners; and concerns over income inequality, environmental degradation, and human rights violations add to a sense of unease and organized outbursts of anger as seen in Seattle and other cities. The lack of broad public conviction in favor of free trade might well, in a time of slow growth or recession, bring a potent political backlash that would result in a reversion to protectionism. To avoid such a future swing away from globalization, steps could be taken to mitigate the discontent of those who do not share in its benefits or who fear losing their jobs. Progressive measures—improved skill training programs, health-care insurance, assured portable pension plans—could build a dike.

Apart from efforts to empower the WTO or other intergovernmental agency to adopt codes of behavior governing labor standards and/or environmental protection, an impressive coalition of diverse groups called the Fair Labor Association (FLA) was formed in 1996 to eliminate or at least diminish sweatshop conditions throughout the world. This organization combines numerous private human rights groups, the U.S. government, and major apparel companies such as Reebok, Levi Strauss, and Liz Claiborne. Many leading American universities, the National Council of Churches, and the Lawyers Committee for Human Rights are among its members. The FLA has adopted a code prohibiting child labor and forced labor, and establishing minimum wages, maximum hours, and decent working conditions. Independent monitoring, including surprise inspections, is part of the agreement. The ability, ultimately, to enforce the anti-sweatshop rules rests with the public; consumers can look for an FLA label that complying companies are authorized to sew into their products. The participating universities are important in maintaining standards, for their logos are authorized only for products bearing the FLA seal of approval.

In contrast to the FLA, another organization, the Worker Rights Consortium (WRC), also gained support among college communities in the U.S. This group's approach to ending sweatshops is to confront and denigrate multinational corporations, not to work with them. The WRC has the support of American unions that favor protectionism and are unwilling to sanction production that takes place in other countries.

A revealing entrepreneurial facet of globalization is described in a book by David Bornstein that shows how new technology empowers people in many countries to deal in new ways with social problems at the grass roots. Education, health, environment, crime, poverty, child abuse, and so forth cry out for reform. Government has often failed to meet the challenge. There are, however, unusual people—activists referred to as social entrepreneurs—who build coalitions to bring about solutions. These innovators promote and market their progressive ideas to tap into mainstream organizations for financial help. New globalized communications and information technology are essential to this effort. An organization called Ashoka: Innovators for the Public identifies social entrepreneurs whom it assists financially with its own funds and that of other foundations.[38]

The economics faculties of leading U.S. universities propounded the benefits of globalization during the final thirty years of the twentieth century. They influenced foreign students from developing nations who subsequently, as government officials and leading businessmen, were largely responsible for the adoption by their countries of free market policies in the 1990s. But economic and financial problems gave rise to doubts about the prosperity that globalization promised. As a result, American economists split into those who continued advocating freer movement of resources of all kinds to advance globalization and those who, impressed by the severe financial and economic difficulties experienced by developing countries, saw the need for ways of alleviating the distress attributed to globalization. The latter scholars consider limits on free trade, ways of avoiding damage from open financial markets, and the need to make regulation more effective. Leaders of both camps agree that capital controls are needed to reduce the impact of surges of short-term lending and investing that have disrupted developing markets.

Three books that examine, evaluate, and prescribe policy recommendations with regard to globalization are Paul Streeten's *Globalisation: Threat or Opportunity?*, Joseph E. Stiglitz's *Globalization and Its Discontents*, and Jagdish Bhagwati's *In Defense of Globalization.*

Streeten sees globalization in terms reminiscent of Dickens' "best of times, worst of times" dichotomy of 150 years earlier. There have been remarkable gains: between 1960 and 1998 some countries realized major improvements in life expectancy, infant mortality, adult literacy, and real GDP per head. But economic restructuring, technological changes, the rush to freer markets, and competition have taken a heavy toll in impoverishment, insecurity, and weakened institutional support systems. The income gap between rich and poor nations doubled over the previous thirty years, and almost everywhere extreme poverty has been increasing rapidly.

Technology has moved ahead in transport, communications, and information, thereby unifying the world to a considerable extent, but the nation state has not been able to keep up with these rapid changes. Some functions of the state need to be transferred upward to an international or supra-national level to match the globalization of technology and private enterprise. National supervision and regulation has become inadequate. "Globalisation has reduced the ability of national governments both to maintain full employment and to look after the victims of the competitive struggle."[39] Streeten calls for global institutions that go beyond those presently in place to deal with many areas including control of the arms trade, a world central bank, progressive global taxation, and a global energy policy. These are matters that are not high, if present at all, on the agendas of world leaders in the early years of the twenty-first century.

Stiglitz, winner of the 2001 Nobel in economic science, is an academic economist who served on the U.S. Council of Economic Advisers and as chief economist and senior vice president of the World Bank. His theoretical work and policy experience have led him to view government and markets as complementary.

Globalization has been highly beneficial by helping countries to grow rapidly. Stiglitz points to export-led growth that raised the living standards of millions of Asians. Much of the developing world has gained access to knowledge and overcome a pervasive sense of isolation. Foreign aid in the form of irrigation, education, and health projects are cited. But proponents of globalization claim too much. They associate it with accepting a model of capitalism made in America, and they insist that developing countries follow it.

While world income rose an average of 2.5 percent annually over the final decade of the twentieth century, there was an increase of almost 100 million people living in dire poverty. One major problem is the asymmetry of trade policy. Poor countries were pressured to eliminate trade barriers while Western barriers were maintained, thereby depriving developing countries of export income from agricultural produce and textiles. Another problem resulted from the lowering of capital market controls. Latin America and Asia received inflows of hot money; when abruptly reversed, the result was collapsed currencies and undermined banking systems.

Stiglitz is critical of the "free market mantra," a central part of what he calls the "Washington Consensus," consisting of views shared by the IMF, the World Bank, and the U.S. Treasury concerning the policies that developing countries should follow. During the last twenty years of the twentieth century the Washington Consensus insisted rigidly on market liberalization, privatization, and fiscal austerity without regard to other vitally needed policies so that they became ends in themselves. The most successful developing countries used globalization to expand exports while taking care that their own trade barriers were not dropped prematurely. They made sure that capital and enterprise were present to provide jobs. The IMF, in Stiglitz's judgment, has blundered by prematurely forcing liberalization and privatization without safety nets or adequate regulatory frameworks.

Stiglitz offers specific reforms to the IMF and the global financial system: intervention to keep short-term capital flows ("hot money") from imposing huge harmful externalities on people who are not lenders or borrowers; bankruptcy reforms and standstills; less reliance on bailouts; banking regulations in developed and less-developed countries; improved risk management by having creditors absorb risks of large real interest fluctuations; and improved safety nets. "We cannot go back on globalization. . . . The issue is how can we make it work."[40]

The eminent economist Jagdish Bhagwati is a prolific contributor to the literature of international economics. He maintains that numerous studies over the past three decades show clearly that trade protection inhibits prosperity for rich and poor countries alike. Globalization, as Bhagwati evaluates it in *In Defense of Globalization*, is unambiguously beneficial. Its critics are viewed as either doctrinaire opponents of capitalism whose minds are closed or people, notably those in nongovernmental organizations, whose intentions to benefit the world's poor exceed their understanding of the issues. Yet Bhagwati recognizes areas in need of reform, notably the problem of short-term capital flows. Developing countries were induced by a "Wall Street-Treasury Complex" to liberalize capital flows which resulted in financial crises in the 1990s. He also wants multinational corporations to adopt higher labor and environmental standards for their plants in developing countries.[41]

The tenet that international specialization and trade are, on balance, always beneficial has long been stoutly defended by mainstream economic theorists. It was noteworthy, therefore, when a Nobel laureate of enormous stature, Professor Paul Samuelson, raised doubts about the benefits to the U.S. of the movement of high-skilled jobs to Asian countries. In a 2004 article that reexamined trade theory, Samuelson declared that comparative advantage does not guarantee net gains from trade.

> Sometimes free trade globalization can convert a technical change abroad into a benefit for both regions; but sometimes a productivity gain in one country can benefit that country alone, while permanently hurting the other country by reducing the gains from trade that are possible between the two countries.
>
> It does not follow from my corrections and emendations that nations should or should not introduce selective protectionism. Even where a genuine harm is dealt out by the roulette wheel of evolving comparative advantage in a world of free trade, what a democracy tries to do in self defense may often amount to gratuitously shooting itself in the foot.[42]

An alarm bell has been sounded by one of the virtuoso players in world financial markets. The billionaire speculator George Soros, who looks at the world economy from the perspective of a hedge fund operator, has warned that global capitalism is inherently unstable and that institutional changes in world government are needed to ward off depression and war. His fear is based on the perception that the acceptance of market fundamentalism, i.e., laissez faire, which existed before World War I has returned. A global political system is required not only to stabilize the global market system by intervening in times of crisis, but also to provide social protection and reduce income inequality.

Nouveau Finance

Rapidly expanding real output—the whole interconnected economic sphere embracing entrepreneurship, research, innovation, investment, production, trade—required the oxygen of finance. The flow of finance certainly swelled, but it also took new forms as the financial markets were to a considerable extent reinvented.

Even before the renewed emphasis on free market policies to spur innovation and growth in the 1980s, traditional financing was to some extent superseded. Corporations previously in thrall to banks for loans began to raise funds by selling short-term debt instruments known as commercial paper to the general public.

Another development, "securitizing" mortgages, greatly expanded the size of the home mortgage market. Financial institutions in the secondary mortgage market buy mortgages from the primary lenders and then, on the basis of these underlying mortgages, issue securities that provide interest and principal payments. The securities are attractive to pension funds and other investors, and thus are able to bring additional funds into the mortgage market.

When banks make large loans they often arrange for other banks to assume a portion of the loan, thereby spreading the risk, a practice called syndication. At the turn of the twenty-first century, syndicated lending expanded and developed a new twist. Loans were divided into smaller segments to be sold to buyers other than banks, often mutual funds. While this development contributes to bank safety, it shifts risk to the non-bank holders of corporate loans. Individual investors who buy mutual funds might thus be taking on more risk than they realize. A latent issue of consumer protection seems present in these circumstances.

The most spectacular financial market phenomenon of the eighties was the great expansion of so-called junk bonds, high-yield, high-risk securities that became notorious when the market for them collapsed. These securities are classified as below "investment grade" by either Moody's or Standard & Poor's, the principal rating agencies. Although they carry a high risk of default, research shows that over an extended time period a large portfolio of them earns a higher return than securities with higher ratings.

Junk bond financing was used in different ways with quite different results. As a vehicle by which small firms could tap into funds to carry out innovations they served a valuable purpose, as was the case in the computer, telecommunications, and cable television industries. The financing of corporate raiders brought about major reorganizations that shook American industry in ways either beneficial or harmful. There were huge opportunities for raiders in acquiring conglomerate corporations. The use of junk bond financing allowed leveraged buyouts of companies whose stock was valued below their worth when broken up. Often the enterprises taken over became more efficient by, for example, uniting struggling branches with other organizations in the same line of business. Inept managers of takeover targets resisted efforts to acquire the companies they managed, but hostile takeovers ousted them in favor of better management. An improvement in the productivity and profitability of American business during the 1990s very likely is due, in part, to the takeovers of the previous decade.

While leveraged buyouts were useful in restructuring undervalued companies, they became a craze. In some cases, unsuitable candidates were purchased at exorbitant prices. Ironically, businesses whose performance improved after being taken over were encumbered by the high cost of acquisition and oppressive debt that consisted largely of junk bonds. Restructuring brought massive white and blue collar layoffs, the misuse of resources, and serious disturbance to communities. The people who arranged the deals also arranged generous fees for cutting them. A kind of madness prevailed as groups of promoters, investment bankers, and company executives feasted on the large funds involved. The Wall Street environment was tainted by conflicts of interest, the misuse of insider information, and market rigging. The success of the corporate acquisitions required a robust economy in which profits rose and assets could be sold at good prices. When the economy slowed at the end of the eighties the precarious junk bond market was hit by a number of major defaults. The years 1989 and 1990 together saw defaults of about $30 billion, and holders of junk bonds experienced substantial losses. When recession began in mid-1990, the wave of takeovers and junk bonds was cited for helping to cause it and for contributing to the savings and loan crisis.

Known as the junk bond king, Michael Milken, who ran a largely autonomous department within the investment banking firm Drexel Burnham Lambert Inc., was sent to jail and fined in 1990 for felonies including illegal securities trading. Thirteen other Wall Street operators were convicted for financial crimes during the eighties.

In reviewing what happened, Herbert Stein observed that blame should not attach to the sale of junk bonds per se, but to the junk bond dealers. It is true that junk bonds are risky, but risk is inherent in capitalism. Investment bankers sold the risky bonds in transactions of extraordinary complexity to pension funds, insurance companies, and savings and loans. The members of the public who invested their savings in these financial intermediaries did not know of the risks involved and did not stand to gain from them, but they would lose in case of failure. The winners of the deals were the investment bankers, fund managers and the lawyers, accountants, and consultants associated with them. It added up to abuse of responsibilities that could have weakened trust in our financial institutions; it constituted the sabotaging of capitalism. It was time for all those leaders of business and politics as well as intellectuals "who consider themselves the champions of capitalism to denounce those who are sabotaging it."[43]

During the long boom of the nineties, junk bonds came strongly back into vogue; by the year 2000 they exceeded $500 billion, about triple the amount of a decade earlier.

The venture capital industry rose to prominence in the U.S. during the eighties. By 1988 venture capital firms managed some $30 billion of investments compared with $3 billion ten years earlier. They are a major provider of equity capital to young companies, especially between the time the enterprise has used up the initial capital of its founders and when it either makes an initial public offer of stock or merges with a larger firm. In addition to pumping money into fledgling firms, venture capitalists contribute management expertise. Indeed, they typically exert substantial control over management decisions. They often protect their investments through convertible preferred stock. As preferred stockholders, they precede common stockholders during a liquidation, and the convertibility feature permits them to acquire common stock in those ventures that become highly successful public corporations. The industry is made up primarily of private investment funds that take the form of limited partnerships.

A study of the venture capital industry in 1989 found "that venture capital was a response to the needs of new businesses with long development cycles and an emphasis on emerging technologies. The demand for venture capital funding emerged since the late 1970s with the rapid expansion of new and small companies in high technology and other manufacturing industries and in technology-related services."[44]

For five years beginning in 1996 venture capitalists seemed, by virtue of their success in quickly amassing almost incredible fortunes, to be financial supermen; newly-minted MBAs rushed to join their ranks. A cluster of them in Menlo Park, California, who launched technology start-ups, made that community widely known; in the 1880s a town of the same name in New Jersey was famous worldwide due to the achievements of Thomas A. Edison who was known as "the Wizard of Menlo Park."

The late 1990s era of fantastic returns stimulated Wall Street banks in 1999/2000 to greatly expand their own venture capital units, even to the extent of shifting resources away from their underwriting activities. Since bank security analysts provide advice to investor customers, an ethical question arises when the analysts' advice contradicts the bank's actions on its own behalf. Banks at times advised others to buy stocks at the same time their venture capital arms were dumping them.

Investors may also be influenced to buy stocks by the optimistic forecasts of corporate chief executives. If based on facts, such forecasts may be credible and useful, but they may be attempts to "talk up" a company's shares based on subjective evaluations, beliefs, or puffery. Disappointed investors who rely on unsubstantiated public projections have no recourse since the passage of the Private Securities Litigation Reform Act of 1995, legislation that protects corporate executives from lawsuits based on their stated views of the company's future performance.

A major development occurred in the way traders participate in the stock market: electronic trading. Prior to 1995 no one traded online, but by 2000 the practice was widespread involving an estimated quarter or more of all individual investors. More striking still was the emergence and popularity of day trading. Day trading, for which many abandoned good jobs, is a vocation, a full-time occupation of trading for the purpose of short-term profit by frequent purchases and sales of stock. Day traders made thousands of trades during a year, and even have been known to make a thousand in a single day. While most day traders conducted their business at home alone with their computer monitor, television set, and newspapers and periodicals, others patronized day-trading shops that provided electronic equipment, information flow, and the companionship of fellow aficionados.

Since day traders darted in and out of the market, they generally tried to identify and exploit short-term momentum in stock prices. Such a mind-set essentially ignores the fundamental factors that determine the success or failure of companies over time. With relatively low trading costs and the exchange of rumors via Internet chat rooms, day trading volume was high and very likely contributed to the volatility of stock prices. Day traders also probably contributed to excessive enthusiasm for Internet stocks and the creation of the financial bubble as the twentieth century ended. Although it seems incredible, a dot-com company providing an auction of empty airline seats came to have a market capitalization greater than that of Delta, U.S. Airways, and United Airlines combined. In the opinion of the distinguished economist and author of *A Random Walk Down Wall Street*, Professor Burton G. Malkiel states, "the legions of day traders are engaged in legalized gambling, and . . . most are likely to fail in this dangerous pursuit."[45] Yet Malkiel also called attention to a silver lining concerning the Internet bubble. The mania for Net stocks is credited with attracting huge amounts of capital and encouraging a multitude of entrepreneurs to the field of communications technology. Risk taking and free capital markets enabled the U.S. to lead the world in this industry. The era of day trading had its dark side; some of the creators of online trading services illegally manipulated trades on the Nasdaq stock market. An investigation by the Securities and Exchange Commission resulted in a settlement in January of 2003 requiring several major miscreants to pay fines totaling about $70 million.

Volatility in the stock market may also have been increased by the practice of rewarding executives and employees with stock options, a device very popular during the last half of the 1990s when stocks were rising. The recipients of options were generally content to hold them for a considerable time as stocks rose, but in a market that hesitates or falls, many options may be exercised and the shares put up for sale, thus feeding any decline in price. This is no minor consideration given that an estimated 4 billion shares of options were granted by Nasdaq-listed companies over a period of four years ending in 1998. The Silicon Valley companies that transformed information technology relied heavily on options to entice gifted people to join their staffs. Stock options contributed to the rise in earnings of "new-economy" companies because they were not, like salaries, considered expenses.

When widespread corporate accounting abuses came to light in 2002, some financial experts cited stock options as a motivating factor. By manipulating financial statements, chief executives could artificially boost company earnings. In response, a rise in the price of their firm's stock enabled them to realize large personal short-term gains by exercising their options. In 2004, the Financial Accounting Standards Board announced that early in 2005 a new rule would require options to be treated as an expense.

Wealth in the scores of billions of dollars was transferred to favored persons by investment banks during the years 1995-2000 soon after the stock of new companies was issued. This occurred when the banks allotted shares comprising initial public offerings (IPOs) to selected clients. Such shares often were worth multiple amounts of the issuing price the next day in the booming market filled with buyers eager to get in on a "hot" new company. This practice, far from competitive pricing, is obviously open to gross abuse and corruption through paybacks. While foreign countries have been urged to adopt transparency in their financial markets to end "sweetheart" deals with a privileged group, the behavior of our own investment banking industry reeked with inefficiency and favoritism.

The Troubles of Organized Labor

Union membership as a proportion of employed Americans fell from its peak of 35 percent in 1945 to 12.5 percent in 2004, a rate only slightly above the 12 percent mark of 1930. Only 8.2 percent of private sector workers were union members, the lowest share since 1901.

By the late 1990s, the makeup of union membership had changed considerably from the days when male manual workers in private sector manufacturing, mining, transportation, and construction were predominant. The new membership profile: 28 percent with college degrees; 56 percent with some college attendance; 42 percent in the public sector; 40 percent were women. The most heavily unionized occupations (55 percent or more) included mail carriers, police and firefighters, commercial pilots and flight attendants, railroad employees, and teachers. Among the occupations with less than 30 percent union membership were coal miners, truck drivers, telephone operators, janitors, carpenters, and nurses. Only about 40 percent of workers who assemble automobiles and manufacture steel carried union cards. Some highly paid people were union members, notably professional athletes and actors; others who are well compensated include airline pilots, some professors, and men and women of the press.

To the consternation of unions and of many employees, corporations have replaced many full-time positions with temporary jobs. Job security and seniority rules, major benefits of unionization, are denied the "temps" who fill these slots. Health insurance and retirement programs, often far more important benefits than the dismissive term "fringe" suggests, fall outside the grasp of this growing employment pool. Companies gain flexibility and cut costs while employees change jobs relatively frequently. The older model of corporate welfare in which companies gained employee loyalty, long-time faithful service, and high productivity from employees who felt a bond with and derived personal identification from their employer in exchange for job security, promotion, and expanded benefits with years of service has largely given way to a more competitive, high-pressure, innovative, less secure working environment.

During 1981, the first year of the Reagan administration, the economy slid into recession. As the rate of unemployment climbed above eight percent at the same time that cutbacks were made in social programs, the leaders of organized labor called attention to workers' discontents by holding a large Solidarity Day rally in Washington, D.C. on September 19. A tone of strained relations had already been set the previous month when the Professional Air Traffic Controllers Organization (PATCO) went on strike. President Reagan responded quickly: controllers who did not return to work after one more day had passed were fired; no negotiations were permitted since a strike by federal employees would be illegal. The majority of controllers were discharged, the union was decertified, and a long period of hiring and training replacements was begun. The government did not relent despite a reduction in air traffic and numerous flight delays. The firing of the air traffic controllers had a lasting effect on the willingness of unions generally to strike due to the threat of replacement workers.

The difficulties of organized labor due to the dynamics of technological innovation and economic liberalization, and to an unsupportive political climate, have been compounded by aggressive antiunion activities by employers. Tough, sophisticated tactics have been used regularly to convince workers to reject unions. Companies hire consultants, generally law firms, who provide specialized knowledge of the intricacies of labor law together with carefully calibrated campaigns to persuade workers that unionization is not in their interest. Each time an employer succeeds in thwarting unionization, the incentive for other companies to develop an anti-union program increases, for they fear competition with union-free rivals. With the help of consultants, firms coach their supervisors on how to convince workers that unions are not worthwhile. They also often threaten to close the plant if it is unionized, a tactic that is illegal, and therefore done in an indirect manner. Even if the union were to make a successful case to the National Labor Relations Board that the law has been violated, the mildness of the penalty and the time it takes for redress may well deter the union from seeking legal recourse.

December 1986 marked the centenary of the founding of the American Federation of Labor, the nation's first sustained national labor organization. The problems that organized labor now faced made it a time of almost desperate reexamination rather than celebration.

The frustration experienced by organized labor in the U.S. was illustrated by the failure of the United Auto Workers (UAW) to organize the Nissan Motor Corporation's assembly plant in Smyrna, Tennessee in July 1989. A bitter campaign tested the ability of the union to organize Japanese-owned plants in this country. After mounting a major effort involving 30 professional organizers, the union was rejected by a 2 to 1 margin. It blamed its defeat on a strong anti-union campaign that created a climate of fear. The company, having used one of the top labor law firms in the South, attributed the outcome to the lack of a good reason for workers to want a union. Wages and benefits were in line with plants that have UAW agreements and well above the average pay in manufacturing plants in middle Tennessee. Not long after this defeat, the UAW was given a symbolic slap when Chrysler Corporation removed the union's president from the company board of directors. Union representation on the board of an American company is a rarity; the UAW was given the seat in 1980 when it made contract concessions to help the struggling company survive.

The ultimate union weapon, the strike, has become semi-obsolete. From the 1950s through the 1970s, the average number of major strikes per year exceeded three hundred, about ten times that of the nineties. Despite tight labor markets, unions have become reluctant to strike or even to threaten to do so. Striking can still be successful when the union has a strongly-felt issue to fight for and the employer is vulnerable to pressure. A case in point was the nationwide strike by 185,000 teamster union drivers and package sorters against United Parcel Service in 1997. A major reason for walking out was the insecurity and unsatisfactory conditions of part-time workers whose numbers had grown to over 50 percent of the company workforce. The union also objected to the proposed substitution of a company pension scheme for the existing industry-wide plan. Although the fifteen-day strike caused much inconvenience, there was empathy with the striking men and women on the part of the public. They were recognizable and friendly regular visitors to homes and businesses. The settlement brought wage increases that were twice as large for part-timers as for full-time employees. The pension plan was not changed. Probably the most significant feature of the agreement was the company's promise gradually to shift ten thousand jobs from part-time to full-time status.

In 1998 and 1999 total union membership rose slightly, giving hope to the labor federation's leadership that the generally downward trend might have come to an end. In California, some 75,000 home health-aid workers were organized, and in North Carolina, the textile workers' union ended a long string of defeats by winning an organizing election at a group of plants that produce towels, sheets, and comforters.

The future success of organized labor depends in part on its ability to recruit members in jobs for which knowledge, especially technical skills, are required. Changes in the structure and competitive conditions of the American economy have contributed to the difficulty of organizing. Manufacturing jobs have declined as laborsaving methods and equipment have been adopted and work has been outsourced to other countries. Large corporations have reduced their own employment levels and have contracted out work to smaller firms. The context for the participants in the modern global marketplace, be they employers or employees, requires quickness, flexibility, and innovation. Traditional unionists have usually concentrated on protecting existing jobs, resisting or adjusting gradually to change rather than adjusting quickly to new circumstances.

Attitudes toward union representation could become more favorable in some areas, however, as a result of the trend by companies to deny workers health and other benefits by designating them temporary employees or dealing with them as independent contractors. The rapidly expanding services sector of the economy contains a large number of poorly paid and sometimes mistreated workers who seem likely candidates for union membership if ways can be found to overcome resistance from management. Among professional personnel, an interesting development occurred in June of 1999 in the medical profession. To countervail the corporate power of health-maintenance organizations, the American

Medical Association voted to create a physicians' union.

In 2005, fifty years after its formation, the AFL-CIO was split by the defection of several unions including two of its three biggest members. A "Change to Win" coalition led by the Service Employees International Union (SEIU) was formed to revitalize the union movement through new and more energetic organizing tactics.

In Britain, trade unions were formidable during the 1960s and 1970s, but the callous strikes that caused the 1978-1979 "Winter of Discontent" made unions unpopular and brought Margaret Thatcher to power. The new prime minister confronted the union movement on economic and moral grounds. To become more competitive in world markets inflation had to be brought under control, and this meant restraining the ability of unions to raise labor costs through their strong bargaining power and aggressive tactics as well as resistance to much-needed better methods of production. Ethical issues concerned the ability of union leaders to call strikes without approval of the rank and file and to threaten workers who continued working with expulsion from the union and therefore loss of their jobs.

Trade unions were regulated in a number of ways including the prohibition of secondary boycotts, known in the U.K. as secondary picketing. Thus, it became illegal for workers not on strike at their company to walk out in support of a strike elsewhere. Secret ballots were required for such major matters as authorizing strikes and the election of officers, referred to by Mrs. Thatcher as "giving the unions back to their members."

But legislation alone was not sufficient to reduce union power and allow for economic revitalization. A dramatic confrontation took place between the government and the National Union of Miners (NUM) under the leadership of Arthur Scargill, a determined Marxist who, following the re-election of the Thatcher government in 1983, deemed another four years of her government to be unacceptable. The NUM was widely viewed as capable of bringing down the government, for its strike in 1974 had triggered the collapse of the Heath administration.

Nationalized in 1947, the high-cost, heavily subsidized coal mining industry needed to be rationalized by closing unprofitable mines and reducing the workforce. The NUM rejected mine closings and Scargill called a strike without a ballot in March of 1984. A long, bitter, and sometimes violent struggle lasted until the union capitulated a year later. During this time there were thousands of arrests. Miners who wanted to work, and their families, were regularly intimidated. To Scargill and other militants, the clash was a major battle in the class war, and they received funds raised on Western European city streets by socialist supporters, and even from Colonel Qaddafi in Libya, and from Afghanistan. The National Coal Board, backed by the government, withstood the disruption and turmoil. As a result, the postwar balance of power between the unions, management, and government was recast.

By 1985 union membership in Britain was 43 percent of all employees, compared with 53 percent in 1980. The number of working days lost to strikes per 1,000 employees fell by roughly two-thirds between 1975-1979 and 1985-1988.

The decline of union influence occurred in Europe generally, not just in Britain. As in the U.S., fundamental changes in the economy were at work including the decline of industries where unions had traditionally been strong, such as shipbuilding and steelmaking, while financial services and electronics expanded. The older, bureaucratic union leaders with strong leftist orientation lost rapport with younger workers.

In Germany, Europe's largest economy, unions were a well-established part of the post-World War II era. From 1970 to 1990 trade union membership held steady at about one-third of all wage earners, and collective bargaining for whole industries was a distinctive feature of the industrial scene. But since national reunification in October of 1990, less than a year after the fall of the Berlin Wall, the strength of unions weakened. By 2000 the proportion of workers who are union members was down to 25 percent. In March of that year, the largest union, IG Metall, concluded a two-year agreement with employers that was about in line with expected German productivity growth. While this bargain continued the fifty year-old pattern of collective bargaining, a shift is under way in Germany toward agreements between companies and their own workers that are more flexible than industry-wide contracts. IG Metall's membership was down to two-thirds of its 1990 level. There is, however, strong growth in a union for workers in the service sector.

Adjusting the Welfare State

As discussed earlier, the welfare state, having developed into an imposing and widely accepted set of institutions during the middle third of the twentieth century, came under fire in the seventies. Political controversy was intense during the next decade and into the nineties. Our purpose here is to identify problems of the welfare state and to explain how it has been affected by the struggle over its size and legitimacy.

That welfare states clearly have limits beyond which they become counterproductive was obvious by the 1980s. Given Sweden's status as the most advanced of all welfare states, it seems fitting to draw on the work of a Swedish economist, Assar Lindbeck, for a synopsis of major limiting factors. Lindbeck identifies three areas: disincentive effects, the role and freedom of choice of the family, individual-state relations.[46]

Welfare states require high taxes which cause resources to leave high-tax for low-tax sectors where marginal social returns are lower, thereby restraining the growth of total output. The administration of welfare state programs and tax collections add to resource costs. Emphasizing the pervasiveness of the disincentive effects, Lindbeck specifies the following: "substitution effects in favor of (1) leisure (recreation) time, (2) lower intensity of work . . . (3) the pursuit of do-it-yourself work, (4) production for barter, (5) occupations with largely non-pecuniary benefits, and (6) the search for tax loopholes."[47] There are also negative consequences for private saving needed for a decentralized, entrepreneurial economy and the plural society and culture that are fostered by it.

Advanced welfare states have succeeded in enhancing economic security and eliminating much economic misery. But in doing so, they have transferred to public institutions important functions that have traditionally been provided by markets and households, notably the care of the sick, the old, and children. In other words, the care of persons, once a prime family responsibility, has moved to the public sector. With high marginal tax rates and with the public sector largely monopolizing vital services, households have less freedom of choice in some important life-situations. In turn, adverse psychological effects, frustration and stress, may result as people experience a feeling of helplessness.

The relationship of the individual to the state changes as the welfare state matures. A high-tax environment encourages the exploitation of tax loopholes and the asymmetrical treatment of assets that rewards financial manipulation rather than productive activity. Citizens are likely to look to government for benefits, thereby giving impetus to ongoing political conflict by competing interest groups. High marginal tax rates and benefits are an inducement to cheating and illegal occupations. There may be an erosion of the general standard of social behavior as citizens come to consider dishonesty justified or necessary to receive appropriate returns for their efforts and risk-taking. In response to cheating and tax-induced manipulation, governments are prone to impose additional intervention by the public bureaucracy. The result, as in Sweden, is a strong "control state" in which resources of the legal system tend to be diverted from fighting crimes against individuals to dealing with economic crimes against the state.[48]

In general terms, the charge against the welfare state was that it had become excessive in size and bureaucratically intrusive into the lives of individual citizens. Expansion beyond some optimum size is counterproductive because anti-social effects outweigh the redistribution benefits.

The public sectors of the advanced industrialized countries increased much faster than the private sectors between the early sixties and early seventies. The very substantial growth of government spending relative to GDP is evident from Table 3.1. Rapidly rising government expenditures were accompanied by a rise in government debt relative to GDP and by a big jump in the share of government expenditures required for interest payments on the expanded debt.

Inflation during the 1970s was attributed by many to the Keynesian policy of countering recessions by stimulating the economy through expansionary monetary and fiscal policies. Keynes, who died in 1946, certainly advocated such an approach, but he also advised budget surpluses in good years. In the post-World War II period until the 1980s, stimulative tonic was popular and applied rather freely, but budget surpluses or balanced budgets were not achieved in prosperous years. A principal objective of the so-called New Right movement that gained in importance in the 1970s and influenced policy in the 1980s was to reduce the size of government. Government was viewed as too big due largely to the pressure for expensive government programs, and because government bureaucracies develop a vested interest in expanding the role of government. Critics charged that while government programs are presented in the public interest, they are promoted by a constituency of professional and nonprofessional service workers who are beneficiaries of the programs through increased employment opportunities.

Controversy continued into the nineties, but the drastic situations predicted by the more ardent opponents of the welfare state did not materialize. Liberal democracies were not endangered. Important changes did take place that can best be understood as part of a comprehensive structural adjustment of the world economic environment. Countries faced with the demands of globalization responded by adopting policies to attract foreign investment and to make their economies more competitive. These include privatization and deregulation, tax reduction, trimming of expenditures on public services and providing them more efficiently, and requiring the able-bodied unemployed to engage in work training and job placement programs rather than simply paying them unrequited financial assistance. The burgeoning of the largely unregulated global economy was of major historical importance for national social policy. It did not, however, result in displacing the welfare state. In a careful study, the British scholar Christopher Pierson found not only that the enormous growth of the welfare state was a remarkable feature of the era following World War II, but that "it remains one of the dominant . . . institutions of the modern world."[49]

Another examination of the evolution of the welfare state makes a clear distinction between developments in Western Europe and the U.S. A Dutch sociologist, Anton C. Zijderveld, observed that while there are many differences between the European countries, as a group their welfare states are quite different from that found in the American states. Between 1960 and 1980 the welfare states in Western Europe became "comprehensive," going beyond social security in the sense of providing insurance against risks beyond people's control, by adding a group of social rights covering not only economic but social and psychological well-being. Such an intensive and extensive welfare state is viewed as "dominating the market, the society, the polity, and the culture, penetrating deeply into the lives of individual citizens."[50]

The American welfare state, introduced by Franklin Roosevelt and expanded mainly by Lyndon Johnson, stayed well short of the comprehensive Western European model; a great gulf existed between the American programs and those of the more extreme welfare states of Sweden and the Netherlands.

Since about 1980 there has been a "waning of the welfare state" in Western Europe so remarkable as to be characterized as a "fundamental transformation." By the end of the nineties, very little support remained for the kind of comprehensive welfare state that was widely accepted twenty years earlier, even among staunch social democrats.

To reduce their deficits, European governments pared expenditures in a variety of ways. Eligibility requirements for some social services were tightened. Contributions to the cost of health and other services by individuals were adopted or increased. The amount allowed for benefits, such as unemployment and child support, was reduced. Benefits paid for unemployment, illness, and children rose less rapidly than the rate of price inflation. Waiting periods were introduced before certain benefits such as sick leave would be paid. Employment levels were lowered in the civil service.

By relinquishing some of its power through deregulation, privatization, and decentralization, the state strengthened civil society, i.e., organizations and institutions largely independent of the state. Nongovernmental organizations serve as mediating structures between the state and private interests. One result of the reforms has been "to bring Europe closer to America sociopolitically and socioeconomically." While clearly the welfare state has survived, a search has been under way for "a socioeconomically and culturally as well as morally sustainable welfare state."[51]

During the 1980s the British private sector increased its role as a provider of welfare. Private hospitals expanded their facilities substantially. Private health insurance coverage almost doubled to just under 10 percent of the population. There was a rise in the percentage of children educated privately, and residential care for older people was shifted somewhat from local government to private suppliers. In response to tax incentives, millions of people dropped out of the state pension program in favor of private pension plans. While the National Health Service (NHS) preserved its patient care delivery based on tax revenue, it was reformed by the creation of an internal market. The demand side consisted of district health authorities and some physicians; services were supplied by various entities, principally hospital and community units organized as self-governing NHS trusts, as well as private and voluntary suppliers. The two sides of the market were linked by contracts that specified treatments including quality standards and prices.

Thatcherism attacked the basic concepts of the welfare state that had grown up in Britain, and its legislation clearly modified it. But despite the crisis atmosphere and dire predictions, the welfare state proved to be resilient, continuing to be large and very active.[52]

In the June 2001 national election, the British Labour Party was returned to power with a majority almost as large as in 1997. This was a notable achievement, the first time the party had retained power with a majority large enough to continue for a full second term. It was also a personal triumph for Prime Minister Tony Blair who, in establishing Labour as a pragmatic, centrist force, was as influential as Margaret Thatcher had been during the eighties. Labour was returned again in 2005, although with its majority much reduced.

The domestic objective of the British government early in the twenty-first century has been to reform public services. Health care, education, and transportation have fallen short of expectations and compare unfavorably with the quality of services in the wealthier countries on the continent of Europe. In creating New Labour, Tony Blair abandoned state ownership, national economic planning, and traditional income redistribution policies. Instead the Third Way, while maintaining state support levels, seeks a more efficient state.

Welfare programs in the U.S. have largely been successful and command popular support, but they have long been the target of a barrage of criticism that they are useless or worse. "Welfare state" has been used as a pejorative term, and "welfare mess" was long a political phrase of choice for some. The traditionally strong belief in rugged individualism clashes with the need for a social "safety net" provided by the state. While government has done much to improve people's lives, a strand in the American ethos sees it as a threat to individual liberty. When people become dependent on government they tend to lose their self-respect, fail to function effectively, and therefore are unable to realize their potential as productive members of society. It is necessary to reconcile this negative view with the persistence and popularity of major welfare state programs.

Observing the American welfare state as a whole, scholars at Yale University discerned sets of reasonably coherent commitments. Two types of income transfer programs are identified: category one provides insurance against falling into poverty; category two aids those who lack opportunity. They therefore suggest that a more accurate description would be an "insurance/opportunity state."[53]

Social insurance payments comprise the great bulk of American social welfare expenditures, the lion's share consisting of Social Security and Medicare benefits. The social insurance concept, developed in the 1930s, is based on the principle that security against life's misfortunes requires assurance of income. Income based on productive employment might be interrupted by vicissitudes of life such as illness, old age, loss of a family breadwinner, or unemployment. Eligibility for the various social insurance benefits is contingent upon the payment of taxes on wages to finance them. In this manner, some degree of income security is available to families based on their prior productive employment.

The second, much smaller, component of the welfare state in the U.S. comprises means-tested assistance to persons in need. Most of this aid consists of in-kind assistance, and includes Medicaid, food stamps, housing benefits, and various types of education aid. The remaining small share of means-tested assistance is distributed in cash; this includes the program called (until 1996) Aid to Families with Dependent Children

(AFDC), and General Assistance, the programs generally regarded by the public as "welfare."

The various programs that comprise the opportunity/insurance welfare state resulted from compromises made by a society that emphasizes the role of the market yet also recognizes the need for government—for while self-reliance is prized, so also is mutual support. Impassioned debate over welfare reflects the sensitivity of the issue and also suggests a lack of clarity about what is involved. "There is a tendency to equate 'welfare' with AFDC, to equate both with the 'welfare state,' and to regard the latter as synonymous with 'antipoverty' programs." But AFDC has been relatively small—on the order of 4 percent of all social welfare spending by the federal government during the eighties. "Welfare" was "a perennial topic of controversy" but was "of very little significance to the fiscal difficulties of the modern welfare state. Because cash assistance programs for the able-bodied poor are so small, whatever 'perverse incentives' they provide, they can have no significant impact on general economic productivity."[54]

Soon after assuming office in 1993, President Bill Clinton proposed a major reform of American health care: the establishment of universal coverage. Like his predecessor some forty-odd years earlier, Harry S. Truman, who repeatedly requested a system of comprehensive compulsory health insurance, he was rebuffed by Congress. But some significant, although less ambitious, benefits were enacted during Clinton's second term. Children's health insurance was adopted, and substantial tax credits for the first two years of college vastly expanded educational opportunities for middle-income families.

The U.S. enacted basic reform of welfare policy in 1996 in The Personal Responsibility and Work Opportunity Reconciliation Act. Cash assistance to the poor had been guaranteed for an indefinite period by the federal government since 1935. Now, under a revised philosophy and structure, stress was placed on individual self-sufficiency with requirements that beneficiaries return to work. In signing the act, Clinton observed that it marked the end of "welfare as we know it."

Under the new law the states gained broad authority over welfare programs: Temporary Assistance for Needy Families (TANF), which replaced AFDC; Supplemental Security Income (SSI); and food stamps. Federal financing for these purposes took the form of block grants, i.e. predetermined lump sums, to the states. The states have almost complete authority to set their own rules for eligibility and benefits within federal guidelines. These mandate that able-bodied welfare recipients become employed within two years or lose benefits. Other provisions of the law place a number of specific restrictions on eligibility. By 2000 the welfare rolls had been cut by over 50 percent, and welfare was no longer a contentious national political issue.

Studies evaluating the results of welfare reform suggest that improvement has occurred, but that a reasonably satisfactory solution to the problem of the poor has not been achieved. Single mothers who are unable to work regularly and do not qualify for public assistance are among those for whom welfare reform has been an ordeal. Large numbers of single mothers have left the welfare rolls and joined the work force but are still straining to get by on marginal or submarginal incomes. Social reformers advocate a number of government steps to improve the lives of single mothers, including better job training, raising the minimum wage, expanding Medicaid, and providing after-school programs for children whose mothers are employed.

A welfare program may provide fewer benefits than the law allows. The U.S. Department of Agriculture reported that in 1998 that only 59 percent of eligible persons received food stamps. Access is often difficult for those who find it hard to negotiate the paperwork and to get appointments with the required state agency. Application forms vary from state to state and range in length from a couple of pages to more than thirty.

However the reform of "welfare" comes ultimately to be judged, it is clear that the American welfare state is an established institution. Its two largest components, Social Security and Medicare, appear to be politically sacrosanct; in the presidential campaigns of 2000 the two major parties were fervent in reciting the mantra "save Social Security and protect Medicare."

In 2003, after fifteen years of discussion, the Medicare program covering 40 million elderly and disabled Americans was reformed in a major way by the addition of federally subsidized prescription drug benefits beginning in 2006 for beneficiaries who buy a newly created insurance policy or who join a private health plan. This measure, taken in response to rapidly increasing use and cost of drugs, is an expansion of health care that received widespread support.

Let us recall what happened to income levels and income distribution in the U.S. following World War II, and extend the time frame to the 1990s. For twenty-six years, 1947-1973, income growth was strong enough for median family income to more than double in constant dollars. Over the next twenty-three years, 1973-1996, income growth fluctuated around a weak upward trend, rising only 5 percent in real terms. The major factor explaining the sudden break in trend was the collapse of productivity growth after 1973. During the earlier, rapid growth period, inequality declined, touching its postwar low point in 1968. "In the 1973-to-mid-1990s period, on the other hand, when both real median family and household incomes were growing slowly, inequality in both distributions were clearly on the rise." The Gini index for families rose from .356 in 1973 to .425 in 1996, a 19 percent increase in inequality; for households the increase was fifteen percent.[55] During the 1990s the Gini coefficient was higher than at any other time since the late 1940s and indicated a rise in inequality of about 13 percent over the half century since the end of World War II.

Good data regarding income distribution in the U.S. before 1947 is lacking, so historical comparison can only be approximate. There is, however, agreement among researchers that inequality was greater during the first four decades than during the second half of the twentieth century. Income inequality appears to have been particularly great in the late 1920s and early 1930s. It lessened markedly during the 1940s, so that by the end of World War II it is estimated to have been lower than at any time earlier in the century. The growth in inequality from the early 1970s into the 1990s did not reach the high levels of the prewar era.[56]

Skill-based technological changes in employment are a prime reason for the rise in income inequality starting in the 1970s. Education became the main determinant of a good standard of living, and the low end of the distribution of family income has a concentration of families headed by females whose education ended in high school. The decline of unions is another factor involved in the growing income disparity. Power shifted away from workers toward managers and stockholders. "Deregulation, globalization, and technology have reduced the typical employee's bargaining power, and no countervailing institution has arisen to exert an opposite force."[57]

The changing pattern of income distribution is shown by the percentage share of aggregate family income received by each fifth and the top 5 percent of families.

Table 4.1

	1st Quintile	2nd Quintile	3rd Quintile	4th Quintile	5th Quintile	Top 5 Percent
1947	5.0	11.9	17.0	23.1	43.0	17.5
1969	5.6	12.4	17.7	23.7	40.6	15.6
1996	4.2	10.0	15.8	23.1	46.8	20.3

Table consists of Bureau of the Census data. The first quintile refers to the 20 percent of families with the lowest incomes. Adapted from Frank Levy, *The New Dollars and Dreams*. The Russell Sage Foundation, 1998, p. 199.

In 1979, according to a Congressional Budget Office study, the top 1 percent of families had incomes 10 times that of typical families. By 1997 that ratio had risen to 23 times as much.

International inequality comparisons have shown considerable difference between members of the Organization for Economic Cooperation and Development (OECD). The U.S. has the most unequal distribution; the least unequal are the Nordic and other northern European countries. A striking finding of an OECD analysis of low-paid employment among member countries is that the U.S., in the mid-1990s, had the highest percentage of workers who are "low-paid," at 25 percent of employed workers. On average, low-paid employment in the majority of member countries was about 14 percent. And the average for Sweden, Finland, and Belgium was only slightly over 6 percent. In this context, low pay is not defined in absolute terms but refers to earnings less than two-thirds of the median for full-time employees. The rationale for using a relative definition is that when people's earnings are some distance below the median they may experience a feeling of social exclusion or deprivation. Since analysis of income differences across nations involves many attitudinal and behavioral factors reflecting variations in culture, it is inherently difficult to judge the desirability of particular distributional income patterns.[58]

Concern about economic inequality in the U.S. was expressed in the media, by politicians, and by the public in the 1980s—highlighted by accounts of child poverty and homelessness. In assessing the disparity of income distribution circa 1990, economist Paul Krugman described a problem with no solution in sight. He observed that in the 1980s the poor became poorer as the rich and the upper middle class were getting much richer. It was a decade of great profits from financial deals. While educated workers gained higher earnings, blue-collar workers experienced a decline in real wages. Given that inequality had risen rapidly, and that extremes of wealth and poverty had emerged, a search for a new policy response might be expected. But poverty, as an issue, "has basically exhausted the patience of the general public." The War on Poverty of the 1960s was waged when incomes were rising steadily and government activism was viewed optimistically. But as poverty failed to decline, it became viewed as intractable. Government as a means of raising the living standards of the poor by helping them financially to become more productive was no longer viewed as credible, and with slow productivity growth of the economy a basic problem, tax increases on the rich ran counter to the policy of stimulating risk-taking and entrepreneurship. "The growing gap between rich and poor was arguably the central fact about economic life in America in the 1980s. But no policy changes now under discussion seem likely to narrow the gap significantly."[59]

The income gap continued in the nineties. It is viewed with complacency by many conservative thinkers who concentrate on increasing aggregate income and, relying on "trickle-down economics," point out that low-income families and households benefit with the passage of time. The country entered a remarkable five-year boom that ended in 2000. Working-class real wages improved at last, but the income gap continued to widen as upper-incomes soared.

Runaway executive compensation was regularly observed and questioned during the nineties. *Business Week* reviewed Graef S. Crystal's *In Search of Excess: The Overcompensation of American Executives* in 1991, noting that the pay of CEOs at America's largest companies was 150 times that of the average worker, while in Japan the ratio was 17 to 1. Crystal's analysis of proxy statements revealed that directors larded executive compensation with restricted stock "that pays off regardless of performance, and he decries the repricing of stock options when poor results send a company's shares into a tailspin."[60] *The Wall Street Journal* regularly took note of soaring executive pay, referring to "the buddy system" of executives and their boards of directors. Observing that there seemed to be no limit to rising CEO compensation, the *Journal* attributed the phenomenon "to boards' intensified pursuit of outside talent, swollen profit, a takeover boom and the lessened uproar about executive pay," with greed in style.[61]

In 1995 United for a Fair Economy, a national independent non-profit organization, was formed to work in coalition with labor, religious, educational, and other groups including investors and business leaders to promote a fair economy. Prime focuses of its attention are the inequalities of income and wealth in the U.S., wide disparities that it deplores and considers potentially dangerous. Some of the findings published by this organization are striking. Whereas in 1980, CEOs made 42 times that of the average worker, in 1999 they made 475 times as much. Top executives made twice as much as the President of the U.S. in 1960 compared with 62 times as much in 1999.

Normally, top pay is supposed to be the reward for top results, but by the late nineties rewards often were showered on CEOs who produced poor results. In 2001, business news stories described lavish settlements for deposed executives of companies that performed badly: a CEO who presided for three years over Lucent received a go-away payment of nearly $13 million; a chief financial officer of Lucent who served for less than a year took a $5 million payoff; and a man who headed Honeywell International for two years left with $9 million plus lavish perks.

The idea that a disproportionate share of income tends to go to a few at the top at this stage of our history has been analyzed in *The Winner-Take-All Society* by Robert H. Frank and Philip J. Cook. In this 1995 book they write of "profound changes" that have already occurred in economic and social life, with more dramatic changes on the way. Some of the changes benefit consumers who gain access to very talented people. But stress is placed on negative consequences.

> Winner-take-all markets have increased the disparity between rich and poor. They have lured some of our most talented citizens into socially unproductive, sometimes even destructive tasks. . . . And winner-take-all markets have molded our culture and discourse in ways many of us find deeply troubling.[62]

Two pithy comments by economists drive home the point of view of those concerned about the trends considered above. "In the theology of capitalism the distribution of wealth, income and earnings are of no consequence. There is no concept of fairness other than that those who produce in the market get fairly compensated by the market."[63] "Whether measured by wages, income or wealth, for 25 years the share of the privileged has increased, and everyone else (a roughly 80 percent majority) has become relatively worse off. We are truly in a second Gilded Age."[64]

Reference was made earlier to Professor Paul Krugman's assessment of the growing disparity of income distribution in the U.S. as of 1990. In 2002, citing congressional and academic studies, he wrote that the rapidly widening income gaps since the 1970s have resulted in a return close to the extremes of the 1920s. A large disproportion in the growth of real family incomes from 1979 to 1997 is clear; while average income grew 28 percent, median family income rose by just 10 percent. It is often argued that great income inequality actually is in the interest of the population as a whole since it is a byproduct of market incentives that raise total national income—a rising tide raises all boats. This comforting belief was not borne out from 1979 to 1997; the lowest fifth of families experienced a small decline in their incomes over those years. Indeed, "large numbers of Americans are worse off economically than their counterparts in other advanced countries."[65]

In a striking journalistic concurrence in June 2005, *The New York Times* and *The Wall Street Journal* each ran extensive multipart series on the growing gap between the rich and the poor and the danger of a loss of social mobility. The *Times* emphasized the extraordinary rise in the incomes of that tiny minority, the "hyper-rich." The top 0.1 percent of income earners averaged $3 million in 2002, the latest year for which the data were available. This constituted a rise of 150 percent in real terms since 1980, far in excess of any other income group. This small group—the top one-thousandth—received 7.4 percent of the national total, twice its 1980 portion. "The share of income earned by the rest of the top 10 percent rose far less, and the share earned by the bottom 90 percent fell."[66]

Analysts who are untroubled by the growing disparities in income distribution point out that almost all segments of society are experiencing some gain in absolute terms. Even the lowest 20 percent of households gained in real terms from 1993 to 2003. Tax cuts that contributed to the extraordinary accumulation of wealth by the few are sanctioned by some economists on the grounds that investment and innovation are thereby encouraged. But those who are concerned, even alarmed, about the trends in the distribution of income and wealth see a threat to the democratic society and warn of the establishment of an aristocracy of inherited wealth. Of total household wealth, 40 percent is now owned by just 1 percent of households. Wealth confers power, and power can be used to control more than goods.

Rise and Decline of Government Spending

In an earlier section it was noted that government spending increased relative to GDP during the twentieth century, reaching more than 40 percent for a group of leading advanced countries by 1980. The Thatcher/

Reagan assault on government spending failed to reverse the trend during the eighties; the ratio continued rising until reaching a peak in the mid-1990s. While it is to a considerable extent explained by military expenditures for wars, hot and cold, and for purchases of civilian services, notably education and health, the rise of the welfare state was central to this phenomenon. From 1960 onward, the greatest growth came in the form of transfer payments and subsidies to the elderly and other groups receiving income support.

As the twentieth century came to a close, governments began to retrench a bit—their expenditures grew less rapidly than total output. Collectively, the apex was reached in 1993. For European Union countries, government spending as a percentage of GDP fell by about 8 percent between 1993 and 2003. Japan was an exception: it increased government spending relative to national output in an effort to overcome economic stagnation.

In the U.S. the peak came in 1992; the rate fell by 12 percent to 2000, then rose by 7 percent to 2003. During President George W. Bush's first term (2001-2004) federal expenditures grew by 33 percent. Even excluding defense and homeland security, the upsurge in expenditures was the greatest in three decades.

Table 4.2
General Government Total Outlays
Percent of GDP

	1987	1993	2003
France	51.9	55.3	54.4
Germany	45.8	49.3	49.4
Italy	50.8	57.7	48.5
U.K.	43.6	45.7	42.8
Netherlands	58.4	56.0	48.6
Sweden	58.3	73.0	59.0
European Union Countries	48.5	52.7	48.4
U.S.	36.7	37.5	35.9
Japan	31.7	34.7	38.3
Total OECD	40.3	43.3	41.2

Adapted from *OECD Economic Outlook*, No. 74, December 2003, p. 208. Data combine accounts for central, state, and local governments plus social security.

Environmentalism

The middle of the twentieth century brought a change in the way humanity sees itself in relation to the physical environment. Traditionally the Earth was viewed as so spacious that people could always escape from a deteriorating natural (or social) environment by moving to another place, as if there were a limitless plane available to inhabit. As the economist and social evolutionist Kenneth Boulding observed, "The image of the frontier is probably one of the oldest images of mankind, and it is not surprising that we find it hard to get rid of."[67] But with the popularity of air travel, and then the coming of the space age, a new image—spaceship Earth—took hold embodying the realization that human activity is limited to a closed sphere. World population, which had grown slowly and fitfully for hundreds of years, rose from about 720 million in 1750, to around 1.6 billion in 1900, and 2.5 billion in 1950. This rapid expansion is attributed mainly to a declining death rate due to the agricultural and industrial revolutions that raised living standards and particularly to improved nutrition, medical care, and public health measures that brought control of epidemic diseases. It then took only forty years, 1950 to 1990, for world population to more than double to 5.3 billion. An estimated 8 billion is in prospect for 2020. The growth of population and of output in industry and agriculture resulted in a tremendous rise in industrial pollution and other waste to be absorbed by air, land, and water.

In the U.S., the environmental movement began after World War II with the move to the suburbs made possible by the greater availability of automobiles, highways, and housing developments as the economy expanded. The transplanted population wanted to enjoy the pleasures of clean air and unspoiled natural surroundings. "However, the reality of suburban life—smog, traffic jams, and strip development—too often left this bucolic fantasy unrealized. At the same time some rural folk watched with dismay as their small towns became urbanized."[68] Strong public support developed in the 1960s for environmental legislation, and a "quality of life" constituency took form that influenced the political parties. A variety of problems became apparent: cities were running out of landfill to take solid waste; toxic waste dumps posed health hazards; water systems were contaminated; food and drink contained pesticides; and rain and smog corrupted the air. Environmental organizations were not entirely new—the Sierra Club (1892) and the National Wildlife Federation (1936) are examples of established groups. But the movement now became wider, deeper, and politically much more potent. Greenpeace,

Friends of the Earth, the Environmental Defense Fund, and the National Resources Defense Fund were politically influential. In 1962 the book *Silent Spring* by Rachel Carson made known to a wide readership the enormous environmental damage done by promiscuous use of pesticides and herbicides. On April 22, 1970, the U.S. celebrated Earth Day with some 20 million people participating in nationwide demonstrations to direct attention to the inability of nature to cope with the rapidly growing amount of pollution. Three months later the Environmental Protection Agency (EPA) was established by an executive reorganization order issued by President Richard Nixon transferring environmental agencies from various departments to the new, centralized agency. The time had come for government to play an important role in environmental protection. Just as the urgent problems of the 1930s were the catalyst for major government intervention; particularly to stabilize the economy, regulate certain key economic activities, and provide a social safety net; government was now needed to meet the newly recognized problem of environmental deterioration that threatened the viability of the earth's ecological processes. Since a collective response was required in the collective interest, its implementation could properly be viewed as a degree of socialism, although that term had become politically incorrect. A problem requiring regulation, or the substitution of collective for individual action, is known as market failure—meaning either that the market system does not efficiently allocate society's resources or that it fails to satisfy goals important to society. One form of market failure arises from naturally produced goods such as ocean fish. Known as "open-access property" or "common property resources," they are available for people to take for themselves. Every fisherman has an incentive to maximize his catch, leading to overfishing. Limits on the amount of fish to be taken are necessary to prevent the depletion and perhaps even extinction of fish species.

An understanding of environmental problems requires the concept of externalities, or external costs. Externalities cause a distortion of market prices because they fail to cover all costs of production. Firms consider only the private cost of production, i.e., the amount they pay for the resources they use. But the production process may involve costs that are borne by members of society other than the producers (and consumers) of a product or service. Since they are not incurred by the primary market participants, they are considered social costs or costs external to the market pricing mechanism. Pollution typically occurs because firms use resources that, to them, are free. Power plants emit pollutants from burning high-sulfur coal: ecosystem destruction results from the release of sulfur dioxide and other contaminants into the air. Clean air, a naturally produced economic good available to all, is appropriated by power companies for use in production along with the inputs they pay for. In the absence of government intervention, the producer has no incentive to economize on the use of clean air. The result is environmental degradation that is systematic, not accidental as, for example, in the case of leakage from foundering tankers.

Given the need for government intervention, what form should it take? Three major strategies are available: "(1) regulation, exemplified by the promulgation of discharge standards; (2) economic incentives in the form of fees (or taxes); (3) permits to pollute that can be bought and sold in markets."[69]

Regulations, or direct controls, are generally regarded as the least satisfactory method on grounds of inefficiency. Complicated regulations must be written; enforcement of them is difficult and expensive. Business firms can fend them off by pressuring legislators, manipulating regulatory proceedings, and going to court where, should they lose, fines are often insignificant. In the case of deadly poisons or some health emergency, a complete ban is necessary, but emissions goals generally can be better met by fees or tradable permits to pollute. Fees encourage firms to find or devise the cheapest way to control emissions. While technical considerations in applying them are detailed and complicated,

> an appropriate fee or tax per unit of emissions will, in effect, put the right price tag on clean air and water—just as the market now puts the right price tag on oil and steel. Once our precious air and water resources are priced correctly, polluters will husband them as carefully as they now husband coal, labor, cement and steel. . . . Those who despoil the environment are forced to compensate society for the muck they spew out . . . [and] there will be less pollution than in an unregulated market.[70]

Emission fees and tradable permits are both ways of forcing polluters to internalize external costs, but by using the market to achieve a limit or cap on emissions, permits to pollute have an efficiency advantage. Public authorities set the overall limit and issue permits for that amount. The cost of reducing emissions is minimized because firms with low marginal cost of abatement make deep cuts allowing them to sell their extra permits to firms for whom the cost of cutting emissions is higher. The market mechanism is thus employed to determine the price of the permits.

The U.S. has had success with a system of trading permits for sulfur dioxide emissions by electric power plants to mitigate the problem of acid rain. Air quality standards adopted in the Clean Air Act of 1970 proved difficult to enforce; an amendment in 1990 instituted the market mechanism. The U.S. has not, however, adopted a tax or tradable permit system to control carbon dioxide, the greenhouse gas (GHG) widely considered to be a major cause of global warming. In the Kyoto Protocol of 1997 the industrial nations undertook collectively to reduce their emissions of greenhouse gases 5.2 percent from 1990 levels sometime between 2008 and 2012. The U.S., which emits more GHG than any other country, has refused to agree to this treaty.

Recognition of a need for combating climate change has grown over the years among American scientists, governments, and corporate executives. Gradually action is being taken. In 2004 eight U.S. state governments brought suit against major utility companies to force them to reduce greenhouse gases. Mandatory limits on carbon dioxide emissions were imposed within the European Union in January 2005 together with a market for trading the right to emit carbon. According to a leading business publication,

> Remarkably, business is far ahead of Congress and the White House. . . . Indeed, there is surprising consensus about the policies needed to spur innovation and fight global warming. The basic idea: mandatory reductions or taxes on carbon emissions, combined with a worldwide emissions-trading program.

By adopting separate rules, the states may induce a movement for uniform national standards. There is a clear precedent in the 1990 amendments to the Clean Air Act.[71]

Decisions concerning the control of mercury illustrate the conflict between scientific finding and political choice. The Environmental Protection Agency found in 2000 that mercury, a heavy substance that precipitates to Earth close to emitting plants, should be rigidly controlled because it is a cause of neurological problems in children. Early in 2004, however, a different administration proposed instead to use the less rigorous system of trading emission rights. As a result, power plant emissions would be reduced by an estimated 70 percent rather than by 90 percent under mandatory regulation. This easing of control suggests the political influence of the power industry.

That the Earth's natural resources are limited and that environmental change needs to be controlled is well understood internationally. Pollution controls and land-use planning regulations are now practiced by most industrialized countries. Regional and international organizations monitor the environment and agreements have been reached to limit damage to it. A notable example of the latter is the 1987 Montreal Protocol by which nations agreed to curtail "use of the chlorofluorocarbons (CFCs) and other compounds that destroy the ozone layer. Companies such as Dupont that produced CFCs ended up profiting from the production of ozone friendly alternatives."[72]

Ecologists have come to recognize the importance of spatial patterns that involve "economies of configuration," a topic examined by economist Robert R. Gottfried. Landowners individually create a pattern of land covers and use that to create ecological relationships of which they are generally unaware but may, over time and space, have important effects. One such comprehensive unit is a watershed, i.e., a land area drained by a given stream system. Since many landowners are involved, the configuration of the whole complex landscape is a result of the interaction of their activities, and

> individual owners acting alone cannot provide the socially optimal mix of ecologically provided goods and services, nor can typical internalizing of externalities. In short, the presence of economies of configuration implies that the market will fail, even when traditional methods of internalizing externalities are applied. Other means have to be found to deal with the landscape-ecological processes.[73]

Landscapes are seen as mosaics that may include forest, field, wetland, and urban areas. The use of individual pieces of land may have environmental impacts, for example, erosion, water quality, and species survival. But "no guarantee exists that a society will produce landscape patterns, nor particular land uses, that will provide the mix of goods and services that the society desires." A sense of urgency about developing appropriate policies exists because "there are limits to the amount of change humans can impose on ecosystems without serious irreversible consequences." A variety of cooperative approaches are under consideration and some have been implemented. Such organizations bring together individual landowners and persons concerned with the environment, private organizations with an interest or stake in land management, and officials and agencies of government. The cooperative approaches require the state to provide a "supportive environment." It can facilitate the formation of organizations and provide funds, technical assistance, and research.[74]

The following summary of a specific land use study illustrates the general problem. Dramatic changes in land use, particularly by urban sprawl and the creation of pine plantations, are reducing the native forests of the southern U.S. As the forests disappear, so too do the important qualities they provide such as biodiversiy, water quality, and wood fiber. To better understand what is happening, a scientific study called a small area assessment was conducted to provide landscape-level information to all those involved in determining land use activities. The study analyzed a portion of the Cumberland Plateau in Tennessee, an area with extensive native hardwood forest tracts consisting predominantly of oak and hickory species. It focused largely on the conversion of native forest habitat to pine plantations. These woodlands provide habitat for neotropical migratory songbirds "and serve as the headwaters to some of the most biologically diverse, freshwater stream systems found in the world."[75] Hundreds of animal species depend for their survival on the resources provided by the forest. Native forests have been cleared and replaced over a period of twenty years with loblolly pine. "There was approximately 14% less area with intact native forest canopy on the Southern Cumberland Plateau in 2000 than was present in 1981." The rate of decrease of native forest area from 1997 to 2000 was almost twice that between 1981 and 1997. "There was 237% more recently cleared forest area present in 2000 . . . than was present in 1981." "Total area in pine plantation increased by 170% (24,947 acres) from 1981 to 2000. . . . Pine plantation and associated lands newly cleared for this purpose were responsible for 74% of native forest conversion." An index of water quality indicated that sites close to logged areas have significantly lower water quality.

While the assessment does not make policy recommendations, it provides a factual basis on which policy-makers may draw. The loss of nutrients in the deforested soil signals the danger of creation of a wasteland. The plateau surface consists of sandy soils sensitive to the removal of nutrients as a result of whole-tree harvesting and acid precipitation. In the absence of some organized control over what is done on the land, irreversible loss of valuable natural resources seems inevitable.[76]

Surge and Excess

The 1990s brought a sustained period of real economic growth accompanied by a spectacular stock market boom and bust. Then came revelations of crass, deceptive, morally repulsive business practices threatening to the efficient functioning of the economy.

The American economy experienced its longest continuous expansion—fully ten years—beginning in 1991, more than twice the length of the average expansion since World War II. It took time for the expansion to gain strong momentum. Until 1996, growth was not impressive and corporate downsizing was commonplace. Then from 1996 to 2000 real GDP grew by more than 4 percent annually while the unemployment rate fell steadily from 5.4 percent in 1996 to 4 percent in 2000 without igniting significant inflation. This excellent performance is largely attributable to high productivity growth resulting from technological advances and strong investment. It had a dazzling effect; as in the 1920s a belief developed on the part of many that a "new era" had arrived making past experience largely irrelevant. Recent history suggested that robust growth with low unemployment would set off an inflationary spiral. Yet now a case was made that a "new, improved" economic system had been developed that could run smoothly for an indefinite time. Furthermore, the American economy acted as a "locomotive" for the rapidly growing global economy.

Investment in hi-tech companies was a powerful driving force for the U.S. economy. Enthusiasm for "new economy" businesses developed into an exaggerated optimism often laced with arrogance and greed. As the stock market boom gained momentum Alan Greenspan, Federal Reserve chairman, warned as early as 1996 of "irrational exuberance," and indeed a bull market ensued that ranks with the greatest in history. Over a five-year period to January 2000, the Dow Jones Industrial Average rose by 200 percent, while the Nasdaq Composite Index peaked in March up 571 percent. The highest flyers were technology stocks such as Microsoft Corporation and Dell Computer Corporation. From the end of 1994 to their peaks, the price of the former was multiplied 16 times and the latter 93 times.[77] The boom in telecommunications, based on fiber optic cable, was especially "hot." Many companies raced to provide fiber optic links to carry Internet data and telephone service worldwide. The resulting plethora of cable lanes overwhelmed the demand of customers causing much confusion, loss, and bankruptcy within the industry. The innovative entrepreneurs brought important advanced technology into use; but, in their stampede, they provided a classic demonstration of the creative destruction theory developed by Schumpeter a half-century earlier. In addition, the downfall of some of the industry's leading firms was accompanied by accounting abuses. Another, perhaps even more egregious case of mania, was the Internet bubble. The mood of exuberance reflected a virtual disbelief in the notion of risk as venture capitalists and entrepreneurs envisioned unlimited growth despite the absence of profits. In the first quarter of 2000, realism pricked the bubble and it burst. In the two years preceding the collapse, startups that set what later seemed fantasy goals, attracted thousands of young, well-educated employees who threw themselves wholeheartedly into the new enterprises relying on stock-option plans to return very rich rewards. Ambition, hubris, greed, and arrogance along with ability and optimism created a climate of unreality that had no tolerance for voices of moderation. The temper of these years was caught in a novel by Tom Wolfe.

> The boom was on, and the banking business had caught fire, and a wonderful giddy madness was in the air. The line officers from Marketing were pushing through loans, their "big sales," with a pell-mell abandon. If you were a referee who insisted on detecting the madness and blowing your whistle, they just ran right over you, laughed at you, made you feel timid and old fashioned. Like every other senior credit officer, Peepgass had signed off on tens of millions of dollars' worth of loans with self-destruct written all over them. . . . In fact, he had been swept up in the madness himself.[78]

During the 1996-2000 period, television channels devoted much time to stock market and other financial news. Wall Street professionals, often quite young men and women, regularly expressed great confidence in the future of the economy and the stock market; it was not uncommon for them to brush aside doubts about the longevity of the good times. However, not all such soothsayers were unencumbered with many years of experience. Wayne D. Angell, a prominent financial economist who had served as a Federal Reserve governor and was now chief economist at Bear Stearns, dismissed the notion of a bubble in an op-ed piece in 1999. He held that the evidence "indicates that we have at last arrived in a new-era economy, one in which information technologies and sound money fuel long-term noninflationary growth."[79] The similarity of this confident statement to the memorably wrong prediction by Irving Fisher seventy years earlier is striking.

Adverse changes in the economy developed rapidly in 2000: the annualized GDP growth rate fell from 5.6 percent in the second quarter to 2.4 percent in the third. Demand for information and communications equipment faltered during the final six months of the year causing capital spending to fall, and the price of high-tech stock plunged by 80 percent. After peaking in the first quarter of 2000, the major stock indexes suffered losses ranging from severe to devastating during that year, and were down again significantly by the end of 2001. In November of 2001, the National Bureau of Economic Research (NBER) declared that the downturn in economic activity had met its criteria for recession the previous March. The economy shrank in each of the first three quarters of 2001, then resumed growth despite the destruction and disruption of the terrorist attacks on the World Trade Center and the Pentagon on September 11. But growth was so slow that the NBER delayed declaring the recession over until, in July 2003, it stipulated that it had ended in November 2001.

The decline and fall of Enron Corp. was the first in a series of financial scandals that undermined public confidence in corporate America and the regulators charged with its oversight. It had long been an article of faith that American financial reports were essentially "transparent," i.e., reliably informative and trustworthy. Suddenly, it became apparent that the management, governance, and accounting practices of some of the largest, most prestigious companies lacked integrity. Official investigations, legislative hearings, and lawsuits were launched to determine to what extent there may have been malfeasance, misfeasance, or nonfeasance in particular instances. As a consequence, investor distrust had a negative effect on stock prices and the flow of funds into corporate investment during 2002.

Two natural gas pipeline companies were merged in 1987 under the name Enteron, presumably carefully selected to convey a favorable image. When the press discovered the dictionary definition of enteron to be alimentary canal, the company's name was shortened to Enron. The organization soon left ridicule behind as it took advantage of newly deregulated natural gas and electricity markets by converting itself into a major trader in those and other forms of energy all across the U.S. and abroad. By making innovative use of arcane financial instruments that it traded on the Internet, it was able to hedge huge futures contracts and expand its trading activities to include a great range of things other than energy, for example, newsprint and fibre optic cable. By 2000, Enron had become a marvel of the "new economy," the seventh largest company in the nation in terms of sales, and praised for its innovations by *Fortune*.

Mighty Enron fell precipitously from its pedestal during 2001—it suffered a large loss and reduced stockholders' equity after its chief executive officer unexpectedly resigned. Charged with massive fraud of its stockholders, the company declared bankruptcy in December, the largest in U.S. history to that time. Once $90, its stock price plunged to just pennies. Thousands of its employees were quickly discharged. Most employees lost the bulk of their retirement savings because company policy had urged them to concentrate their 401(k) assets in Enron stock.

The way Enron had been managed came as quite a revelation following its filing for bankruptcy. Profits from trading had been much exaggerated. Most remarkable was its use of off-balance sheet partnerships for the purpose of reporting phantom profits and disguising major losses. Some of its officers enriched themselves enormously—most notably, the chief financial officer who made $30 million via the partnerships.

And while encouraging employees to continue to buy company stock, top executives were selling. CEO Kenneth Lay, who had been advised of financial problems and tricky accounting, realized over $200 million from such sales. Enron's executives had developed a corporate culture of pushing their business practices to the limit, eventually beyond what the nation's laws and mores allow.

Enron's financial manipulations were carried out with the advice and approval of the Arthur Andersen accounting firm which served it as both auditor and financial consultant. Because of its complicity in the Enron debacle as well as other allegations of impropriety, Andersen lost its credibility and many important clients dropped it. In one respect, its fall was more poignant than Enron's. Enron was young and flamboyant, and it eagerly embraced risk. Andersen, begun as a small firm in 1919, grew steadily based on competence and reliability until by 2001 it was a giant of the industry with 85,000 employees in 84 countries. In June 2002, the firm was found guilty in a jury trial of obstructing the Securities and Exchange Commission in its investigation of the fall of Enron. The decision was a climax to a series of allegations of improper conduct extending over several years. It had been fined $7 million by the Securities and Exchange Commission in 2000 for permitting fraud at Waste Management Corporation.

The 2002 conviction was overturned by the U.S. Supreme Court in 2005. Although the firm was not exonerated, the government's case was found to have failed to show a "consciousness of wrongdoing." Drastically reduced in size and still fending off lawsuits, the firm's prospects remained poor.

In 2000 another of the major global accounting firms, KPMG, was charged with tax-fraud by arranging questionable tax shelters. It settled with the U.S. government by agreeing to pay $456 million in fines and adhere to many conditions, including closing its tax advisory service for private clients. A particularly notable aspect of the proceedings was that seven former partners were charged with fraud. The prospect of long prison sentences, as well as fines, applied to executives personally, provides a stronger incentive to circumspect business conduct than penalties levied against abstract corporate entities.

Additional scandals came to light in succeeding months including leading-edge companies such as Dynegy, QWest, WorldCom, and Global Crossing. A variety of practices were used to inflate sales and profits and all allegedly involved executive self-enrichment. WorldCom used the simple deception of treating operating expenses as capital expenditures to inflate profits by billions of dollars.

The emphasis on acquisition of wealth by whatever means and without restraint was certainly not historically unique. For example, in 1904 the young Winston Churchill spoke words that seem well suited to the situation a century later.

> No one seems to care anything but about money today. Nothing is held of account except the bank account. Quality, education, civic distinction, public virtue seem each year to be valued less and less. Riches unadorned seem each year to be valued more and more. We have in London an important section of people who go about preaching the gospel of Mammon, advocating the 10% commandments, who raise each day the inspiring prayer "Give cash in our time, O Lord."[80]

Literally dozens of investigations into conflicts of interest were undertaken by prosecutors and regulators. As in the relationship between Andersen and Enron, major accounting firms provided auditing services to corporations while simultaneously serving as consultants. Auditing calls for rigorous adherence to the spirit and letter of accountancy rules, whereas consulting may involve bending those rules to enhance profits and/or siphoning funds to insiders. To please a client the auditor may approve what ought not to be approved. Corporate CEOs and CFOs (chief financial officers) may view accountants the way J. P. Morgan regarded lawyers when he said he didn't hire lawyers to tell him what he could do but to tell him how to do what he wanted to do.

Stock analysts are supposed to evaluate stocks objectively and give clients honest opinions, but they may instead fashion recommendations to win investment-banking business for their Wall Street financial institutions. A related practice known as "spinning" occurs when securities firms make available a portion of a highly desirable IPO by simultaneously adding it to brokerage accounts of selected corporate executives at below market prices. The executives, chosen for their power to direct business to the securities firms, sell ("spin") the shares when the IPO is introduced into the market thus turning a quick and easy profit. The National Association of Securities Dealers (NASD) has rules against such behavior by its members and conducted its own investigations. The opportunities for payoffs to corporate executives, accountants, analysts, and investment bankers were enormous during the late 1990s boom.

Government regulation of the financial services industry was pathetically inadequate. When Arthur Levitt, chairman of the Securities and Exchange Commission, proposed tighter regulation of accountants, Congress refused to act. The political influence of the major accounting firms prevailed. Congress also took steps to free management from constraints. In 1995, legislation was adopted to restrict investor lawsuits against executives; in 1996, the telecom industry was deregulated; in 2000, trading in over-the-counter derivatives was entirely deregulated. It was in the business sectors that were turned loose in the 1990s where the greatest abuses occurred.

Between the autumn of 2001 and the summer of 2002, a remarkable change took place in the attitude of the public, Congress, and the Bush administration regarding the regulation of business. At the end of July 2002, President George W. Bush signed into law the "Sarbanes-Oxley Act" (Corporate Responsibility Act), legislation that he praised as providing the most significant business reforms since the Great Depression. Only a latter-day Nostradamus would have predicted in 2000 that after a year and a half in office the president would vigorously endorse such comprehensive federal regulation, having promised in his presidential campaign an administration committed to further reduction of government interference in business.

The new legislation provides for the creation of a Public Company Accounting Oversight Board to enforce professional standards, ethics, and competence for the accounting profession. Accounting firms that audit publicly traded companies are prohibited from providing certain specified consulting services, thereby removing the temptation to be lax on accounting issues to protect lucrative consulting fees. They may continue to advise on various other matters. Corporate responsibility is increased and corporate financial disclosure made more useful. Penalties for corporate wrongdoing are increased. The Securities and Exchange Commission is given additional funding to strengthen its investigative and enforcement powers.

Another major problem, corrupt advice given by security analysts at leading Wall Street firms, was not dealt with by the reforms of Sarbanes-Oxley. As noted briefly above, the heart of the matter is that the pay and bonuses of research analysts depended on their effectiveness in bringing business to the underwriting divisions. The very organization of the securities firms created strong incentives for analysts to dupe investors. Investors relied on the advice of security analysts who, perversely, were remunerated for their influence in gratifying corporate investment banking clients. During the "bubble" years of the late 1990s, analysts overwhelmingly favored "buy" over "sell" recommendations. Their strongly bullish positions avoided giving offense to companies their investment banking colleagues might be courting. It has been shown that they promoted securities to the public that, in private, they considered sure losers or "junk." There were some analysts who, for sound reasons, advised the sale of certain securities and were then sacked for their candor.

After eighteen months of intensive investigation by the New York State attorney general's office and the Securities and Exchange Commission, an agreement was reached in December 2002 between them and the leading Wall Street brokerage firms. It provides for fines of $1 billion plus $450 million for independent research reports by firms not engaged in investment banking to be available on line to customers of brokerage firms.

The culture of a major portion of America's financial institutions is, to use a current locution, morally challenged. In an article on investment banking, *The Economist* made this observation: "Even banks with the least tarnished reputations seem riddled with conflicts of interest, perverse incentives and greed."[81]

In 2003, for the third consecutive year, corruption was revealed to be widespread in a major sector of American business. This time it was the respected mutual fund industry, long free of scandal. Mutual funds are required by the Investment Company Act of 1940 to be run in the interest of their shareholder investors. They had grown enormously large as repositories for savings by a myriad of small investors attracted by the financial management and diversification of assets they offer. With some $7 trillion in assets, they served as great intermediary conduits of funds into the capital market. Fund managers violated their fiduciary duty, skimming off fund profits by engaging in trading practices detrimental to their client investors. It is instructive that it was the state regulators of New York and Massachusetts, rather than the nation's chief financial regulator the Securities and Exchange Commission, that discovered the illegal behavior. Presumably, the latter agency failed in its duty due to pressure and persuasion by the industry it was supposedly regulating and/or by being starved for funds to carry out its responsibilities. There is no doubt that better enforcement of existing laws is needed and that new rules may be found necessary. The governance of mutual funds is also in need of reform. Private sector competition did not prevent insiders from fleecing many millions of investors on a regular basis.

Also in 2003, currency traders were added to the roll of financial professionals apprehended for illegal practices. Federal authorities charged forty-seven persons with fraud in the foreign currency exchange market after an eighteen-month investigation in six states. This complex, decentralized, and loosely regulated market has a daily volume of a trillion dollars.

Alfred Marshall, the great neoclassical economist of the late-Victorian and Edwardian eras, expressed a hope for "a wider understanding of the social possibilities of economic chivalry." His assessment of business ethics seems, in a sobering way, apropos of our current problem.

> It is true that many of the largest fortunes are made by speculation rather than by truly constructive work: and much of this speculation is associated with anti-social strategy, and even with evil manipulation of the sources from which ordinary investors derive their guidance. A remedy is not easy, and may never be perfect. Hasty attempts to control speculation by simple enactments have invariably proved either futile or mischievous: but this is one of those matters in which the rapidly increasing force of economic studies may be expected to render great service to the world in the course of this century.[82]

When *The Economist* magazine was founded in 1843 it took a firm stand in favor of trade and free enterprise, a creed to which it has been faithful. In its 160th anniversary issue (June 28, 2003), its editor reported good news and bad news. The good news was that capitalism had just had its best few decades ever. The bad news was outrageous abuse of capitalism by capitalists. Reform of the way corporations are controlled was urged to correct abuses and avoid long-term loss of confidence in financial markets. Government as well as private sector reforms and regulatory enforcement of rules is required to provide supervision and control of corporations by responsible owners. The system has suffered not only from illegal activity but also from owners delegating control to managers who serve their own interests.

Among changes that have recently been adopted by private sector institutions are rules by the New York Stock Exchange and the Nasdaq Stock Market requiring listed firms to have a majority of the members of their boards of directors from outside the company. This is intended to end cozy relationships between CEOs and board members and to foster independent-minded directors.

Over a long period of time there have been repeated exposures of large-scale corrupt business practices that have been followed by public policies to suppress them. Legislators and regulators need to be highly motivated and backed by public opinion, for they seem to have a Sisyphean task rather like that of providing improved antibiotics to deal with the mutational adaptability of disease strains.

Notes

1.   *The Wall Street Journal*, May 3, 1999, p. A22.
2.   Margaret Thatcher, *The Downing Street Years* (Hammersmith, London: Harper-Collins, 1993), p. 7.
3.   Hugh Heclo, "Reaganism and the Search for a Public Philosophy," in John L. Palmer, ed., *Perspectives on the Reagan Years* (Washington, D.C.: The Urban Institute Press, 1986), p. 46.
4.   Peter F. Drucker, *The New Realities* (New York: Harper & Row, 1989), p. 61.
5.   *The Economist*, January 3, 1992, p. 15.
6.   Yergin and Stanislaw, *op. cit.*, p. 114.
7.   Thomas L. Friedman, *The Lexus and the Olive Tree* (New York: Farrar Straus Giroux, 1999), p. 40.
8.   Data from the International Finance Corporation cited in *The Wall Street Journal*, October 2, 1995, p. R4.
9.   Yergin and Stanislaw, *op. cit.*, p. 13.
10. Robert K. Massie, *Peter the Great* (New York: Wings Books, 1980), p. 824.
11. *The Economist*, July 9, 1999, p. 57.
12. *The Wall Street Journal*, June 12, 1998, p. A9.
13. *The Economist*, June 29, 2002, p. 65.
14. Arthur Seldon, *Capitalism* (Oxford: Basil Blackwell, 1990), p. 126.
15. *Journal of Comparative Economics*, December 1990, passim.
16. *The Wall Street Journal*, June 30, 1988, p. 22.
17. *The Wall Street Journal*, November 2, 1987, p. 1.
18. *Business Week*, January 16, 1995, p. 41.
19. Yergin and Stanislaw, *op. cit.*, pp. 352-353.
20. Clyde Prestowitz, *Three Billion New Capitalists* (New York: Basic Books, 2005), p. 110.
21. Ira C Magaziner and Robert B. Reich, *Minding America's Business* (New York: Vintage Books, 1983, orig. 1982), p. 255.
22. Charles L. Schultze, "Industrial Policy: A Dissent," *The Brookings Review* (Washington, D.C.: The Brookings Institution, Fall, 1983), p. 9.
23. Andrew Pollack, "America's Answer to Japan's MITI," *The New York Times*, March 5, 1989, Section 3, p. 1.
24. Michael E. Porter and Hirotaka Takeuchi, "Fixing What Really Ails Japan," *Foreign Affairs*, May/June, 1999, p. 77.
25. Erik Guyot, *The Wall Street Journal*, September 27, 1999, p. R20.
26. Adam Segal, "Is America Losing Its Edge? Innovation in a Globalized World," *Foreign Affairs*, November/December, 2004, p.8.
27. Prestowitz, *op. cit.*, pp. 16, 19, 131, 132, 211.
28. *The Wall Street Journal*, October 17, 2000, p. A22.
29. Thomas L. Friedman, *op. cit.*, pp. 91, 115.
30. An "edited executive summary" of recommendations is given in *Foreign Affairs*, November/December, 1999, pp. 169-183.
31. Benjamin M. Friedman, *The New York Review of Books*, July 15, 1999, p. 42.
32. Anthony Sampson, *The Money Lenders* (New York: The Viking Press, 1981), p. 16.
33. From Kevin Maney in *USA Today* cited by Thomas L. Friedman, *op. cit.*, p. 111.
34. Anthony Bianco and Wendy Zellner, "Is Wal-Mart Too Powerful?" *Business Week*, October 6, 2003, pp. 102, 106.

35. As reported by Joseph Kahn, *The New York Times*, May 7, 2000, Section 3, p. 4.

36. *The Economist*, June 24, 2000, pp. 81-83.

37. John Kenneth Galbraith, *American Capitalism; the Concept of Countervailing Power* (Boston: Houghton Mifflin, 1952), Chapters 9, 10.

38. The book by David Bornstein, *How to Change the World: Social Entrepreneurship and the Power of New Ideas* was reviewed by William J. Holstein in *The New York Times*, February 22, 2004, Section 3, p. 6.

39. Paul Streeten, *Globalisation: Threat or Opportunity?* (Copenhagen: Copenhagen Business School Press, 2001), p. 35.

40. Joseph E. Stiglitz, *Globalization and its Discontents* (New York: W. W. Norton, 2002), p. 222.

41. The capsule summary given here is derived from an essay by Richard N. Cooper in *Foreign Affairs*, January/February, 2004, pp. 152-155, that discusses Jagdish Bhagwati, *In Defense of Globalization* (New York: Oxford University Press, 2004).

42. Paul A. Samuelson, "Where Ricardo and Mill Rebut and Confirm Arguments of Mainstream Economists Supporting Globalization," *Journal of Economic Perspectives*, Volume 18, No. 3, Summer 2004, p. 142.

43. *The Wall Street Journal*, February 23, 1990, p. A10. Herbert Stein, a distinguished business economist and student of American business culture, was chairman of the Council of Economic Advisers in the Nixon administration.

44. Yolanda K. Henderson, "The Emergence of the Venture Capital Industry," *New England Economic Review*, July/August, 1989, pp. 64-78.

45. *The Wall Street Journal*, August 3, 1999, p. A22.

46. Assar Lindbeck, "Limits to the Welfare State," *Challenge*, January/February, 1986, pp. 31-36.

47. *Ibid.*, p. 32.

48. *Ibid.*, p. 36.

49. Pierson, *op. cit.*, p. 208.

50. Anton C. Zijderveld, *The Waning of the Welfare State* (New Brunswick: Transaction Publishers, 1999), p. 3.

51. *Ibid.*, pp. 2, 4, 96.

52. David Gladstone, *The Twentieth-Century Welfare State* (New York: St. Martin's Press, 1999), p. 91.

53. Theodore R. Marmor, Jerry L. Mashaw, and Philip L. Harvey, *America's Misunderstood Welfare State: Persistent Myths, Enduring Realities* (New York: Basic Books, 1990), p. 31.

54. *Ibid.*, pp. 57, 84, 86.

55. Ryscavage, *op. cit.*, p. 48.

56. *Ibid.*, pp. 155-156, 187.

57. Frank Levy, *The New Dollars and Dreams* (New York: The Russell Sage Foundation, 1998), p. 189.

58. Ryscavage, *op. cit.*, pp. 165, 169, 177.

59. Paul Krugman, "The Income Distribution Disparity," *Challenge*, July/August 1990, p. 6.

60. *Business Week*, November 18, 1991, p. 20.

61. *The Wall Street Journal*, April 13, 1994, p. R15; April 12, 1995, p. R1.

62. Robert H. Frank and Philip J. Cook, *The Winner-Take-All Society* (New York: The Free Press, 1995), p. 5.

63. Lester Thurow, *Shifting Fortunes* (United for a Fair Economy, pamphlet, 1999), p.1.

64. Juliet Schor, *Ibid.*, p. 3.
65. Paul Krugman, "For Richer," *The New York Times Magazine*, October 20, 2002, pp. 65, 67, 76.
66. *The New York Times*, June 5, 2005, p. 1.
67. Kenneth E. Boulding, *Beyond Economics* (Ann Arbor: The University of Michigan Press, 1968), p. 275.
68. Marc K. Landy, Marc J. Roberts, and Stephen R. Thomas, *The Environmental Protection Agency* (New York: Oxford University Press, 1990), p. 22.
69. Leonard Ortolano, *Environmental Regulation and Impact Assessment* (New York: John Wiley & Sons, 1997), p. 159.
70. Alan S. Blinder, *Hard Heads, Soft Hearts* (Reading, MA: Addison-Wesley, 1987), p. 140.
71. *Business Week*, August 16, 2004, pp. 60, 64, 69.
72. Molly O'Meara, "The Risks of Disrupting Climate," in *The World Watch Reader on Global Environmental Issues* (New York: W. W. Norton, 1998), p. 53.
73. Robert R. Gottfried, *Economics, Ecology, and the Roots of Western Faith: Perspectives From the Garden* (Lanham, Maryland: Rowman & Littlefield, 1995), pp. 86, 132.
74. *Ibid.*, pp. 19, 89, 136.
75. Landscape Analysis Laboratory, *An Assessment of Forest Change on the Cumberland Plateau in Southern Tennessee* (Sewanee, TN: The University of the South, 2002), p. iii.
76. *Ibid.*, pp. vi, vii.
77. *The Wall Street Journal*, October 16, 2000, p. 1.
78. Tom Wolfe, *A Man in Full* (New York: Farrar Straus and Giroux, 1998), p. 239.
79. *The Wall Street Journal*, February 3, 1999, p. A22.
80. Roy Jenkins, *Churchill* (New York: Farrar, Straus and Giroux, 2001), p. 86.
81. *The Economist*, November 29, 2003.
82. Marshall, *op. cit.*, p. 719.

5

Recapitulation and Inferences

The capitalist system of today is widely acknowledged to be firmly established and likely to endure indefinitely. Viewed in long-run historical perspective, however, it is a relatively new phenomenon. And in the light of humanity's tortuous past it seems wise to avoid overconfidence concerning future developments.

The hunting period of early history had communistic elements, and vestigial communism continued into the pastoral period. In primitive societies land was sometimes held in common. The economies of these societies were not remotely capitalist systems, but their ritualized trading practices may have contained the seeds of market forces.

The ancient civilizations of Babylon, Egypt, China, and India contained niches of early private enterprise, as did Classical Greece and Rome. The work of farmers, laborers, craftsmen, transporters of goods, and merchants was vital to their societies' achievements, but they were under state control. Economic actors had supporting rather than leading roles.

For a thousand years after the fall of the Roman Empire, Europe was economically and politically fragmented. Conditions for the development of economic activity were generally unfavorable during this long quasi-interregnum in the evolution of civilization. Trade and capital markets managed to survive although economic activity for profit, especially trading and lending, were discouraged by religious dogma intended to suppress or control activities deemed sinful and to maintain a strict hierarchical social order. Eventually, rising population led to the movement of people from manorial estates to towns where manufacturing and commercial activities flourished. Enterprising merchants worked closely with craftsmen in organizing, financing, and marketing products. Scientific discoveries led to innovations in production, for example, power machinery that increased productivity. Contact with the East through the

181

Crusades stimulated European commerce. It has been shown that some religious orders were important in accumulating capital and investing in manufacturing and agriculture. They also contributed to social stability, continuity, the rule of law, and the development of useful skills. In general, it seems fair to say that after a millennium had passed since the end of Roman hegemony, the elements of nascent capitalism had established a firm beachhead, the perimeter of which was steadily widening.

From the time of Christopher Columbus to that of Adam Smith, powerful forces—the Renaissance, rise of the nation state, voyages of discovery, and the Protestant Reformation—changed the way the world worked. Knowledge was gained by exploration, observation, experimentation, and testing as a more secular and pragmatic view of life gained relative to a theological interpretation of mankind's place in the cosmos. Trade expanded greatly, new markets opened, many important innovations were introduced. The Protestant Reformation with its emphasis on individualism encouraged hard work, diligence, saving, investment, and business enterprise. Profit making became fully compatible with a Godly life. Large as well as many small enterprises brought capitalists to the fore. Simultaneously, the various nation states that dominated large areas under monarchical rule competed for the world's resources. Private enterprise was not allowed to run free but was required to produce and trade so as to contribute to the strength of the nation and its rulers. Economic life was under comprehensive government regulation by tariffs, subsidies, and prohibitions, as well as by monopoly grants to favored subjects. It was taken for granted during this age of Mercantilism that if economic activity was not controlled the nation's resources would be frittered away. But while the political elites justified their controlling authority as necessary to their nation's power, they were also able to benefit personally from the self-serving way they used it. The term "crony mercantilism" seems an apt label for their behavior.

Beginning in Britain during the second half of the eighteenth century, building on the accretion of knowledge, skills, and capital of preceding centuries and propelled by major new technological achievements in manufacturing, full-blown capitalism took off into sustained growth that supported a rapidly increasing population with rising per capita income. The emergence of capitalist attitudes and behavior in the British North American colonies is an intriguing subject of historical research given the successor country's unique history as a "new" society in the New World. The break from traditional ways to modern enterprise was part of the ferment of the American Revolution.

Leading British and French intellectuals preceded Adam Smith in advancing the case for a free market economy, but it was Smith's *The Wealth of Nations* that most profoundly influenced his and later generations to accept it. Smith presented a highly persuasive comprehensive theory of how a free market system automatically achieves economic growth, making the population wealthy and the nation strong. To realize this great "natural" benefit, the burdensome Mercantilist restrictions had to be removed. Smith had come to economics as an outgrowth of his profession as a moral philosopher. As fully as he praised self-interest in motivating people to work, save, invest, and reap profit from their efforts and abilities, he realistically identified harmful results of economic power. Government was to be limited but not banished in Smith's view of a just and prosperous society. Indeed, he specified clearly three major roles for government and left open the full range and extent of government activity to be determined empirically.

During the century from the end of the Napoleonic wars to the onset of World War I (1815-1914), industrial capitalism spread and grew, transforming the economies of the West. The capitalist ethos of the world of business also permeated the broader culture encompassing government, religion, and academia.

Economic growth and development brought great benefits and generated an optimistic view of continued human progress. At the same time, however, there was a distressing aspect of the changes brought by industrialization. Industrial production required the recruitment of a large labor force to operate machines, and this resulted in urban slums. Work in factories, mines, and mills was often dangerous and unhealthy, with long hours and child labor. These conditions meant a mean, miserable life made even worse when economic conditions caused layoffs and reduced wages. In response, trade unions took root and the socialist movement began to offer an alternative form of social organization to replace laissez faire capitalism. Social reformers studied the conditions, brought them vividly to the attention of better-off strata of society, and presented plans for improvement. Modern socialism thus grew in reaction to industrial capitalism.

Karl Marx viewed capitalism as a major historical era that brought enormous progress but was destined to be superseded by a new phase, socialism. Eventually that too would be replaced as historical forces brought about a final stage, communism, when humanity would achieve peace, justice, and plenty.

Marx analyzed the business cycle, saw the growing concentration of economic power, and recognized the key roles of technology and innovative entrepreneurship. However, his predictions of increasing impoverization of labor, elimination of the middle class, and a falling rate of profit have not been fulfilled. Although Marxist prophecies failed and his theories proved wrong in important respects, Marxism had a great impact on world events for over a century. Socialism became a political force in Europe when the German Social Democratic Party was formed in 1875 and was soon emulated in other countries. Socialist political influence gradually increased during the decades to 1914. The strength of the socialist movement is clear from the reaction of the German government which responded in two ways: repression and concession. The latter approach brought about the first comprehensive welfare state as an antidote to socialist agitation. While its rhetoric was radical, the Social Democratic Party was reformist in practice.

In Britain, the socialist movement only very gradually became active politically. Shortly before World War I the British Labour Party was formed around a core of trade unions. Union workers were reluctant to adopt a socialist philosophy at this time, but by the end of World War I socialism became a basic tenet of the Labour Party. Also, in the years just before the war the British government, following the German precedent, adopted its first version of the welfare state. This step resulted from a combination of middle-class studies of social conditions and working-class pressure for reform.

The last third of the nineteenth century in the U.S.—the Gilded Age—brought powerful corporations that treated their workers harshly while huge fortunes were amassed by "captains" of industry and finance. Laissez faire prevailed and periods of severe economic depression were endured. The Socialist party, founded in 1901, gradually grew for the next decade and a half as workers in certain cities and in various rural areas sought a means of achieving a better life. Some ameliorative legislation blunted the expansion of this nascent workers' party. A reform movements known as Progressivism had an important impact at both the federal and state levels of government.

As World War I loomed, the European socialist movements solemnly pledged not to fight in a "capitalist" war. When war came, their resolve quickly succumbed to fervent nationalism. Not so for the Socialist party in the U.S. which did oppose the war, a stand that resulted in government repression and public antipathy that rendered it impotent for over a decade.

The economic/political paradigm of the pre-World War I era was transformed during the two decades following the end of the conflict. Communism became entrenched in the Soviet Union, and fascism was adopted in Italy, Germany, and Spain. The broad appeal of socialism after World War I is apparent by the inclusion of its name in the titles of the Union of Soviet Socialist Republics and German National Socialism, in both cases to cover brutal dictatorships that were the antithesis of democratic socialist ideals. In sharp contrast, the Scandinavian countries did adopt democratic socialist policies that enabled them to avoid the problems of low production and high unemployment that plagued the major market economies. The U.S. enjoyed a prosperous decade during the twenties but plunged into deep depression in the thirties. In response, the New Deal administration introduced various socialist measures to supplement and support traditional American capitalist institutions. As in other Western countries, faith in capitalism was weakened and its survival seemed in doubt to many. When the nineteen thirties ended and the world became engulfed in World War II, the need to mobilize economic resources for military purposes meant that the market mechanism was largely suspended. The end of hostilities in 1945 opened the way for a fresh start in economic policy.

The immediate postwar period of recovery and adjustment saw a variety of economic policies in different countries. In the U.K. a Labour government of six years (1945-1951) implemented partial socialism that included a moderate form of economic planning to guide the economy on the basis of collaboration between government and the private sector. This experience in planning had disappointing results. Selected major industries were nationalized, but again there was disappointment as the goals of efficiency and economic growth were not achieved. There were major reforms in social services, the most important being the establishment of the National Health Service.

After its defeat, Germany was divided between the Soviet Union and the Western allies. Attention here is on the western zones of occupation that became the new nation of West Germany in 1949. In the immediate postwar years the economy, hard-pressed to recover from the devastation of war, was beset by hyperinflation and black markets. In 1948 currency reform and the removal of rationing and price controls were followed by remarkable improvement in economic performance. With aid from the Marshall Plan, the "German economic miracle" transformed the new nation into a prosperous land. It developed what became known as a social market economy based on balance between the free market and government intervention that did not involve economic planning.

France opted for national economic planning and a relatively large nationalized sector of the economy. Planning took the form of targeting investment and production for selected heavy industries but not for individual firms. The state used regulatory and financial means to guide business decision making. The first plan, covering six years, was considered successful. In succeeding decades the results of state influence on the economy became less and less satisfactory, and in response planning fell out of favor.

When the U.S. emerged from World War II, it did not embrace national economic planning or nationalization of industry but returned to its traditional reliance on the market. It did retain the reforms of the New Deal era and explicitly adopted a philosophy of government responsibility for maintaining a high level of employment and output. The economic paradigm introduced by John Maynard Keynes in 1936 provided the theoretical basis for the use of monetary and fiscal policies to promote economic stability and long-term growth.

By the middle of the twentieth century, capitalism had been modified in ways that reduced its reliance on laissez faire and incorporated elements of socialist doctrine. The term mixed economy was used to characterize the blend of policies. Considerable antipathy to capitalism remained following the excesses and failures of capitalist economies before World War II, but there were also intellectuals who praised capitalism and, in particular, extolled the entrepreneurs who provided the creative energy for the innovations that brought advances to society.

Government programs that constitute the modern welfare state were gradually adopted by European countries following the example set by Germany in the eighteen eighties. The severe depression of the nineteen thirties brought the U.S. into the fold. By the post-World War II period, the welfare state had become a major feature of the Western world. It reached a peak of acceptance during the nineteen sixties.

During the twentieth century, use of consumer debt grew rapidly as installment purchasing and credit cards became widely used along with sophisticated advertising and impulsive buying. Business also expanded the use of debt as the practice of leveraging increased. The early capitalist ethos that emphasized duty, responsibility, and self-discipline gave ground to an attitude of greater hedonism, quicker gratification of desires, and corporate focus on short-run earnings, stock price increases, and emoluments. Thus, important changes occurred in capitalism's value system and behavior practices.

The American labor movement, having become powerful during the thirties and forties, was brought under federal regulatory laws following World War II. Over the next several decades a collection of federal and state laws were adopted to provide protection to workers in such areas as safety, privacy, and civil rights. After 1945 the union movement very gradually lost strength as membership fell relative to the size of the growing work force. Structural changes in the economy and employer resistance largely account for this trend.

Union membership in Britain expanded rapidly in both absolute and relative terms from the late sixties through the seventies. In an attempt to cope with persistent inflation while pursuing a macroeconomic growth policy, government sought cooperation from unions and management. Unions were to exercise restraint in wage demands in exchange for restraint by management in product pricing. Employees joined unions in order to be represented during the negotiation of "incomes policies." After some initial success the policy collapsed; massive strikes caused serious disruption of production including essential government services. In response there was a fundamental shift in policy following the election of a conservative government in 1979.

Postwar Germany embraced a policy that significantly strengthened the roles of workers in economic decision making. One was a collective bargaining system involving unions and employers' associations that determined wages and other matters regionally or nationally. Another gave workers a voice in a wide range of company policies through works councils. Such councils, of different degrees of influence, were adopted by many countries in Western Europe.

The Western mixed economies that combined a predominantly private sector market mechanism, Keynesian-inspired government macroeconomic policies, various degrees of government ownership and regulation, and the welfare state, performed well during the years 1950-1975, an exception being Britain where growth was slow.

During the 1970s a combination of heightened inflation and stagnation (soon conflated into "stagflation") called into question the viability of the mixed economy model. To encourage faster economic growth, a policy shift toward greater market freedom was begun in the U.S. during President Carter's administration. Prime Minister Margaret Thatcher in 1979 and President Ronald Reagan in 1981 assumed office explicitly dedicated to renewed emphasis on capitalism. A reduction in the role of government in the economy was not limited to the U.K. and the U.S. but came into vogue throughout much of the world.

The process of privatization of industry began quite suddenly in Britain in the early eighties and was quickly emulated in other countries. The British Labour Party abandoned its commitment to state ownership in 1995 under its new leader, Tony Blair. By the latter part of the nineties, the privatization drive largely played out because the leading candidate industries had been privatized and because of a reaction against disappointing results from privatized monopolies and abusive management practices.

Government deregulation, a high priority of the Reagan administration, was relatively minor in its overall impact. Initial reductions in regulation at the federal level were offset by later increases in the areas of environment, public safety, and consumer protection. State governments became more assertive in some areas when federal regulations were reduced. Yet the fervent anti-regulatory attitude in influential political and business circles contributed to a costly breakdown of sound financial practice. In the late 1980s lax enforcement of government oversight induced by political pressure together with mismanagement, embezzlement, and fraud led to insolvency of savings and loan associations. About $300 billion in public funds were needed to reimburse insured depositors.

During the final two decades of the twentieth century strong competition together with growing criticism of longstanding regulatory practices in the huge telephone and electric power industries resulted in considerable deregulation of those sectors. Major new technical and organizational changes transformed the communications field in the freer market environment. Electric power deregulation promised to deliver lower cost energy to consumers, but by the turn of the twenty-first century the bloom came off the rose of energy deregulation as the manipulation of markets resulted in power shortages and high prices.

In response to a slow rate of economic growth in the 1970s, a long debate took place in the U.S. during the eighties over the need for a national industrial policy. At the time, the rapidly growing Japanese economy, guided by government, was seen as a serious rival to the American model. Advocates of an American industrial policy viewed it as necessary to promote investment in strategic industries, and they proposed formal cooperation by business, labor, and government to promote competitiveness. Opponents of an industrial policy argued that it would be counterproductive, even disastrous, and that Japanese ascendancy was far from assured. The debate spent itself with no new policy being adopted. Nevertheless piecemeal government programs continued to be employed when they were considered necessary for national security.

The 1990s brought a remarkable change of fortune for both the U.S. and Japan. The former forged ahead with a surge of innovation and investment that culminated in a historic boom during the second half of the decade. In stark contrast, Japan suffered a collapse of what was now seen as a "bubble economy" and sank into a prolonged period of economic sluggishness.

In the wake of the fall of the Berlin Wall in 1989 and the disintegration of the Soviet Union in 1991, the Communist ideological competition to capitalism evaporated. Acceptance of market forces brought a new phase of capitalism called globalization. Yet the swing in the direction of lais-sez faire policies did not eliminate the welfare state or the acceptance of a role for government in the areas of environment, health, and safety. The new order carried with it the serious danger that the global financial system might veer out of control due to sudden flights of capital.

By the end of the twentieth century, rapid advances in information technology and communications went hand in hand with greater open-ness in economic relationships across national borders. Trade increased in a highly competitive climate, capital was raised and flowed in abun-dance across boundaries along with ideas and skills that accelerated the growth of world output. These dynamic developments made the concept of globalization ubiquitous in international economic discussion. While the fruits of this progress were widely acknowledged and praised, there were grave reservations expressed over poverty rates, glaring income inequality, and damage to the environment. Anti-globalization groups mounted protests at meetings of international organizations such as the World Trade Organization and gained the attention of their leaders. In the early years of the twenty-first century, globalization was viewed as very beneficial but reforms are needed. Getting international agreement on reform measures and implementing them would be politically very difficult to achieve.

Financial innovations increased the flow of funds through intermedi-aries during the latter part of the twentieth century. Commercial paper provided a way for corporations to raise funds by bypassing banks. Mortgages were "securitized" to expand the home mortgage market. In the 1980s, the junk bond market played a major role in the expansion of corporate debt with the proceeds often used to take over corporations through mergers and acquisitions. Takeovers are credited with increasing the productivity and profitability of American business. Junk bonds also were used to fund small "cutting edge" firms in the computer, telecommunications, and cable television industries. But serious problems emerged. Firms purchased at exorbitant prices were subsequently burdened by huge debt obligations. Leveraged buyouts became excessive resulting in poor use of resources, employee layoffs, and disrupted communities while the promoters and investment bankers who arranged the takeover deals reaped enormous fees. Conflicts of interest, misuse of insider information, and market rigging on the part of Wall Street deal makers were revealed. When economic activity slowed late in the eighties the holders of junk bonds lost heavily. Unsuspecting and ill-informed small investors who had relied on the advice and reputations of well-known financial firms suffered losses they could ill afford. A number of prominent financial figures were found guilty of illegal conduct. Respected leaders of the business community in America viewed the abuses as damaging to the capitalist system.

The venture capitalist industry came to play a leading role in the U.S. in the eighties, pumping money into fledgling firms and providing them with management expertise. Venture capitalists nurtured small firms that required considerable time to bring new technologies to viability. In the early nineties overexpansion resulted in a sharp decline in this industry, but then a rebound brought record financing highs in the late nineties. A great concentration of investment in internet companies created enormously great stock values that gave the industry a brief incandescence until the crash of 2000.

Another phenomenon of the last few years of the twentieth century was the introduction of electronic or online trading of securities. To take full advantage of gains in the rapidly rising stock market many enthusiastic investors chose to devote themselves full time to trading online for short-term profit. Their high volume of trading was largely a form of gambling that contributed to market volatility and the development of a bubble as stock values became detached from company earnings.

This was also a time when stock options became very important in rewarding company executives and employees to supplement or even substitute for salaries. They were not treated as expenses, thus contributing to company earnings, profits, and share prices. The case for stock options is strongest as a motivating factor in attracting bright young people to work in emerging high technology businesses in the hope of becoming very rich in a short time. With a stock market reversal of fortune, however, the cashing in of options exerts downward pressure on stock prices and may make them worthless. Critics argued that stock options siphon profits from stockholders who buy stock at present market value, that they serve as motivation for accounting abuses to exaggerate company profits, and that they are company expenses and should be recorded as such in corporate accounts.

The power of organized labor in the U.S. suffered a major decline from the middle to the end of the twentieth century. Gradually the makeup of union membership changed: male manual workers in heavy industry became relatively fewer while service workers including government employees were among the groups showing gains. Corporations replaced full-time with temporary workers who are denied the major benefits of job security, seniority, health insurance, and retirement programs. As unions were held in check in the last two decades of the twentieth and the early years of the twenty-first century by an increasingly competitive global economy and vigorous employer resistance they became less aggressive.

The decline of union strength in Britain was dramatic after 1980. Trade unions had a strong political orientation, particularly in the coal mining region. The coal miners' union defied the government, and after a fierce struggle the union was defeated. Legislation was adopted to curb the power of the union movement, so that the post-World War II balance of power between the unions, management, and government was changed. This was part of a trend of shifting influence in European countries generally.

The welfare state, widely accepted and implemented after World War II, became highly controversial by the seventies and was modified in important ways during the last third of the twentieth century. During the sixties and seventies the public sectors of advanced industrialized countries grew faster than their private sectors. Government debt rose relative to GDP, and the problem of inflation grew. In its more highly developed forms, as in Sweden, the welfare state came to be considered excessive in size and bureaucratically intrusive into the lives of individuals. Its negative effects on production could outweigh its beneficial redistributive effects. A movement to reduce the size of government succeeded in making the welfare state less comprehensive and generous. Although diminished, the major welfare programs were not abandoned. The changes occurred amid a structural adjustment of the world economic environment required by the powerful force of globalization.

Welfare reforms adopted in the U.S. in 1996 shifted responsibility for certain programs from the federal to the state level of government and required greater individual self-sufficiency. The two main social programs, Social Security and Medicare, remained intact. There are, however, continuing concerns about their costs and coverage.

Income in the U.S. was more equally distributed from about 1940 to 1970 than in the earlier and later decades of the twentieth century. Concern over a trend toward greater inequality began to be expressed during the 1980s and continued into the twenty-first century. The compensation of top-level American corporate executives increased relative to average worker pay by amounts that scandalized monitoring organizations. Not only has income inequality increased, but there has also been stagnation or worse for the bottom fifth of American families.

Over the course of the twentieth century, the role of government in allocating resources increased dramatically. Before World War I, government expenditures were only ten percent or less of total national output. By the mid-nineties they ran about 50 percent in European Union countries and about 37 percent in the U.S. There was a slight reduction at the end of the century leaving the ratio on the order of about four times higher, on average, compared with a century earlier.

World population growth over the last 250 years has been unprecedented. Increases in industrial and agricultural production have raised living standards far beyond previous experience. But along with abundant output the problems of pollution, overuse of natural resources, and overcrowding emerged and by the middle of the twentieth century resulted in public and political concern sufficient to make environmental protection a duty of government. It had become clear that the market system could not be left alone, that it failed to preserve indispensable ecological standards.

To understand and to devise solutions for the problem of pollution, the concept of externalities is essential. Government policies may take three main forms: regulation, fees, or marketable permits to pollute. Policy choices involve consideration of how best to achieve effective results at least cost. Also, to protect and preserve the Earth's natural resources, land-use planning regulations are needed. In the absence of public policies to guide land use in desirable ways the ecosystems of the world may be irreversibly damaged.

Strong capital expansion and rapid productivity growth brought about a remarkable boom in the U.S. in the 1990s. Financial success fed optimism about the future and morphed into overconfidence that a "new era" of sustainable growth had arrived. Led by investment in hi-tech industries, the stock market surged higher and higher as speculative fever took over from realistic evaluation. A sharp reaction occurred in 2000 as capital spending and GDP declined and the stock market plunged—most severely in the previously high-flying technology sector. The economy was in a shallow recession for much of 2001 but then began a slow recovery hampered by the effects of the devastating terrorist attacks on the World Trade Center and the Pentagon on September 11, 2001.

Accompanying the desirable technical and business innovations of the nineties, the lure of enormous fortunes to be quickly made fostered the development of financial innovations used to exaggerate and deceive. Beginning with the collapse of Enron Corp. in 2001, a series of corporate failures brought to light practices ranging from lax to nefarious on the part of corporations. As in earlier times, it again became obvious that the free market system was open to abuses that require social control. With the efficiency and integrity of the capitalist system and the way it is perceived at stake, reforms were adopted by the federal government and by private sector institutions.

Leading thinkers concerned with human well-being in the broadest sense recognize the crucial importance of the role of government as the instrument necessary for maintaining the interests of society as a whole. It seems appropriate at this point to bring some of their insights into consideration with respect to the relationship between capitalism and socialism.

The big questions of freedom, democracy, self-interest, and social justice were addressed in 1944 by the American theologian/social philosopher Reinhold Niebuhr in a book concerned with the future of democratic civilization. These questions were of much concern as war against totalitarianism was reaching its climax and in light of the severe social problems that had preceded the war; these were still fresh in the national consciousness.

Niebuhr warned that "giving simple moral sanction to self-interest" was a mistake. He believed that self-interest is a very powerful force but dangerous when asserted without regard to broader communities. He called attention to an aspect of Adam Smith's doctrine that is often overlooked. Despite his concept of a pre-established social harmony that transforms self-interest into mutual service, "Smith does not hesitate to make moral demands upon men to sacrifice their interests in the wider interest." While capitalism was given a theoretical justification, as it matured and developed a vast corporate structure its ideology embraced economic freedom but ignored the "moral idealism which informed it." "The idea that economic life is autonomous and ought not to be placed under either moral or political control is an error. . . . The propagation of this error has caused great damage in modern life." Niebuhr concludes that the passion for freedom and the passion for order need to be properly balanced.

> Since freedom and community are partially contradictory and partially complementary values in human life, there is . . . no perfect solution for the relation of the two values to each other. This means that the debate on how much or how little the economic process should be brought under political control is a never-ending one.[1]

Soon after the collapse of Communist regimes in 1989 and 1990, in a major statement of the Catholic Church's social doctrine, Pope John Paul II emphasized the importance of balance between market freedom and state regulation. Marxist criticism of capitalist bourgeois societies for commercialization and alienation of human existence is rejected because Marx based it on a materialist foundation considered by him to be rectifiable only in a collective society. Still, history shows that alienation—and "loss of the authentic meaning of life"—is a reality in Western countries. The problem of consumerism is given careful attention. It catches people "in a web of false and superficial gratifications" that cause alienation. Alienation also occurs in work under competitive conditions in which the worker is considered "only a means and not an end." Closely related to consumerism is the ecological problem. There is "senseless destruction of the natural environment" as the resources of the earth are consumed in an excessive and disordered way.

John Paul II credits the market mechanism for providing "secure advantages" in resource allocation and meeting consumer preferences, then adds a caveat:

> these mechanisms carry the risk of an "idolatry" of the market, an idolatry which ignores the existence of goods which by their nature are not and cannot be mere commodities. . . . It is the task of the State to provide for the defense and preservation of common goods such as the natural and human environments, which cannot be safeguarded simply by market forces.

The danger exists "that a radical capitalist ideology could spread" which blindly entrusts the solution of problems of marginalization, exploitation and alienation "to the free development of market forces"[2]

A sophisticated, ambitious, and influential analysis of societal trends was presented by Francis Fukuyama, a professor of international political economy who once served as the deputy director of the U.S. State Department's policy planning staff, in his 1992 book *The End of History and the Last Man.*

Before discussing Fukuyama's thesis, which was presented as the Cold War ended, it is interesting to consider another bold view—that of John Kenneth Galbraith, in his *The New Industrial State,* published in 1971 when the Cold War was a paramount concern. Galbraith advanced the idea of convergence of industrial societies. The reason was that large-scale production required much capital, advanced technology, and therefore elaborate organization. As a consequence, prices would need to be controlled and markets regulated; planning would replace the market. That capitalism and Communism would therefore converge he thought fortunate because it would end the belief that conflict was inevitable due to irreconcilable differences. Twenty years later the conflict did end, although not in the manner expected by Galbraith.

Fukuyama also considered convergence to be inevitable although he called it homogenization. The causal factor was modern natural science which makes for unlimited wealth creation. "This process guarantees an increasing homogenization of all human societies, regardless of their historical origins or cultural inheritances." As the societies are increasingly connected through globalization and a shared consumer culture they evolve toward a system known alternatively as economic liberalism, free market economics, or capitalism. As the argument proceeds, the "process" is promoted semantically to "the Mechanism," defined as "a kind of Marxist interpretation of history that leads to a completely non-Marxist conclusion." Economics is only part of the story. Another important element is a strong human desire for personal recognition that is increasingly demanded as people become wealthier and better educated and informed. People demand free government as well as free markets. Liberal democracy has clearly become the preferred choice of people throughout the developed world. It encompasses economic liberalism broadly defined, for there are large public sectors in all contemporary capitalist states.

What Fukuyama means by the "end of history" is that Western liberal democracy has triumphed; mankind has reached its highest wisdom. He relies on "the autonomous power of ideas," the approach of the German philosopher Hegel that Marx rejected. The idea of liberal democracy developed by English and French thinkers of the seventeenth and eighteenth centuries has proven itself to be the best idea.

Within liberal societies there is and will continue to be tension between two desiderata: liberty and equality.

> Every society will balance liberty and equality differently, from the individualism of Reagan's America or Thatcher's Britain, to the Christian Democracy of the European continent and the social democracies of Scandinavia. These countries will be very different from one another in their social practices and their quality of life, but the specific tradeoffs they choose can all be made under the broad tent of liberal democracy, without injury to underlying principles.[3]

Ten years after publishing *The End of History and the Last Man*, Fukuyama made the following statement: "The great free-market revolution that began with the coming to power of Margaret Thatcher and Ronald Reagan at the close of the 1970s has finally reached its Thermidor, or point of reversal." That swing in policy was a reaction to the rapid growth of the modern welfare state, but for many it began to evolve into libertarianism, i.e., "an ideological hostility to the state in all its manifestations" that constitutes an overreaching of the free-market revolution.[4]

The market mechanism developed slowly over the course of history and gradually insinuated itself into economies that were dominated by tradition or directed by powerful rulers. In modern times as it gained practical ascendancy in the West it also acquired theoretical sanction. A capitalist ideology of (almost) complete laissez faire rose to dominance; its apogee can conveniently be placed between the American Civil War and World War I (1865-1914). Except for strictly limited functions, intervention by the state was viewed as anathema. An English philosopher and pioneer sociologist, Herbert Spencer, provided the famous phrase "survival of the fittest" to condone mass destitution alongside extraordinary wealth for the barons of industry, finance, and commerce. Known as Social Darwinism, this complacent view of the way the world works held that the human race would be improved by the process of natural selection.

The harshness of capitalism gave rise to a reaction in the form of socialism. In essence, socialism emerged as a means by which industrial workers could gain some improvement in the basic conditions of life. Socialist theory then developed to provide an alternative system that some of its advocates believed should or would replace capitalism. Intense ideological and political/economic/military struggles raged during most of the twentieth century. At the end it became clear that capitalism had not only survived but was widely seen to be the most successful way of generating economic growth and development worldwide.

Yet the so-called "triumph" of capitalism is an overstatement as is the "death" of socialism. Socialism is no longer considered a likely substitute for or challenge to capitalism. Indeed, the term has almost disappeared from public discourse. Yet a comparison of capitalism in 1900 with what it has become in the twenty-first century shows remarkable changes.

Today the state has many roles it did not have a century ago. It has responsibility to restrain corporate monopoly power. It has responsibility to use monetary and fiscal policy to maintain employment, output, and economic growth. It has responsibility to maintain honesty and fair dealing in securities, in corporate accounting, and in corporate governance. It has responsibility for providing an array of social services and benefits summed up in the phrase "welfare state." It has responsibility for regulating pollutants that cause environmental damage. It has responsibility for providing public safety and consumer protection regulations. It is needed to finance basic scientific research. Public expenditures are a much greater share of national output now than a century ago.

The core concept of capitalism is private ownership of the means of production employed in the context of a free market. It is driven by an individualist philosophy. The core concept of socialism is collective (state) guidance and control of economic life. Capitalism excels at providing incentives and opportunities for work, saving, and investment. It is based on liberty. Socialism excels at providing ways of mitigating excesses of capitalism that cause economic fluctuation, personal insecurity, and hardship. It is driven by an ethos of fairness, compassion, and justice that strives to provide opportunities for the disadvantaged and a less unequal distribution of income and wealth than results from market forces.

Capitalism has endured—triumphed—historically because its virtues of freedom and dynamism are indispensable for the fulfillment of human potential. Yet experience demonstrates that unrestrained capitalism is not viable. In the absence of communal constraints, its excesses, and social imbalances become serious problems. Experience has also demonstrated socialism to be unacceptable when it is the dominant form of social organization. It stifles initiative and results in economic stagnation. A combination of capitalism and elements of socialism is needed to achieve the benefits and to avoid the drawbacks associated with both the market and the state. Socialism, having failed to displace capitalism, has become in practice its junior partner. Essentially, it is a silent partner whose name is generally unspoken but whose meliorating influence is undeniable. Together they provide a balance that mirrors the psychological balance between our private and social proclivities. Each is an antidote for the other's faults.

For an appropriate tension and balance to exist between the private sector and the government, it is imperative that they be separate in terms of loci of power. While separation is implicit in the model of a democratic society, it cannot be taken for granted, the point emphasized by President Eisenhower in his farewell address warning against the formation of a "military-industrial complex." If influential private groups acquire enough influence in government to make it in fact, if not in law, the instrument of such groups, then the system as a whole would be transmuted into corporatism (fascism).

The ongoing problem is that of determining the nature and extent of the appropriate role of the state in a changing society. It is clear that democracy-cum-market mechanism promotes creativity and material enrichment. It is clear also that collective control is necessary to some degree to meet society's aspirations for reasonable stability and fairness. Paradoxically, while they have traditionally been viewed as conflicting ideologies, their mature relationship may be seen as symbiotic.

Notes

1. Reinhold Niebuhr, *The Children of Light and the Children of Darkness* (New York: Charles Scribner's Sons, 1944), pp. 25, 26, 76, 151.
2. John Paul II, *On the Hundredth Anniversary of Rerum Novarum*, Encyclical Letter, May 1, 1991 (Washington, D.C.: United States Catholic Conference), pp. 73, 78, 79, 82.
3. Francis Fukuyama, *The End of History and the Last Man* (New York: The Free Press, 1992), pp. xiv, 131, 293.
4. *The Wall Street Journal*, May 2, 2002, p. A14.

Author Bibliography

Degen, Robert A. *The American Monetary System; A Concise Survey of Its Evolution Since 1896.* Lexington, MA: Lexington Books, D.C. Heath and Company, 1987.

———. "United States Recessions and Selected Imports," *The Canadian Journal of Economics and Political Science* (Vol. XXV, no. 2, May, 1959).

———. Introduction to Part III, "Monetary and Financial Aspects." In Weintraub, Sidney and Marvin Goodstein (eds.), *Reaganomics in the Stagflation Economy.* Philadelphia, PA: University of Pennsylvania Press, 1983.

Index